IMAGES
of America

AFRICAN AMERICANS IN LAFAYETTE AND SOUTHWEST LOUISIANA

On the Cover: **SUNDAY GAMES.** In Lafayette, Louisiana, a favorite pastime on a Sunday was to go to the park to see various baseball teams compete with each other. During the late 1940s, African American teams filled the park with excitement. This photograph features the Heymann Porters baseball team. The group's sponsor was Henry Herbert Heymann, and Heymann Park is named in his honor. (Courtesy of O.C. "Dan" Guillot Collection at the Lafayette Clerk of Court Office and Louis J. Perrett, clerk of court, Lafayette Parish.)

IMAGES
of America

AFRICAN AMERICANS IN LAFAYETTE AND SOUTHWEST LOUISIANA

Sherry T. Broussard

ARCADIA
PUBLISHING

ISBN 978-0-7385-9110-0

Published by Arcadia Publishing
Charleston, South Carolina

Printed in the United States of America

Library of Congress Control Number: 2011933005

For all general information, please contact Arcadia Publishing:
Telephone 843-853-2070
Fax 843-853-0044
E-mail sales@arcadiapublishing.com
For customer service and orders:
Toll-Free 1-888-313-2665

Visit us on the Internet at www.arcadiapublishing.com

In memory of my husband, Roosevelt Broussard,
and the trailblazers of southwest Louisiana

Contents

ACKNOWLEDGMENTS

The historical book *African Americans in Lafayette and Southwest Louisiana* is possible because of the contributions of information and pictures provided by the families of southwest Louisiana. The book would not have been possible without the support, encouragement, and participation of persons and organizations listed. Every possible precaution has been taken to make sure the book is as accurate and as error-free as possible. Thanks and appreciation are expressed to the following persons for interviews, information, and pictures: Thelma C. Alex, Leroy and Zelma Banks, Etta Pearl Brew, Donald Burnette, Margaret Young, Nelda Broussard, Evelyn and David Zehner, Enrica Singleton, Rita Stemley, Amater Traylor, Mary LaFontaine, Merline Herbert, Ike Jones, L. Dugas Jr., Clayton and Stella Burgess, Eula M. Dell, Joseph Dennis, Juanita Thibeaux, Reva Monroe, Alvirda Thomas, Adofo Harmon, Phyllis and Lyle Mouton, Loretta Perrot, Bernadette Rubin, Mervin Harmon, Marilyn Malveaux, Margaret G. Guidry, Denris Mouton, Paulette Green, Alvin Bethard, Linda W. Cockrell, Kevin Williams, John W. and Cecile Joseph, Edward Sam, Nelson Abrams, Albert J. Glaude, Alex and Hazel Taylor, Nathan Williams Sr., Sidney Williams Jr., Evelyn Syrie, John and Marlene Broussard, J. Kennedy Green, Gwen Harris, Jane Vidrine, Louis J. Perret (Lafayette parish clerk of court), Edith G. Dupré Library Archives and Special Collections, and the Lafayette Diocese Archives and Research Department. It is important to learn the history and culture of a people and to share the history with others to build a strong foundation of living for future generations. Black history, rich with achievements of ancestors, great-grandparents, grandparents, and parents, contains a wealth of information that should encourage others to achieve great accomplishments in life. It is a story worth telling, a story worth hearing, a story worth writing, and a story worth reading. Thanks to everyone in southwest Louisiana for allowing the author to give a place in history for the people, places, and events that have shaped the lives of African Americans in southwest Louisiana. This book serves as guiding light to achieve greater things. Special thanks goes to Arcadia Publishing for publishing the book.

INTRODUCTION

Southwest Louisiana includes the parishes of Lafayette, Iberia, St. Martin, St. Landry, Acadia, Cameron, Evangeline, St. Mary, Jeff Davis, Allen, Beauregard, Calcasieu, and Vermilion. The people who live in this region of the state are somewhat heterogeneous—some speak French, most are Catholic, but they describe themselves by various ethnic identities. The terms African American and black are used in the book to refer to the unity of the people in the area. The focus is on the shared culture, rituals, and customs, such as in the foods that are eaten, religious and social events, and the music that captivates and stirs the soul. The book features black people in church leadership, as educators, as entrepreneurs, and as entertainers. It begins with the church, a significant part of the lives of the people. The black church is the foundation upon which African Americans build their hopes, dreams, and futures. No other entity as the black church has the power to give peace and comfort in times of sorrow, to give food and shelter from the storms, and to give vision to create businesses, organizations, and schools. Many of the black churches were built during Reconstruction and date back to the mid-1800s.

Amazingly, because of the stamina of the people who were members of the church, several of the churches are in full operation today and more than 100 years old. The churches all share the essence of serving as schools for black children of the day and for serving as meeting places to discuss politics, social and housing problems, farming, voting, and civil-rights issues. The churches were sometimes destroyed by vandals, fires, storms, and floods but were rebuilt and continued to provide protection and serenity. The predominant faith in Lafayette and in southwest Louisiana is Catholic; however, a variety of others are also a part of the southwest communities. African Americans participate in these religions, and some are members of all the various denominations. Because of the strong religious influence throughout the state, Louisianans are known for their generosity and help in times of disasters at home, across the United States, and abroad. The weather is sometimes devastating and causes such natural disasters as hurricanes, tornadoes, and floods. The stores in Lafayette keep a large donation drop box or bin for food items to be collected and donated to local food banks all year long. The black church is the heart of the people. Its members band together to care for one another and to help in sickness, in personal crises, in feeding the less fortunate, in serving as role models, and building schools and other facilities, such as the church fellowship halls. The black church helps to heal sad and broken hearts, care for elderly members, and provide such community services as health-care information, elderly services information, and tutoring programs for the youth.

The black church opens its doors to all people and is one of the richest cultural experiences of peoples' lives. It is the foundation, the heart, and the soul of black people and others who care to worship and share in joy, uplifting spiritual words, harmonious music, and a religious experience like no other. From the beating of the drums, to the keys and cords of the piano and organ, to the stringed instruments and voices that resonate so powerfully with songs of praise and worship, the black church serves as a beacon of hope for all who enter its doors. The ministers, preachers, and priests who deliver words of encouragement, through their Bible teachings and sermons, provide comfort for the mind, body, and soul. In many towns and rural areas of southwest Louisiana, the black church was the first school.

Although educating black children was not an important issue to majority-race citizens of the day, black churches served as schools for many citizens in this book, who grew up in a segregated time. Back then, there were no public schools for black children in mainstream Louisiana and in a lot of places across America. The men and women of that era built their own schools on their own land and served as principals and teachers to educate the children. Some people even opened their homes as schools and taught black children to read and write, and they provided their own transportation for the kids. They even shared their homes with some students who lived in rural southwest parishes to complete their high school education in Lafayette at Paul Breaux High School. Students lived with family members and friends until they graduated from high school. Men and women of earlier times were farmers, cooks, housekeepers, seamstresses, barbers, beauticians, pastors, teachers, principals, and business owners. They were committed and thus provided services to meet the needs of the people of southwest Louisiana. The schools were located in churches, old houses, backs of general stores, and later in primarily one-room schoolhouses with children of various ages in the same room. Education, however, was important to most citizens in early Louisiana, and many parents took extra housekeeping work, baked and sold pies, and worked longer hours doing low-paying jobs to send their children to college. Visionary leaders, such as Booker T. Washington, Mary McLeod Bethune, Pinckney Benton Stewart Pinchback, and many others, not only realized the importance of a good education but also built colleges and universities for black children so that they would have a place to further advance their education. In doing so, they needed these students to bring what they learned back to their communities and improve conditions there. Some of the children became educators, business owners, civic leaders, and entrepreneurs.

At one time in southwest Louisiana, people could find many black businesses at the almost every corner of the predominately black areas of the city of Lafayette and other smaller communities. Those included beauty shops, barbershops, cafés, nightclubs, motels, restaurants, and funeral homes. In earlier years, other businesses included hat shops, dry cleaners, hotels, shoe shops, dress shops, watch-repair shops, community stores, and other types of businesses. Some of those businesses exist today in similar and varied forms, such as washaterias, bookstores, flower shops, lawn services, self-contractors, exercise clubs, and beauty-supply shops. These people are determined and have maintained their businesses despite many economic hardships. It started when many black people became landowners during Reconstruction and after the Emancipation Proclamation that freed the slaves. Many slaves also worked on and for property that they would later own, and others received large pieces of land from previous masters. The land remained in the hands of many families for several generations, being handed down from one generation to the next. The promised "40 acres and a mule" was not seen by most African Americans, yet some wealthy white and black landowners donated land for churches and schools for black citizens in southwest Louisiana.

Today, African American entrepreneurs are busy and involved in many various enterprises, such as the food industry, automotive shops, health clubs, day-care centers, specialty food items, clothing stores, magazine publishing, art studios, and black-owned banks and credit unions. They also own radio stations, apartment and rental properties, restaurants, farms, car-washing services, and antique shops. Leadership, values, commitment, and vision are components that lead to a successful community. Citizens with ideas and ideals create opportunities for advancement in business and in life. Such citizens often have the financial means to create wealth not only for themselves but also for others. Many individuals have added to the success of Louisiana, and their contributions are still flourishing today. *African Americans In Lafayette and Southwest Louisiana* tells part of the history of some citizens, but the story is immense and constantly evolving with contributions of African Americans ranging from business to the arts and outlets from festivals to zydeco music, ensuring that the black community will continue to enrich Louisiana, America, and the world.

One

THE GLORIOUS CHURCH

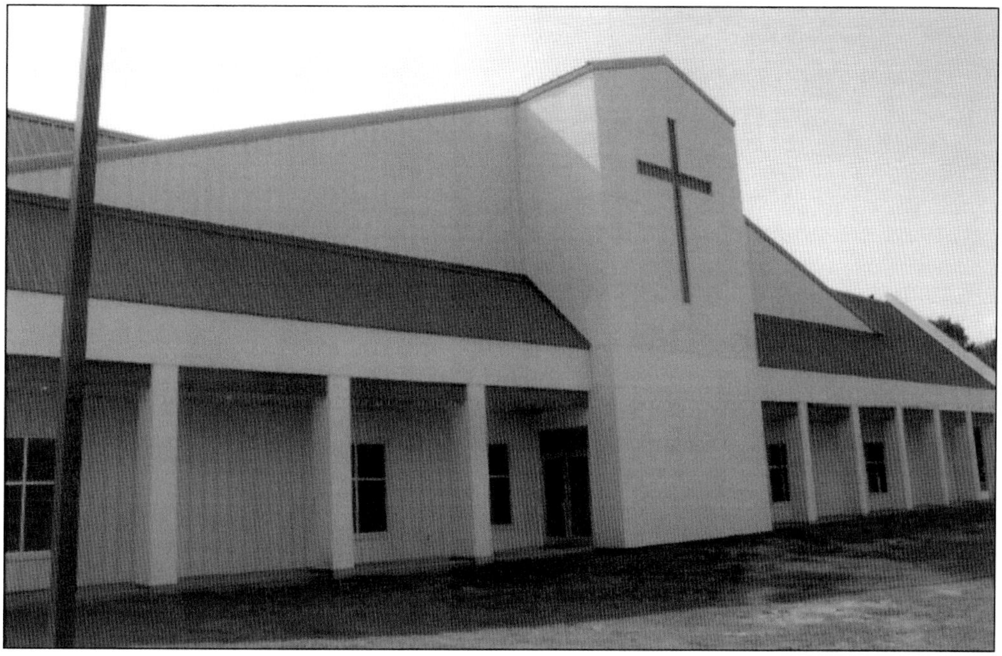

OLDEST BLACK BAPTIST CHURCH (LAFAYETTE PARISH). Organized in 1878, Good Hope Baptist Church is the oldest black Baptist church in Lafayette and is located on Willow Street. Dr. Ricky E. Carter is the current pastor of the church and has served since 1992. With his leadership, membership has increased, and a new church was built and relocated from Magnolia Street to Willow Street. Rev. T.J. James was the first pastor of the church. Pastors G. Oliver and F. Hamm were the next to serve the church. Incorporated in 1912, Rev. Albert R. Butler served as pastor of the church for 45 years. The land was donated by Alexander Mouton, a citizen of Lafayette and governor of Louisiana. The original church was located on Polk and Congress Streets. It was not only used for religious purposes but also as an educational institution. Classes were held at the church until the city (formerly Vermilionville and currently Lafayette) provided a school for black children in 1896. (Courtesy of Paulette Green.)

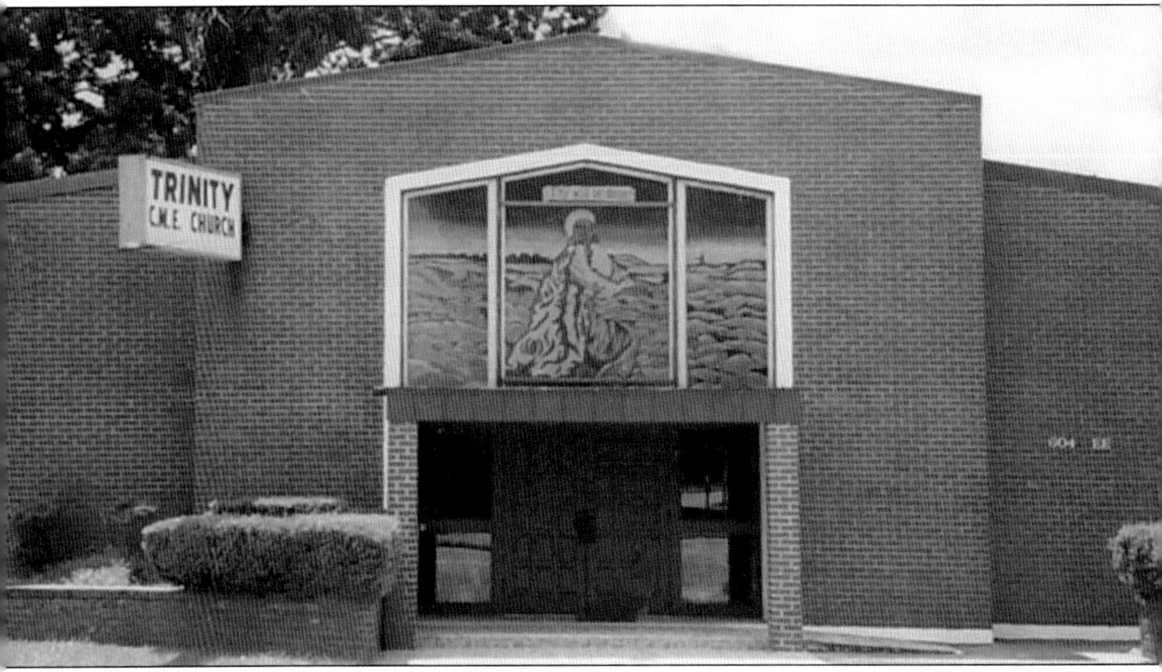

TRINITY CME CHURCH (LAFAYETTE PARISH). Established in 1872, Trinity CME Church is located on Lee Street in Lafayette. The current pastor of the church is Rev. L. Dugas Jr. Gov. Alexander Mouton personally appeared before the duly sworn and commissioned recorder for Lafayette Parish and declared that he wished to aid in the promotion of religion and morality among the black population there. He donated lot 235 in the old corporation of Vermilionville (Lafayette) to the Colored Methodist Episcopal (CME) Church. The parties understood that the land was to be used exclusively for erection of a church, a parsonage, or a public school. The parties also agreed that if the land was used for any other purpose it would revert, at no charge, to the donors or their heirs. The first church edifice, a small-framed building, was erected on the lot. The church prospered and grew, and trustees Paul Breaux and Mitchell Foote (on behalf of the membership) purchased the land in 1883 for $100, which is where the current church building sits. (Courtesy of Ike Jones.)

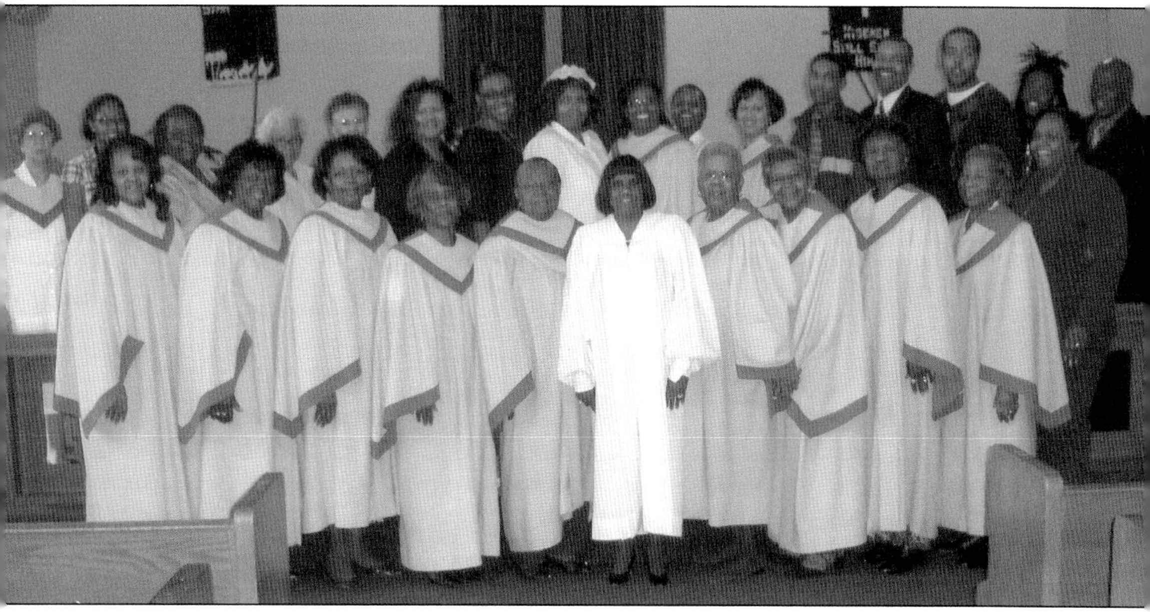

TRINITY CME CHURCH MASS CHOIR (LAFAYETTE PARISH). Mathilda Martin (center, in the white robe) is the director of the church's mass choir. Martin is also the director of the children and youth choir and the missionary choirs. The mass choir frequently performs in the community for various events. It performed for the celebration of the installation services for Dr. Joseph E. Savoie, president of the University of Louisiana at Lafayette, in 2008. (Courtesy of Ike Jones.)

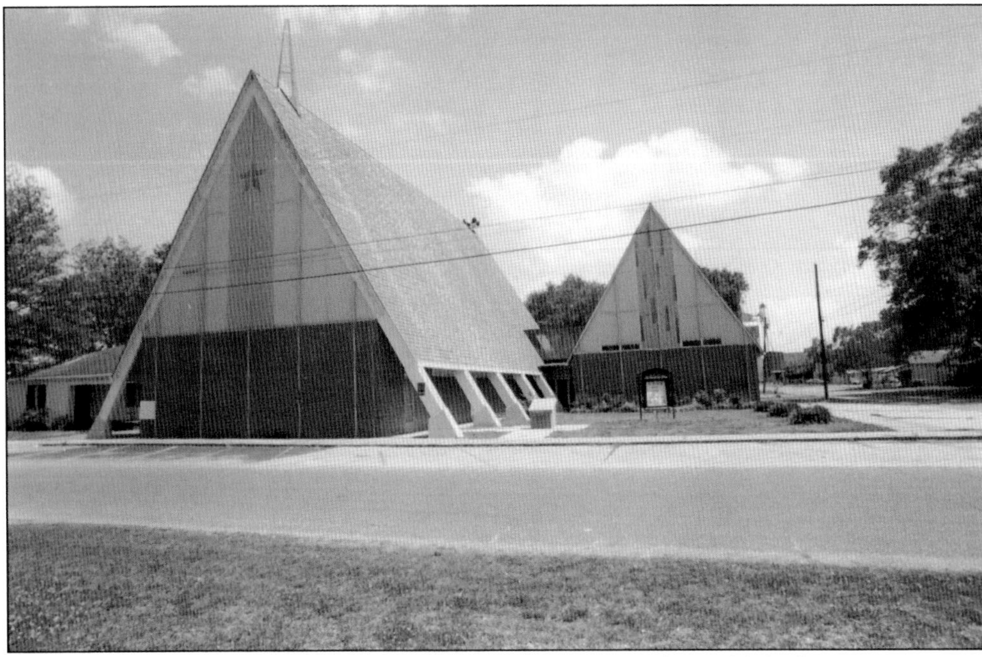

Morning Star Missionary Baptist Church (Acadia Parish). Established in 1899, Morning Star Missionary Baptist Church is located in Crowley, Louisiana, on the corner of Avenue B and Third Streets. The current pastor of the 112-year-old church is Rev. Donald R. Burnett Sr. Reverend Burnett is an active, humble, spiritual pastor and has served in the following capacities: assistant dean of Christian education, Louisiana Baptist Convention; instructor at the Louisiana Baptist Congress of Christian Education; and dean seminar II, division III. The church was organized in 1899 by former slaves who loved God and the black Baptist Church. Rev. Joseph Barker was the first pastor. He was succeeded by Rev. H.C. Ross. Under the leadership of Pastor Ross, the church experienced much growth and development. Ross was a visionary pastor and served as president of the Seventh District Baptist Association. He received an honorary doctor of divinity degree from Leland Baptist College. Ross was pastor of the church for 34 years until his death in 1946. H.C. Ross Elementary School is named in his honor. (Courtesy of Margaret Young.)

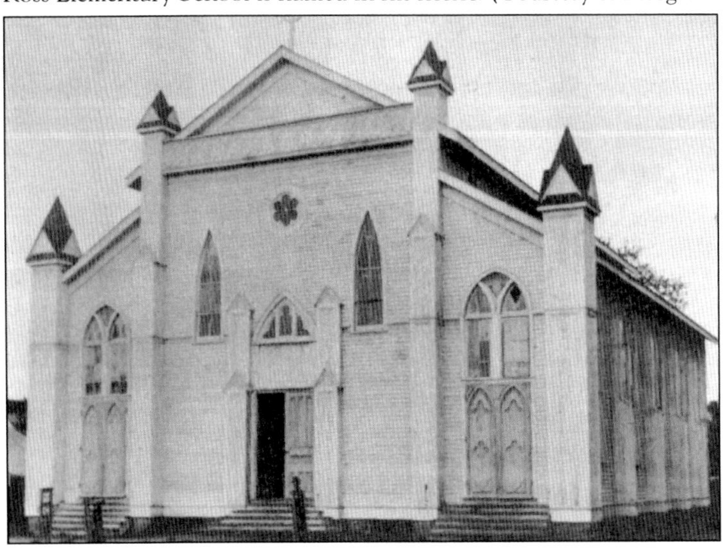

Original St. Paul Catholic Church (Lafayette Parish). St. Paul Church is 100 years old and is located on Simcoe and St. John Streets in Lafayette, Louisiana. The original St. Paul Catholic Church pictured here was built in 1911 and eventually destroyed by a storm. (Courtesy of Louis J. Perret, clerk of court, Lafayette Parish.)

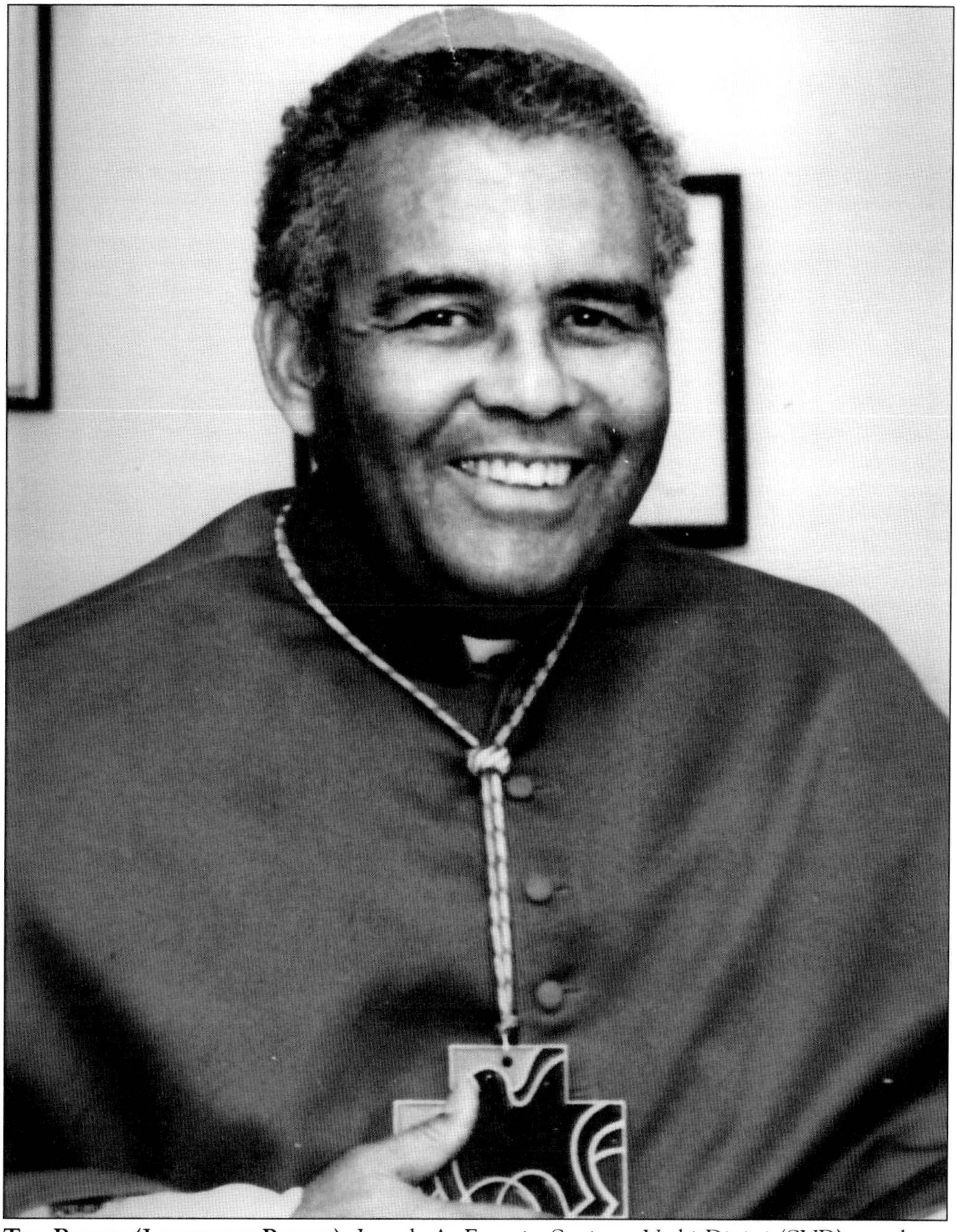

The Bishop (Lafayette Parish). Joseph A. Francis, Societas Verbi Divini (SVD), was born and raised in Lafayette. He completed his education and served as a priest for the Society of the Divine Word Missionaries for 46 years. Francis was appointed and served as bishop in Newark, New Jersey, for 21 years. Bishop Francis was one of three African American priests to become bishops from Louisiana. (Courtesy of Louis J. Perret, clerk of court, Lafayette Parish.)

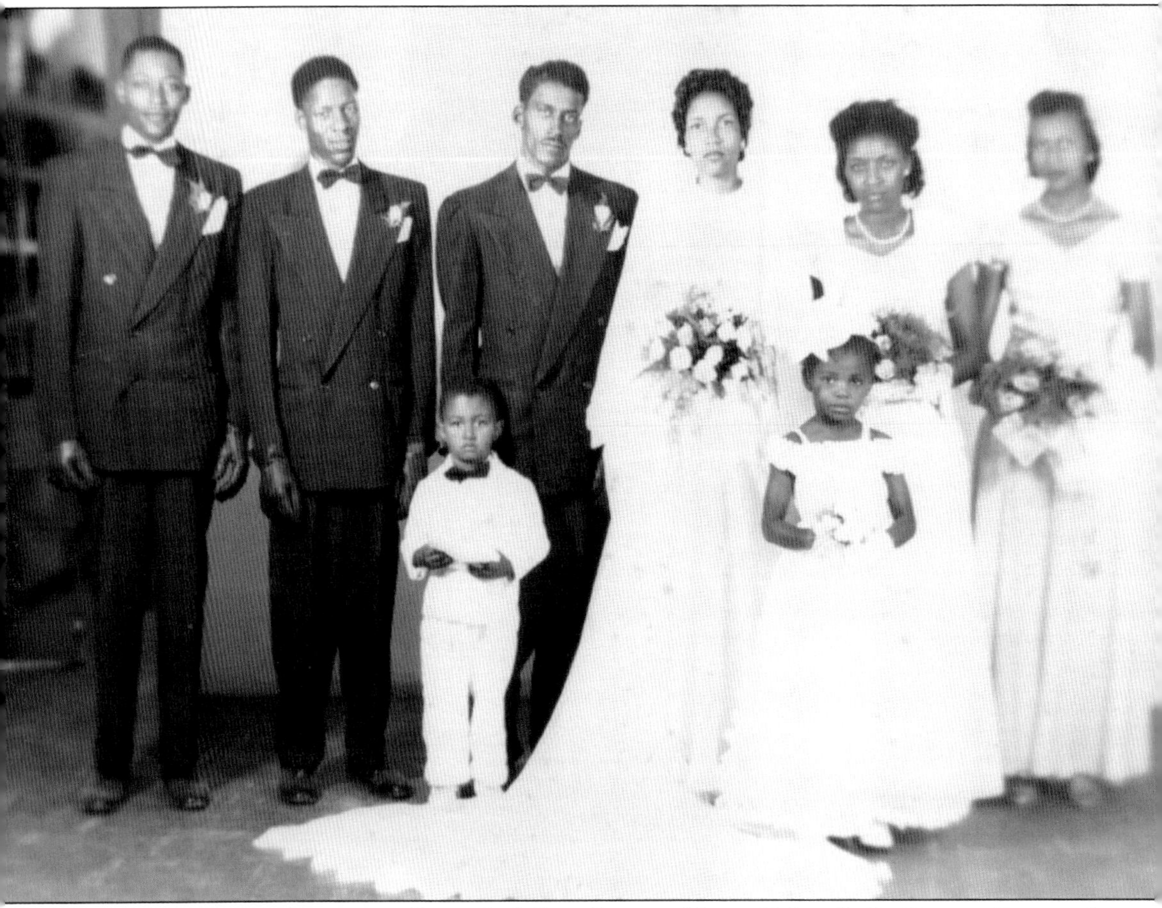

WEDDING, 1948 (LAFAYETTE PARISH). Gilbert Broussard Jr. and Mary Della Clement Broussard were married on September 25, 1948, at St. Paul's Catholic Church. The couple has been married for 62 years and has two daughters, Shelia and Deborah. Standing from left to right, members of the wedding party are Vernon Dugas, Wilfred Dugas, Gilbert (groom), Mary (bride), Viola Sonnier, and Ella Glaude; the ring bearer is a member of the Hayes family, and the flower girl is a member of the Johnson family. (Courtesy of Deborah Broussard.)

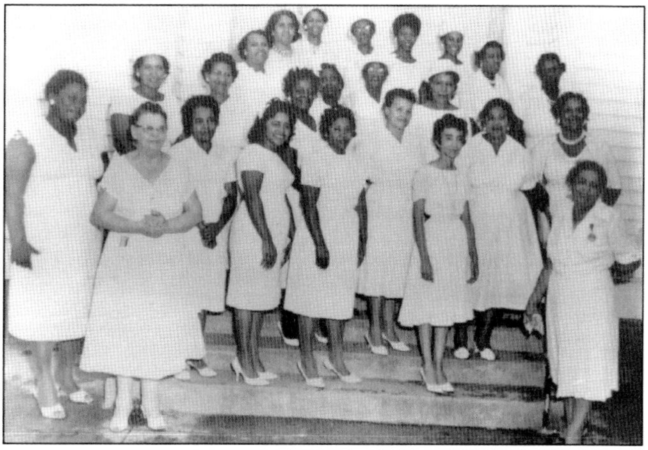

Ladies Auxiliary (Lafayette Parish). Pictured here are members of the Ladies Auxiliary of Peter Claver at St. Theresa Court, No. 11. They represented St. Paul's Catholic Church. (Courtesy of Louis J. Perret, clerk of court, Lafayette Parish.)

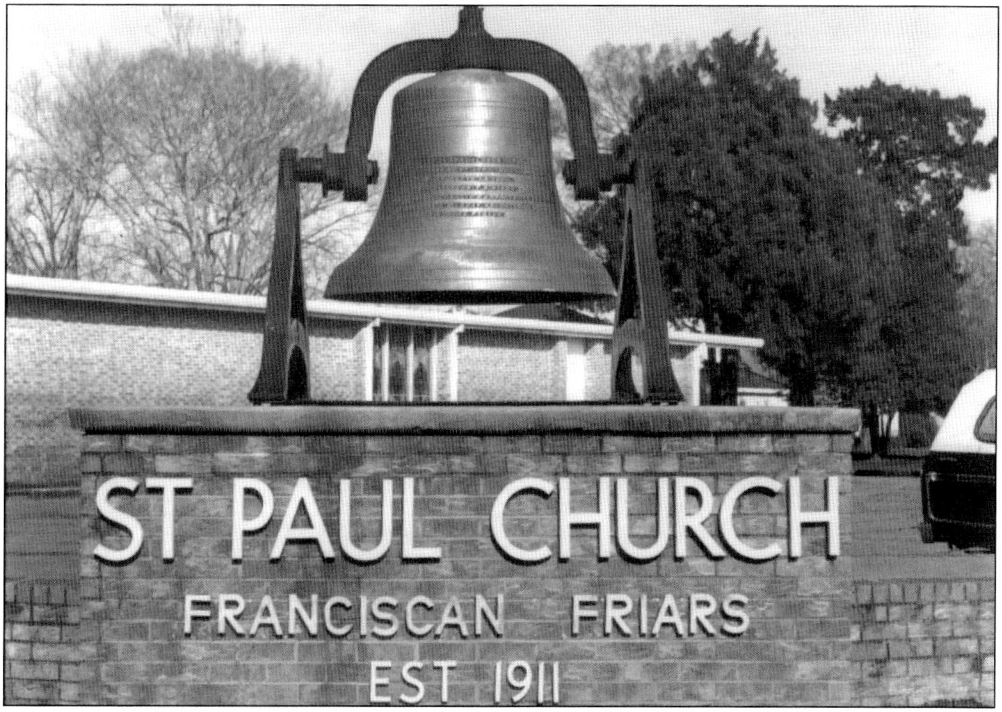

The St. Paul Catholic Church Bell (Lafayette Parish). The church bell represents the journey members of the church took to build their own place of worship. Because people did not have a church home of their own in the early years, they worshipped at St. John's Cathedral, where they sat in the rear because of segregation; they received Holy Communion after all of the white parishioners were served. The current pastor at St. Paul's Catholic Church is Robert Seay, Order of Friars Minor (OFM), who was the first African American priest to serve full-time at a predominately black parish. The bell was given to St. John's Cathedral as a gift of appreciation for allowing black citizens to participate in Mass services. When St. Paul's members built their own place of worship in 1911, and the bell was returned, and it presently hangs in a tall tower, ringing electronically. (Courtesy of Evelyn Zehner.)

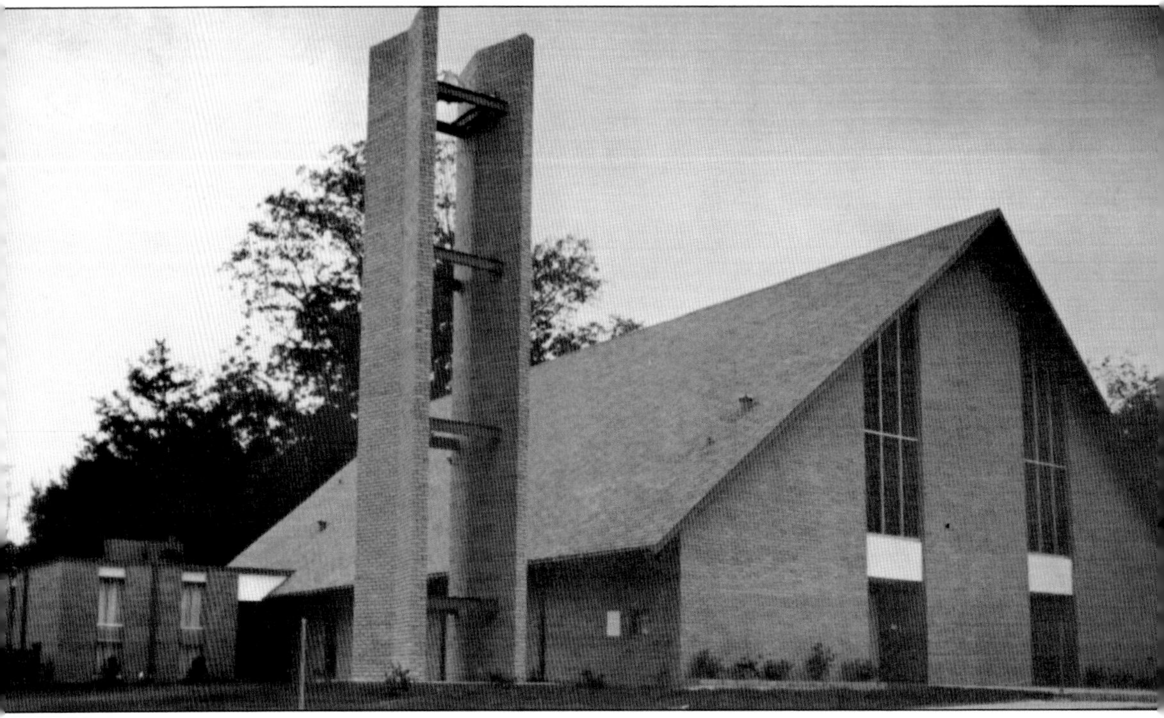

LITTLE ZION MISSIONARY BAPTIST CHURCH (ST. LANDRY PARISH). Little Zion Missionary Baptist Church (formerly named Opelousas African Baptist Church) is 144 years old. The church is located in Opelousas, Louisiana, on the original land where the first church was organized on June 29, 1867. The church began in a blacksmith's shop with a congregation of 16 members under the leadership of Rev. J.P. Davenport. Rev. Charles E. Bryant is the current pastor of the church. He is a graduate of and teaches at Southern University in Baton Rouge, Louisiana. Under his leadership, the church and the community have advanced in educational opportunities for the people. Twelve pastors have served the church through its many years of Christian service. (Courtesy of Eula M. Dell, historian.)

Marking History (St. Landry Parish). This historical marker denotes some of the important dates of the Little Zion Baptist Church's history. The church is located in Opelousas, Louisiana. An acre of land was donated by the police jury of St. Landry Parish for the purpose of building the church on August 20, 1869. The natural stream bordering the church ground on the west side was used for baptisms in the early years of the church. The current building pictured on the previous page was built in 1968. The church also served as the first Negro High School until the 1950s. (Courtesy of Eula M. Dell, historian.)

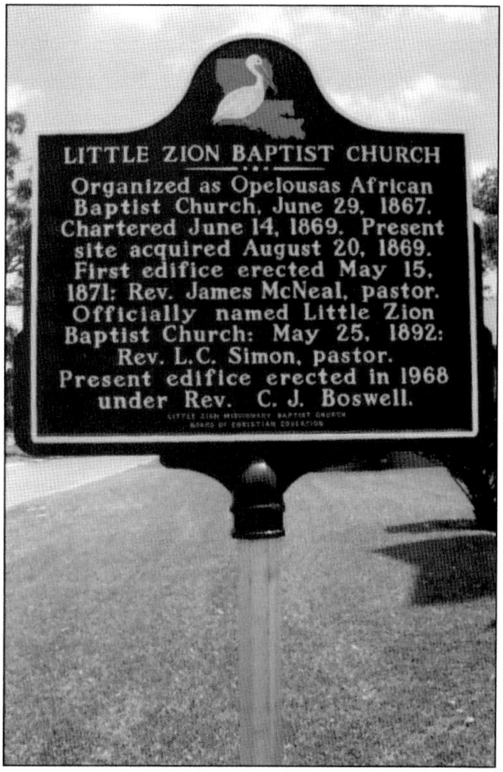

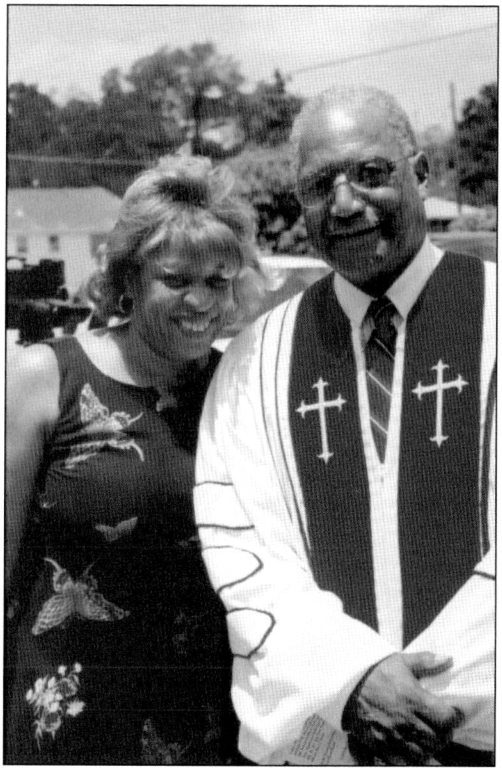

Installation of Church's Historical Marker (St. Landry Parish). Pictured here are Anna Simmons, the first female African American mayor of Opelousas, Louisiana, with Rev. Charles Bryant, pastor of Little Zion Baptist Church, at the celebration of the installation of the church's historical marker. Reverend Bryant is the current pastor of the church and has served since 1994. (Courtesy of Eula M. Dell, historian.)

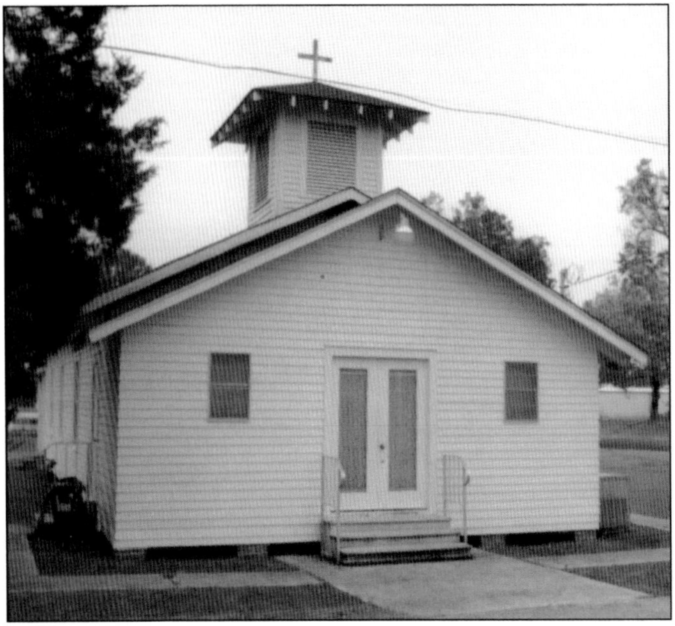

Original Bethlehem Baptist Church (St. Martin Parish). Established in 1876, Bethlehem Baptist Church is located in Breaux Bridge, Louisiana, and is 144 years old. Founded on property donated by the Anderson family, early baptisms at the church were held at Bayou Teche. The church served as a school to educate black children from grades first through seventh until it was severely damaged by the storm and flood of 1927. The building was destroyed, and church records were lost. (Courtesy of Thelma C. Alex.)

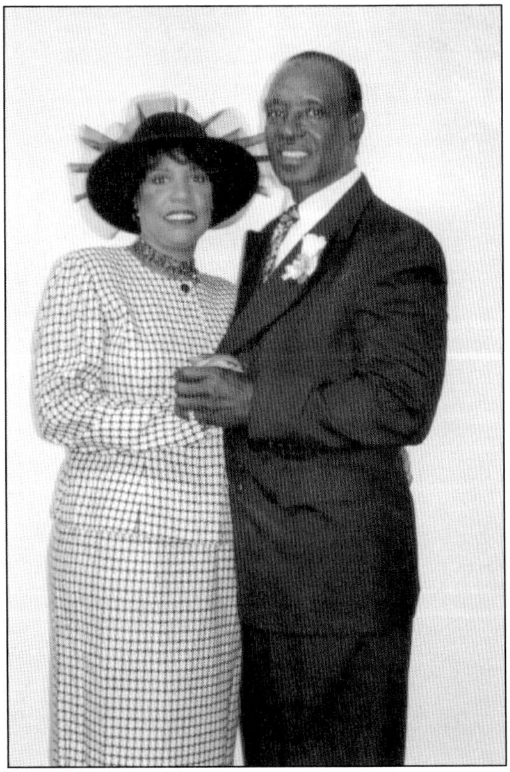

Bethlehem Baptist Church in Breaux Bridge, Louisiana (St. Martin Parish). Pictured here are Rev. Leroy Banks Jr. and his wife, Zelma Banks (first lady of the church). Banks is the current pastor of Bethlehem Baptist Church. Under the leadership of Reverend Banks, who became pastor in June 2003, a new edifice was built in 2008, and the church was relocated to Latiolais Road in Breaux Bridge, Louisiana. The new church has a baptismal pool, a large worshipping sanctuary, and a large kitchen and dining area. (Courtesy of Rev. Leroy Banks Jr.)

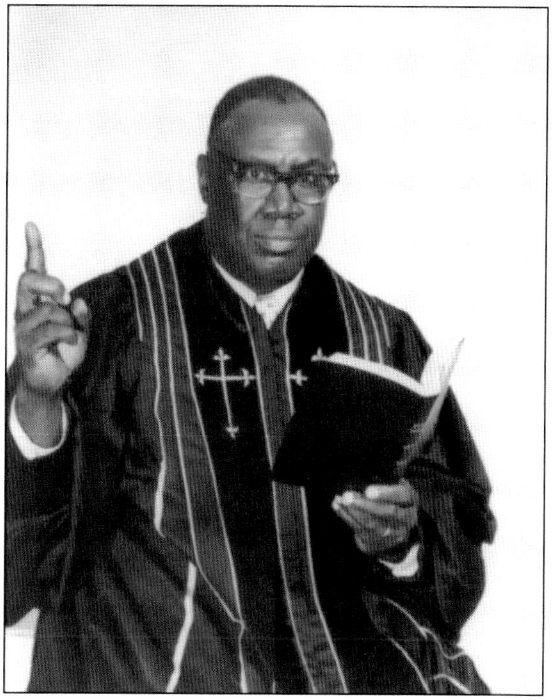

Rev. Livingston Alex (St. Martin Parish). The church's history shows that one of the longest-living pastors, Rev. Livingston Alex, grew up in Bethlehem Baptist Church and served as pastor from 1959 until his death in 1998. At the beginning of his career, Reverend Alex was paid a sum of $2.50 per month as pastor of the church; later, he earned a sum of $27.80 per month. Many of his duties included preaching, teaching, carpentry, lawn care, and cemetery care. Reverend Alex was a science teacher and taught chemistry, biology, and physics in Lafayette and St. Martin Parishes. In 1995, Breaux Bridge honored him by declaring Livingston Alex Day and presented him with the key to the city. (Courtesy of Thelma C. Alex.)

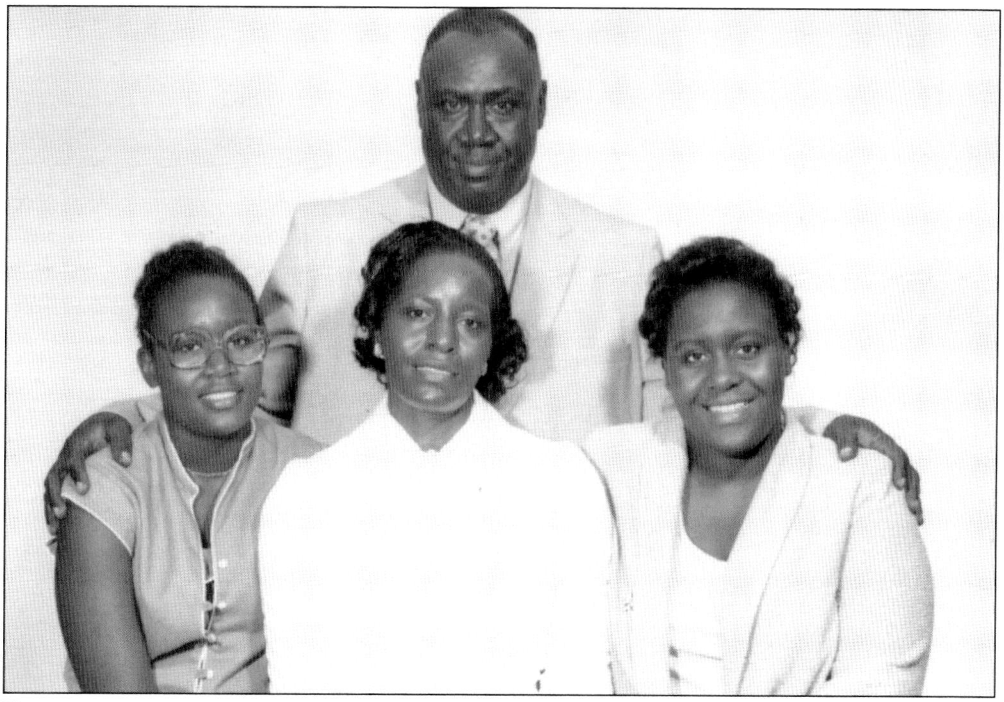

The Livingston Alex Family (St. Martin Parish). Pictured are Rev. Livingston Alex (deceased) with his wife and former first lady of the church, Thelma C. Alex, and their daughters, Yvette Alex (left) and Joslyn Alex. Thelma is a retired school librarian and was the owner of Alex's Day Care Center. Yvette is a doctoral instructor of political science at Indiana University, and Joslyn is a Louisiana attorney. (Courtesy of Thelma C. Alex.)

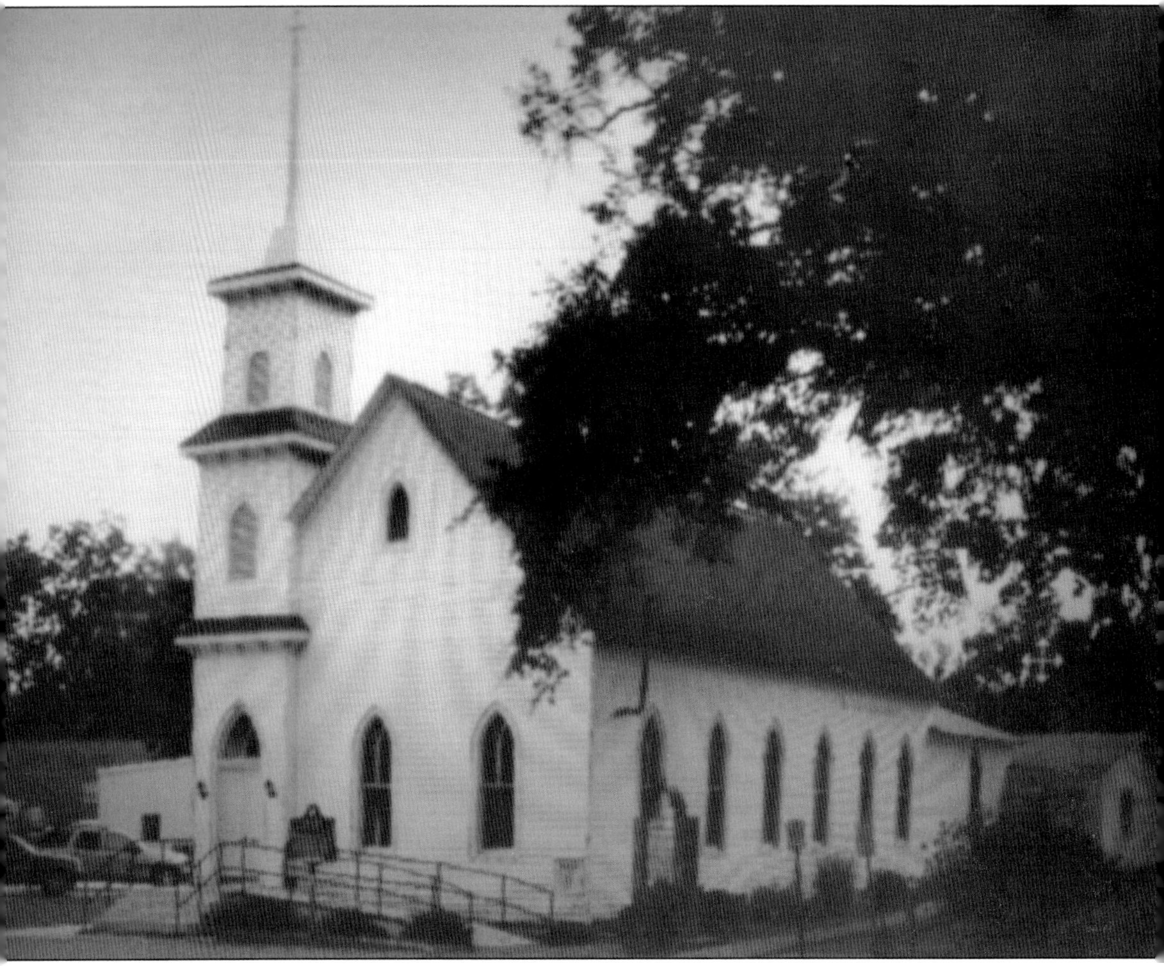

St. Mary Congregational Church (Vermilion Parish). Located in Abbeville, Louisiana, St. Mary Congregational Church is 140 years old. The land was purchased in 1884 from Nickson and Trahan according to courthouse records. Boston Connor, James Robinson, and John Joiner were church trustees present at the sale of the land. Paul Joiner, August Norbert, and Mack Joiner were church deacons who were also present. The church was organized in 1885 under the auspices of the American Missionary Association (AMA) in New York City. After the Emancipation Proclamation, people who believed in the human rights and dignity of mankind moved to the South and began to establish schools and churches for the freed people of color. The congregational churches basically followed Calvinist, Puritan, and congregational beliefs, where in freedom, Congregationalists supported each other in the work of Christ through denominational structures. St. Mary Congregational Church served as the first school for children in Abbeville, Louisiana. Rev. Kevin Williams is the current pastor of the historical church. (Courtesy of Rev. Kevin Williams.)

HISTORICAL MARKER (VERMILION PARISH). The historical marker located in front of St. Mary's Congregational Church denotes the year that the church was established and the name of the first pastor, Rev. James A. Herod. The church is located in Abbeville, Louisiana. (Author's collection.)

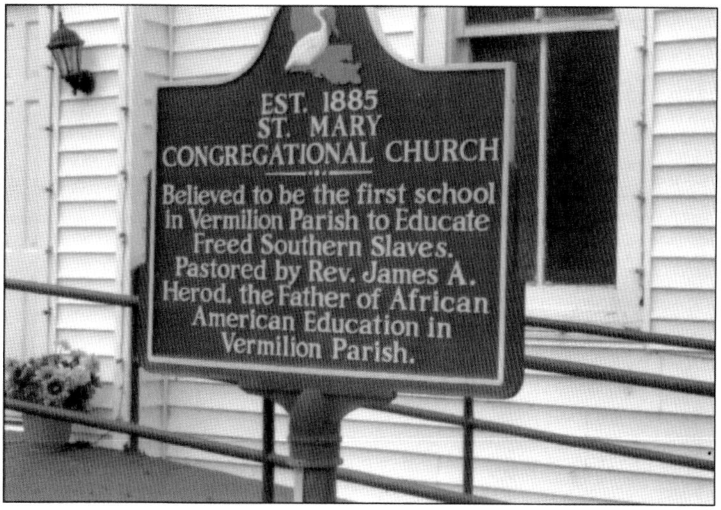

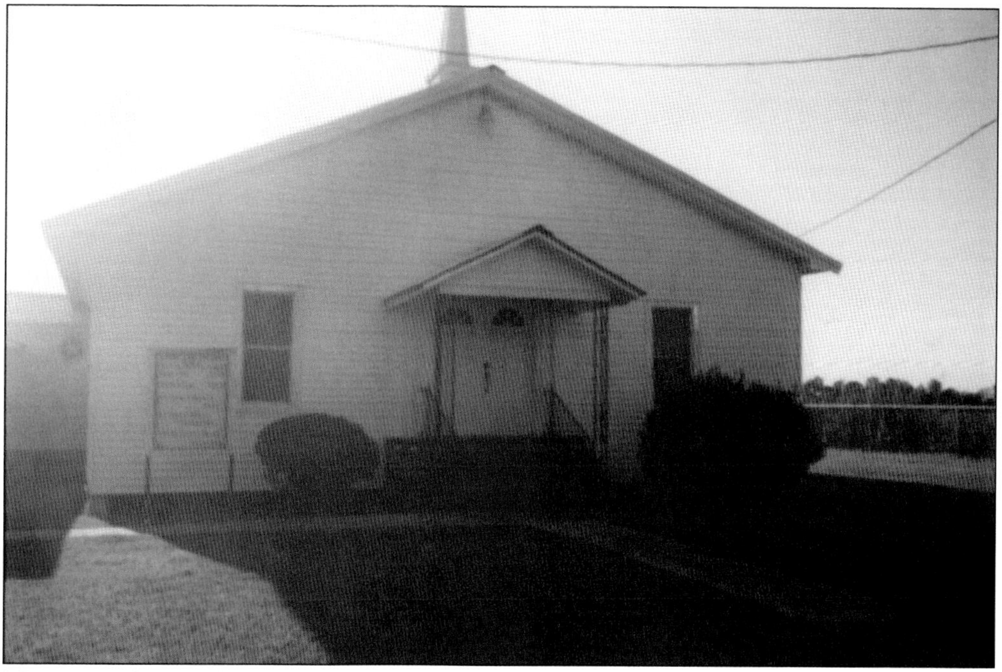

MARYLAND CHAPEL CHRISTIAN METHODIST EPISCOPAL CHURCH (ACADIA PARISH). Established in 1870, Maryland Chapel Christian Methodist Episcopal Church is located in Branch, Louisiana, and is formerly known as Plaquemine Burlee. It is believed to be the first settlement in Acadia Parish. The land was donated by Jessie Clark, a white landowner. The church served as the first school for black children. The church also has its first female minister, Maggie C. Banks, who was licensed by her husband, Jessie C. Banks Sr., who is elder and pastor of the 131-year-old church and serves a membership that continues to grow in leadership and in spirit. The church is a part of the New Orleans district of the South Louisiana Conference of the Fourth Episcopal District, which is comprised of Louisiana and Mississippi. (Courtesy of Reva Monroe.)

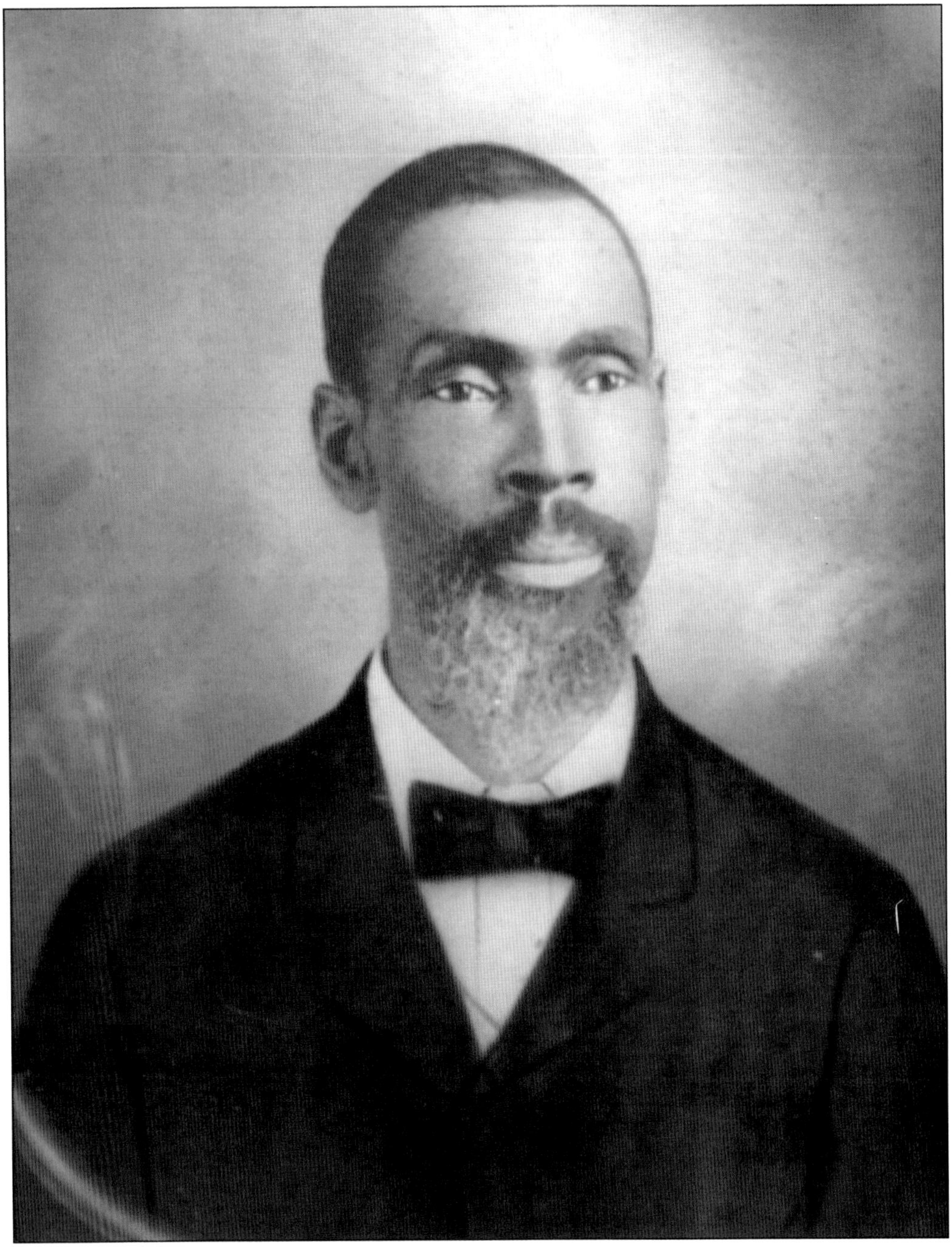

REV. JOHN BERRY LIVINGSTON (IBERIA PARISH). During the tenure of Reverend Livingston, Mount Calvary Baptist Church grew from 18 to 180 members. The church has had only five pastors from 1875 to the present: J.B. Livingston, F.M. Boley, H.M. Jones, Larry W. Norbert, and Jason R. Tolliver. The church was used as a school to educate black children in New Iberia when no public schools were available for them. In 1902, he named his home the Field Street School. Finally, the Iberia School Board built a school in West End Park and named the school J.B. Livingston Elementary in honor of Reverend Livingston. It no longer exists, but the memories remain in hearts of the students who attended the school. (Courtesy of Gwendolyn D. Loud.)

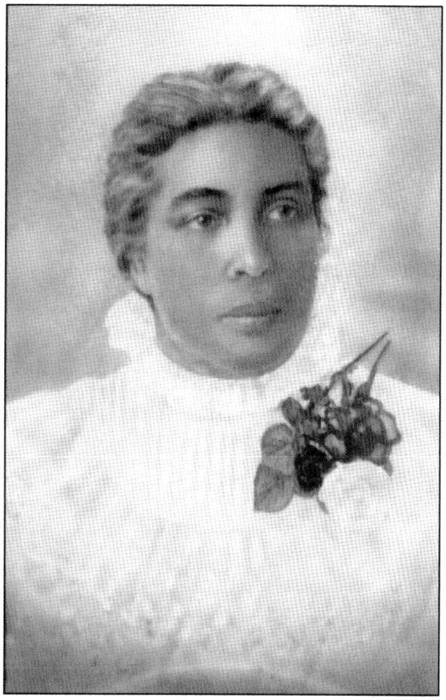

First Lady of Mount Calvary Baptist Church (Iberia Parish). Sister Livingston, wife of Pastor Livingston, married John Berry in Freetown, Louisiana, in 1871. Pastor Livingston had to wait for her hand in marriage because her parents said that she was too young. Later, the couple became the parents of nine children: six girls and three boys. She and Pastor Livingston opened their home as a school for black children on the west side of New Iberia. In 1902, he named his home the Field Street School. Their daughters actually taught other black children in New Iberia to read and write. (Courtesy Gwendolyn D. Loud.)

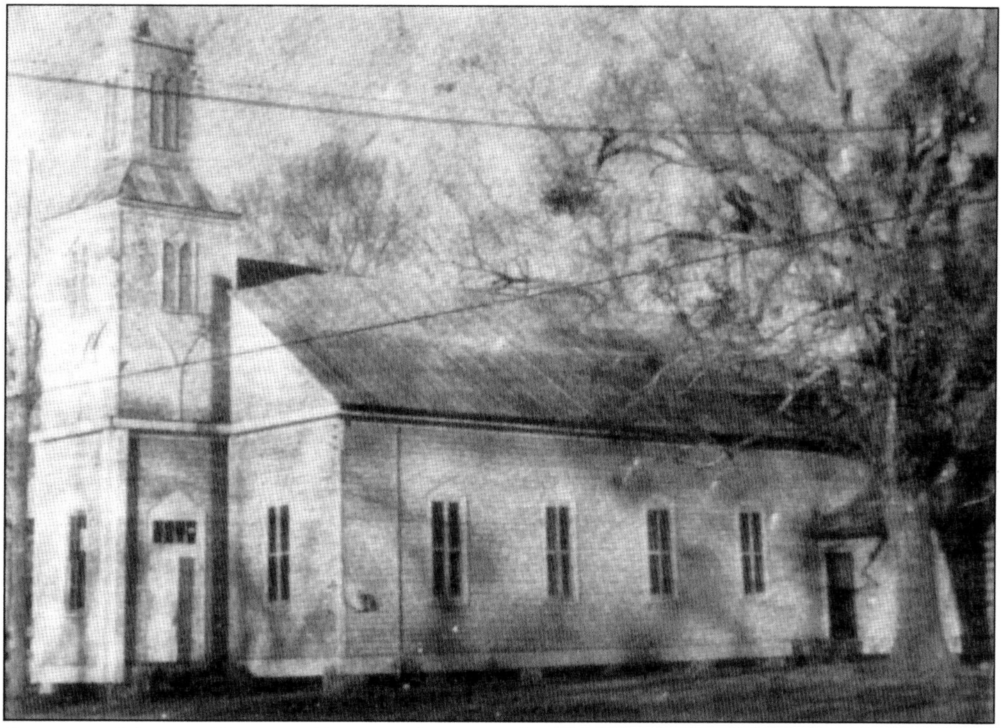

Original Mount Calvary Baptist Church (Iberia Parish). Established in 1875 with a membership of 18, Mount Calvary Baptist Church is one of the oldest churches in New Iberia. The first pastor was Rev. John Berry Livingston. Pastor Livingston also organized and was president of the Sixth District Missionary Baptist Association. Livingston served the church for 44 years until his death in 1922. (Courtesy of Gwendolyn D. Loud.)

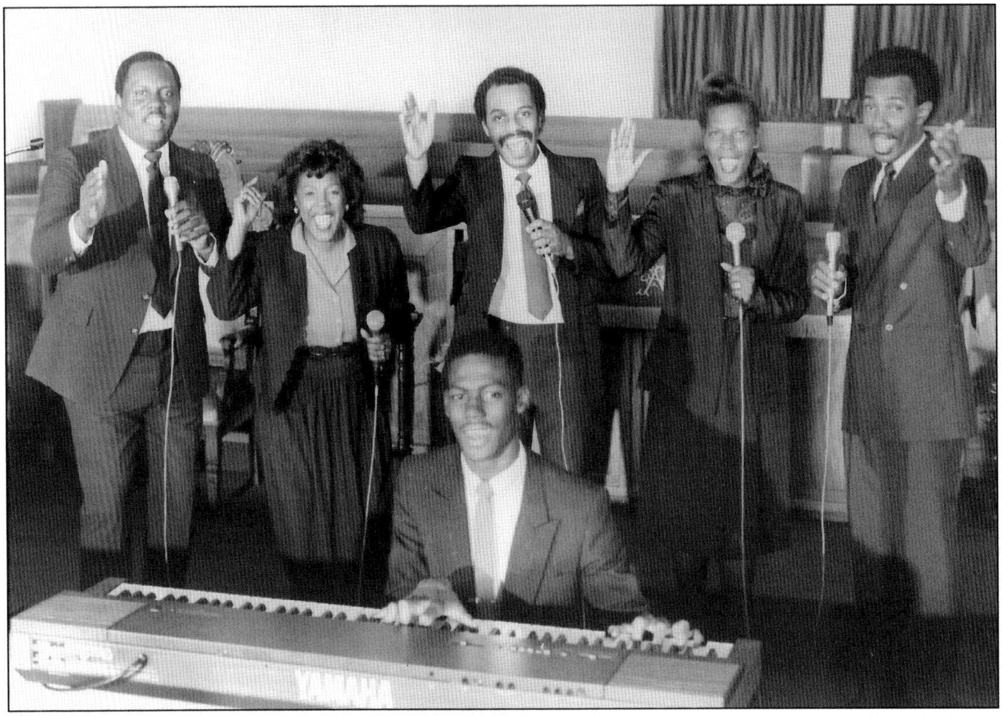

Revival (Lafayette Parish). A look back shows a phenomenal inspirational band whose performances delighted audiences in churches and other places where it performed gospel and other spiritual songs. The band performed at the Vatican in Rome, Italy. Some of the members pictured here include Sylvia M. Cluse, John Freeman, and John Nezey. (Courtesy of Edith G. Dupré Library Archives and Special Collections.)

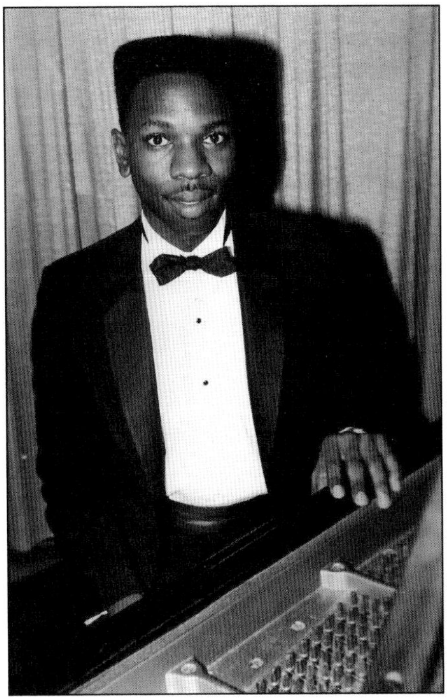

Master Musician (Lafayette Parish). Clark Joseph was born, raised, and educated in Lafayette, Louisiana. He was destined to be a grand musician, and his instruments of choice are the piano and organ. His educational accomplishments include earning Bachelor of Music and Master of Music degrees in piano performance from the University of Southwestern Louisiana. He also received his Master of Science in education from Fordham University in New York City. He conducts and participates in music workshops and seminars throughout the world, and since 2006 he has been a guest lecturer at Southern Methodist University's Perkins School of Theology in the Sacred Music Division. Joseph's musical renditions have touched and inspired the lives of children and adults. (Courtesy of Edith G. Dupré Library Archives and Special Collections.)

Two

Education Heroes and Schools

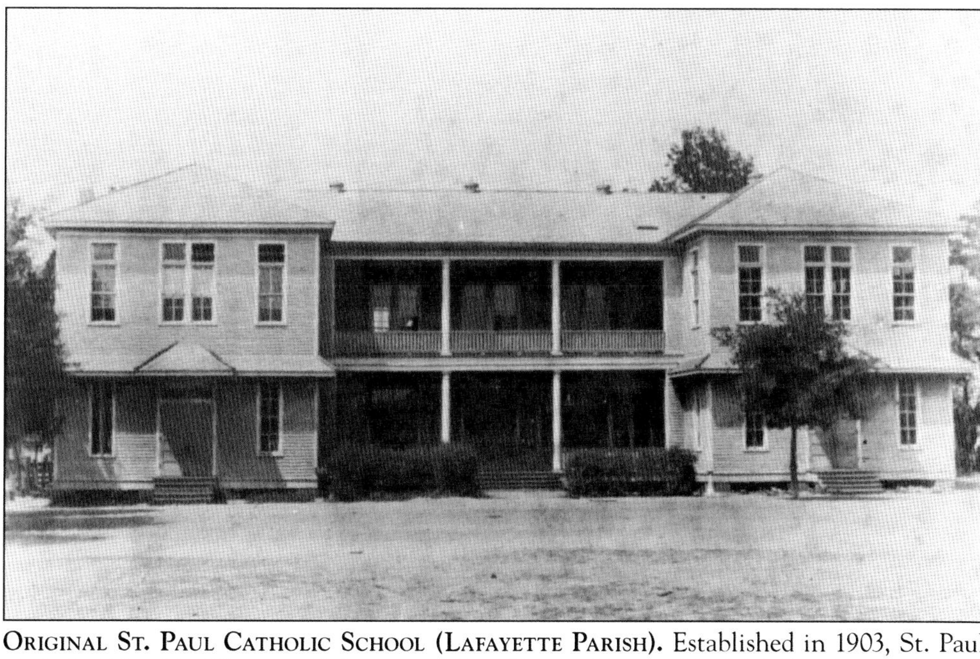

Original St. Paul Catholic School (Lafayette Parish). Established in 1903, St. Paul Catholic School is 108 years old. It was established by the Sisters of the Holy Family in Lafayette, Louisiana. The school pictured here served as both an elementary and high school. It was torn down to make way for a new school. Later, the school changed its name from St. Paul Catholic School to Holy Family Catholic School. The convent that was home to many of the Sisters of the Holy Family is being renovated to create a larger and more modern library for students. The current principal of Holy Family School is Rogers Griffin. (Courtesy of Louis J. Perret, clerk of court, Lafayette Parish.)

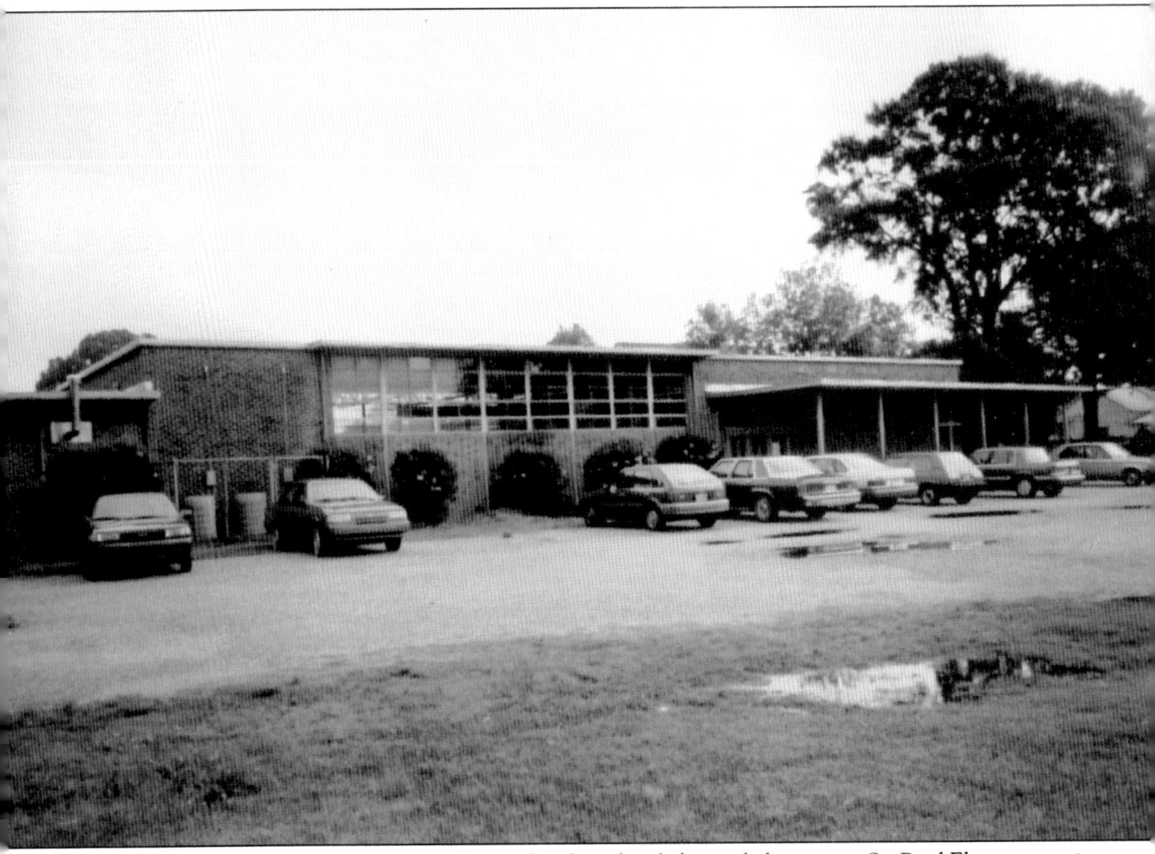

Holy Family School (Lafayette Parish). The school, formerly known as St. Paul Elementary, is over 100 years old and continues to be staffed by lay teachers because of the diminishing faculty of the Sisters of the Holy Family. The school, supported by parents, the church, and the community, is growing and enrollment is increasing. Rogers Griffin is the current principal of the school. (Courtesy of the Lafayette Diocese Archives and Research Department.)

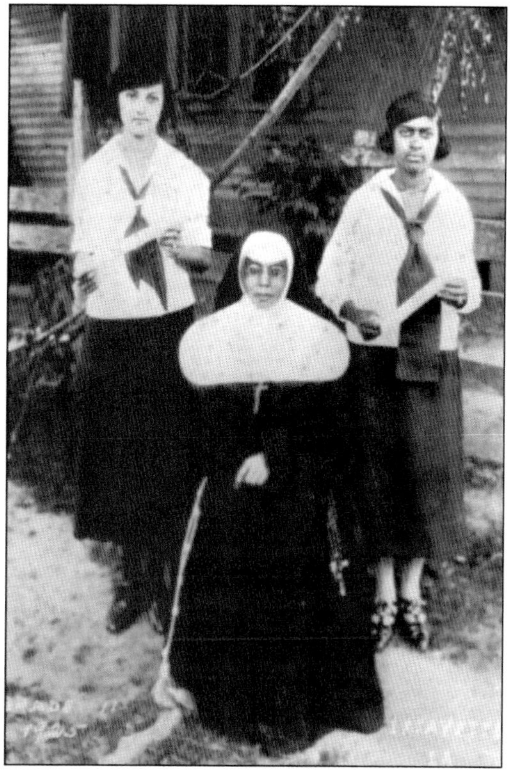

St. Paul School High School Graduates (Lafayette Parish). Pictured here are the first high school graduates of St. Paul High School in 1925. From left to right are Consuella Alexis, Sister Mary Borgia (principal), and Irene Jacquet. The students received teaching certificates in Pitman shorthand and speed-typing courses. (From the O.C. "Dan" Guillot Collection, courtesy of Louis Perret, clerk of court, Lafayette Parish.)

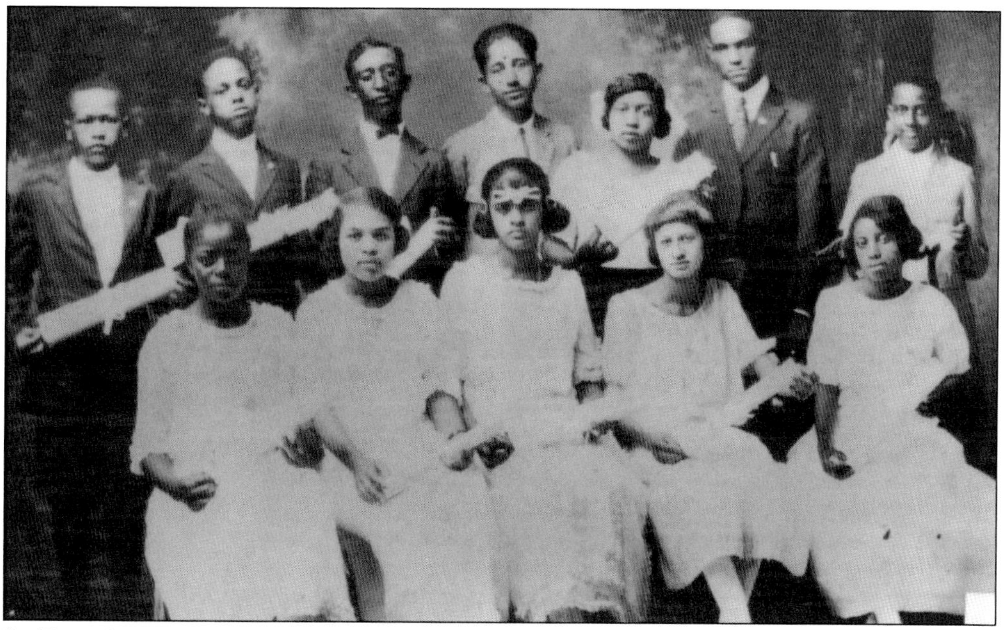

St. Paul Catholic School and Elementary School Graduates (Lafayette Parish). These students graduated in 1923. Pictured from left to right are (first row) Roberta E. Johnson, Ophelia Jones, Zola Amond, Gertrude Claiborne, and Martha Brown; (second row) Kermit Patty, Gabriel Jacquet Jr., Felix Mouton, Victor Broussard, Zoe M. LeBlanc, Robert Green, and Earl Jacquet. (From the O.C. "Dan" Guillot Collection, courtesy of Louis Perret, clerk of court, Lafayette Parish.)

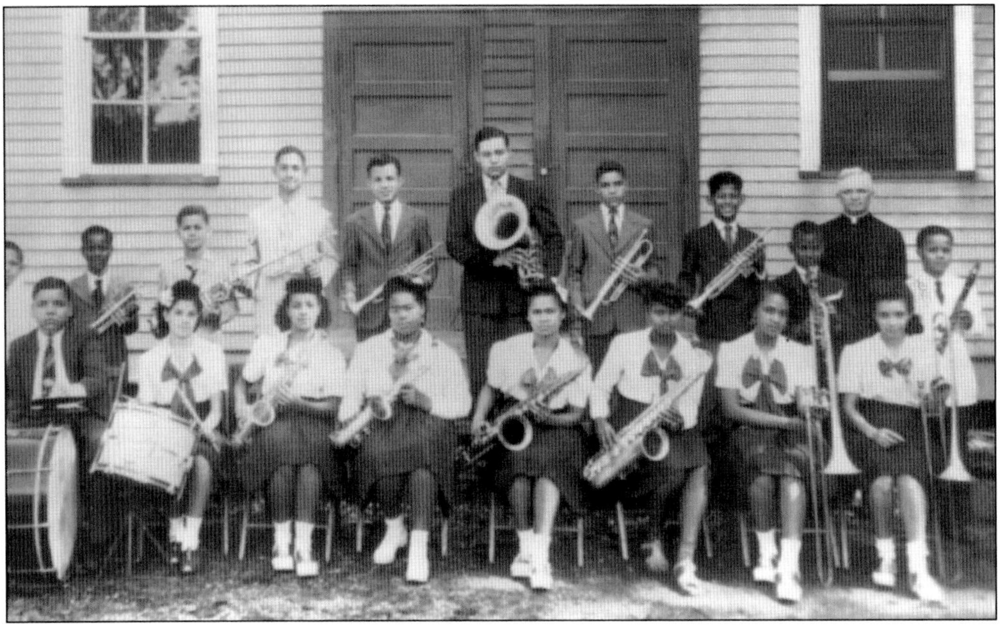

St. Paul Catholic School Band (Lafayette Parish). The St. Paul Catholic School band shows some prominent citizens when they were students. Curt Mouton (first row, far left) is seated with the drums. His musical career spanned more than 50 years. He served as organist for St. Anthony's Catholic Church in Lafayette. Norman C. Francis (second row, fifth from the left) is the longest-serving university president of an American college, Xavier University of Louisiana located in New Orleans, and has been in the position for 43 years. He is the first lay president of the black Catholic university. Dr. Francis was born and raised in Lafayette. He is also the first African American student to graduate from Loyola University New Orleans. He earned his law degree from Loyola University Law School in 1955. In 2006, he was awarded the highest civilian award, the Medal of Freedom, by Pres. George W. Bush. (Courtesy of Louis J. Perret, clerk of court, Lafayette Parish.)

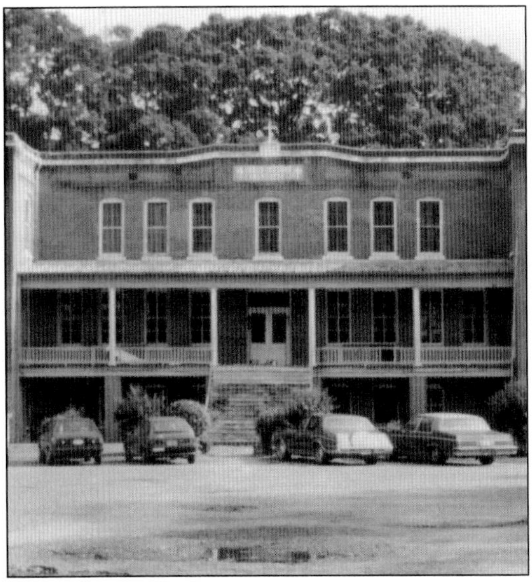

Black Catholic High School (Lafayette Parish). Holy Rosary Institute (HRI) was founded by Fr. Phillip Keller and staffed by the Sisters of the Holy Family. It was the only black Catholic boarding school in America. Later, the school became coed with both males and females attending the school. The dorms were then removed from campus. The school was recently returned to the Sisters of the Holy Family by the Lafayette Diocese. A group of alumni students is working tirelessly to restore Holy Rosary as a vital part of the community. The school is historically preserved and contains a wealth of history about some of the world's best leaders and educators. (Courtesy of the Lafayette Diocese Archives and Research Department.)

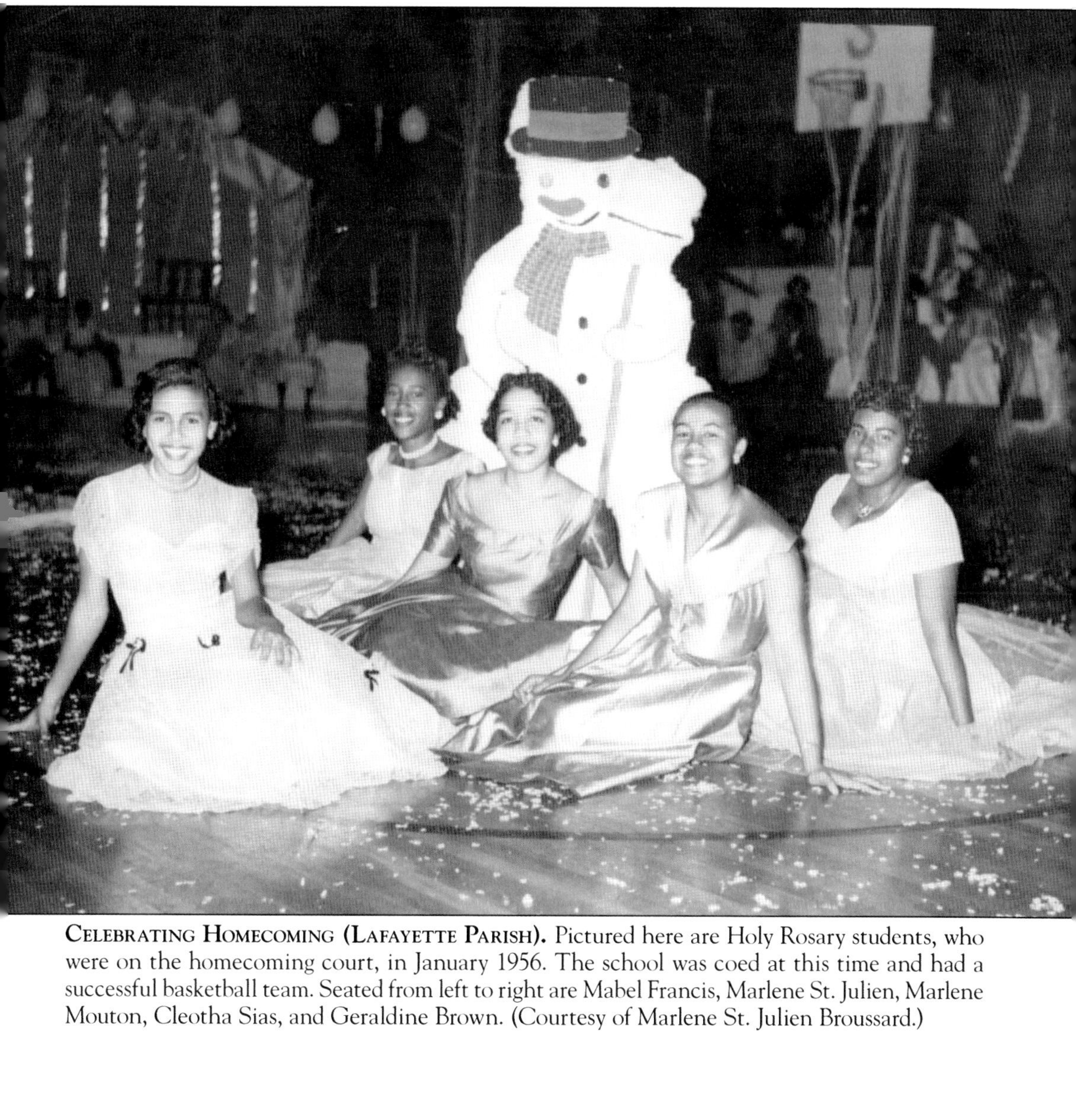

CELEBRATING HOMECOMING (LAFAYETTE PARISH). Pictured here are Holy Rosary students, who were on the homecoming court, in January 1956. The school was coed at this time and had a successful basketball team. Seated from left to right are Mabel Francis, Marlene St. Julien, Marlene Mouton, Cleotha Sias, and Geraldine Brown. (Courtesy of Marlene St. Julien Broussard.)

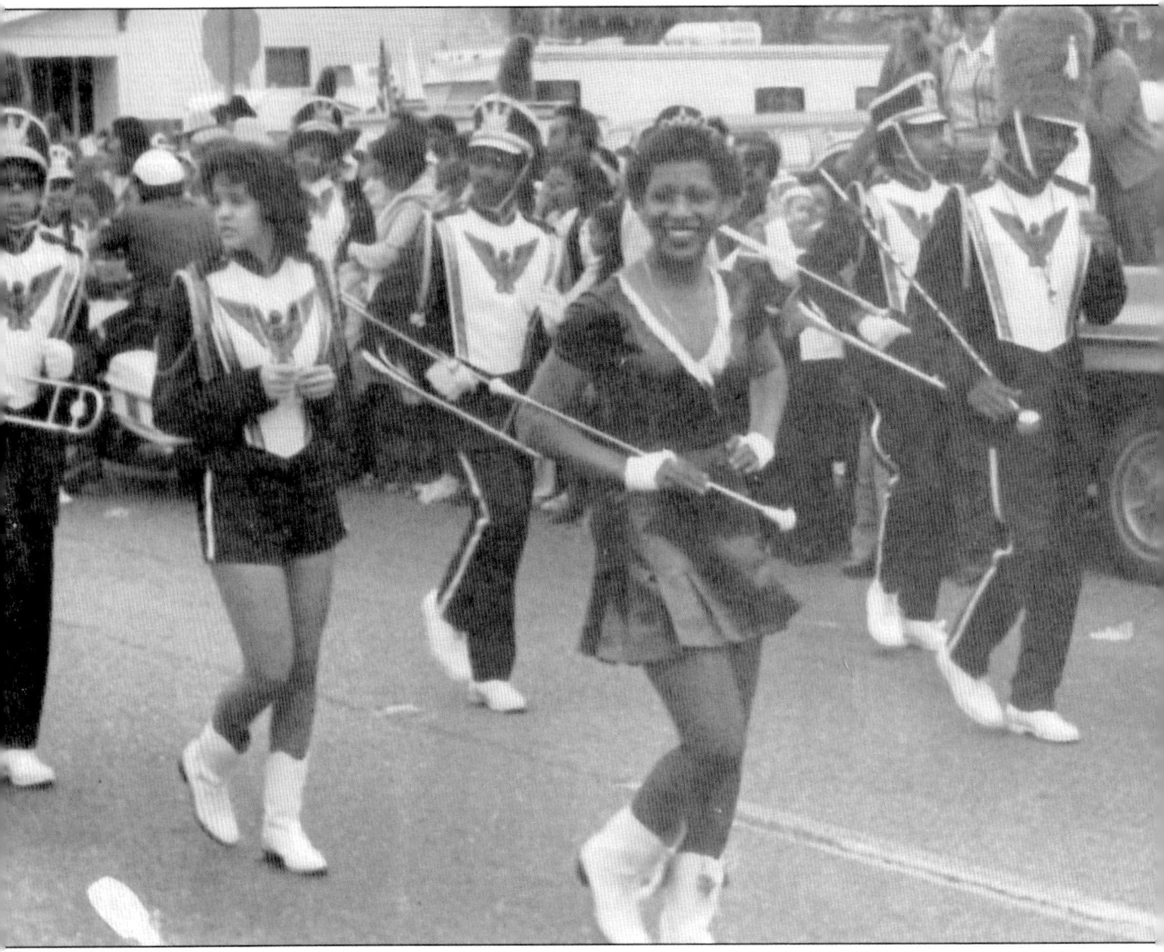

A Look Back (Lafayette Parish) at the Holy Rosary Institute Marching Band and Majorettes. Marching band (Lafayette) members at Holy Rosary Institute practiced long hours and marched in various parades sponsored by the school and the community. The band had a drum major, majorettes, and band members who played their instruments and thrilled crowds with music and dance performances at parades. (Courtesy of the Lafayette Diocese Archives and Research Department.)

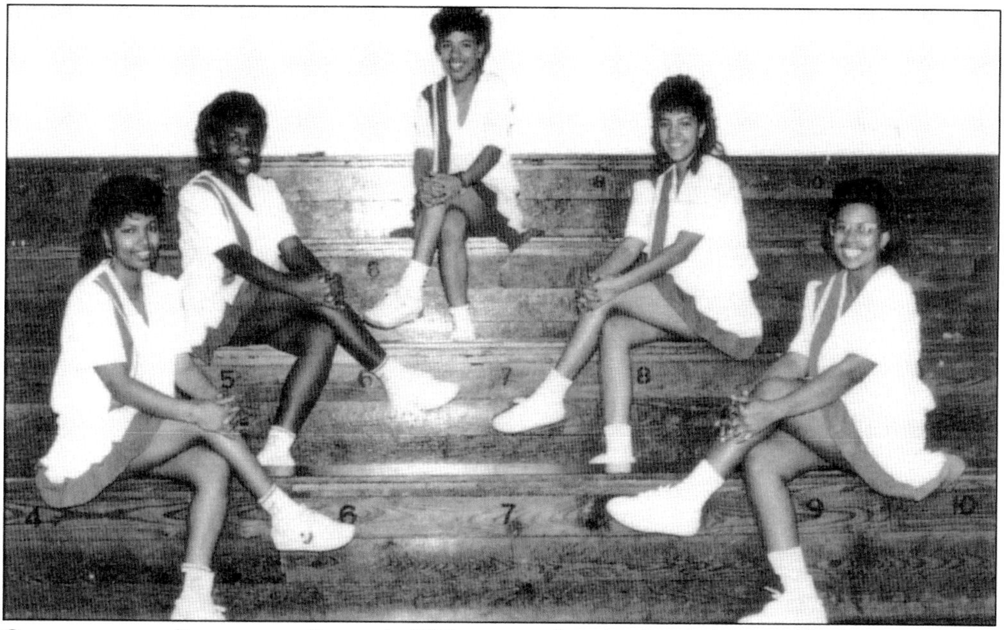

Cheerleaders (Lafayette Parish). HRI varsity cheerleaders led spirit-filled crowds at the basketball games during the school's brighter days. (Courtesy of the Lafayette Diocese Archives and Research Department.)

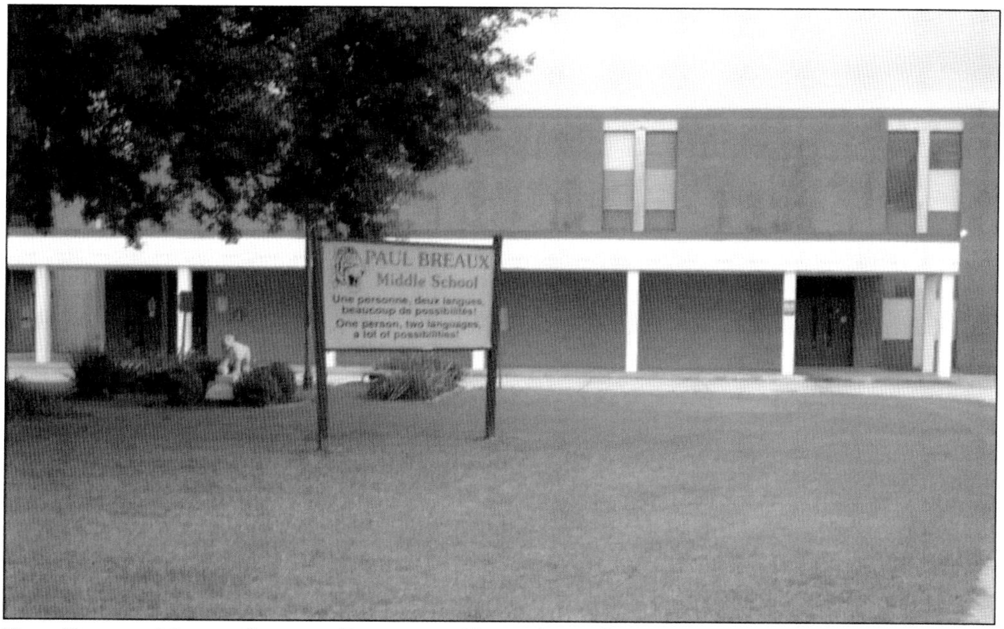

Paul Breaux Middle School (Lafayette Parish). Paul Breaux, a Tuskegee graduate, was an educated man who wanted schools for black children in Lafayette Parish. He worked tirelessly to secure sites for these schools. The early classes were located in an old donated Southern mansion and in local churches. He built a school and later the school board constructed the first black public high school in Lafayette, naming it in honor of Breaux. He was married and the father of two children. He was a member of Trinity CME Church and served on the board of trustees. (Author's collection.)

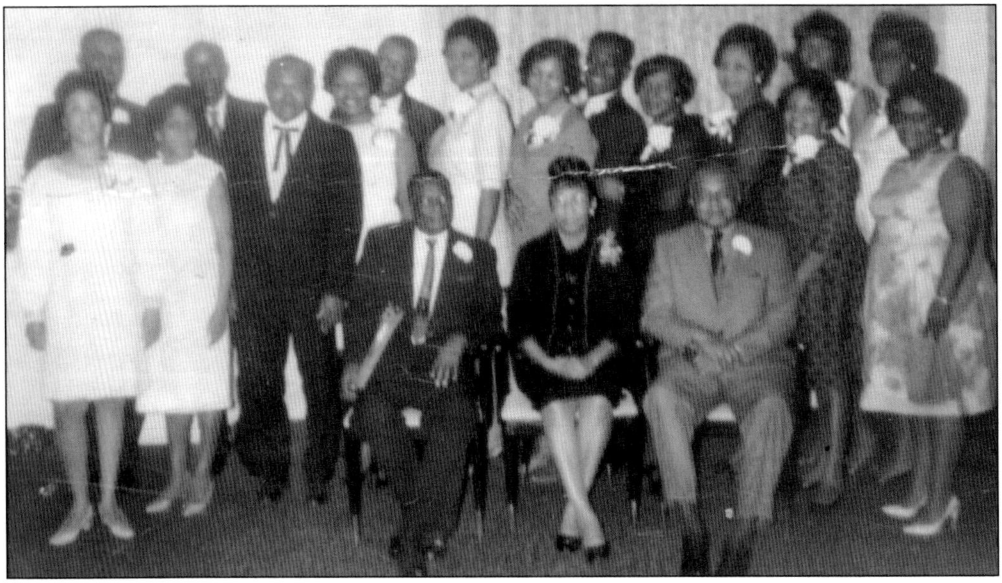

School Memories, Paul Breaux High School Faculty (Lafayette Parish). Lloyd Foote (seated, far right) was the last principal to serve at Paul Breaux High School. W.D. Smith preceded him as principal. Several of the past students, ranging from age 70 to 90, live in Lafayette today and treasure the school and their memories. The school exists today but is a middle school arts academy. The yearbook, the *Paulian*, presents a story of school clubs, sports teams, cheerleaders, and marching bands that produced educators, attorneys, politicians, and community leaders. (Courtesy of Louis J. Perret, clerk of court, Lafayette Parish.)

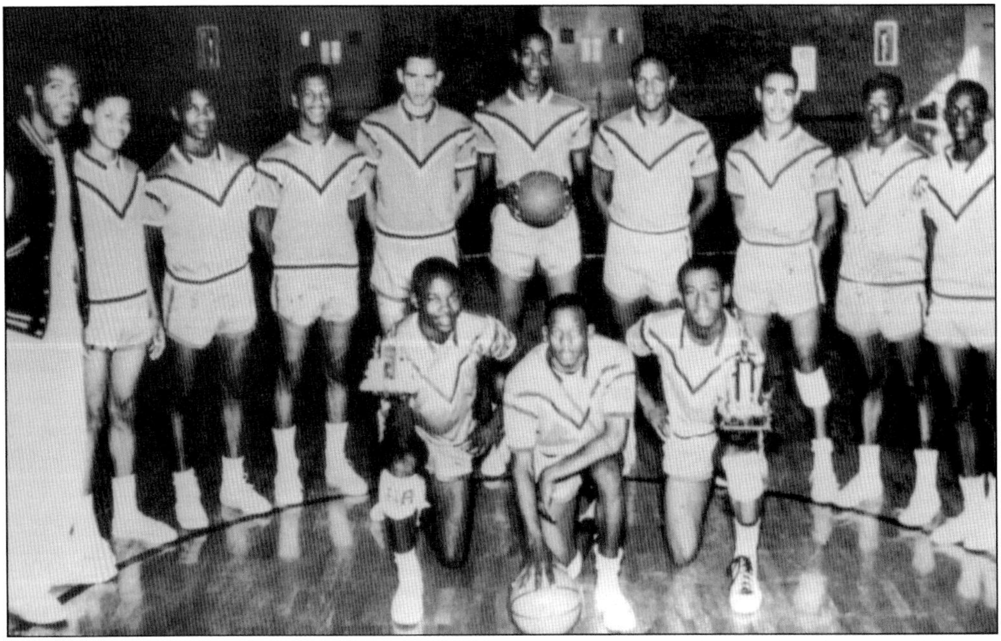

1961–1962 Basketball Team at Paul Breaux High School. Jimmy Singleton and Ernest Nabors were two of the first basketball coaches for the team. The team played local schools as well as schools in other southwest parishes. They were quite successful and won many trophies. (Courtesy of Louis J. Perret, clerk of court, Lafayette Parish.)

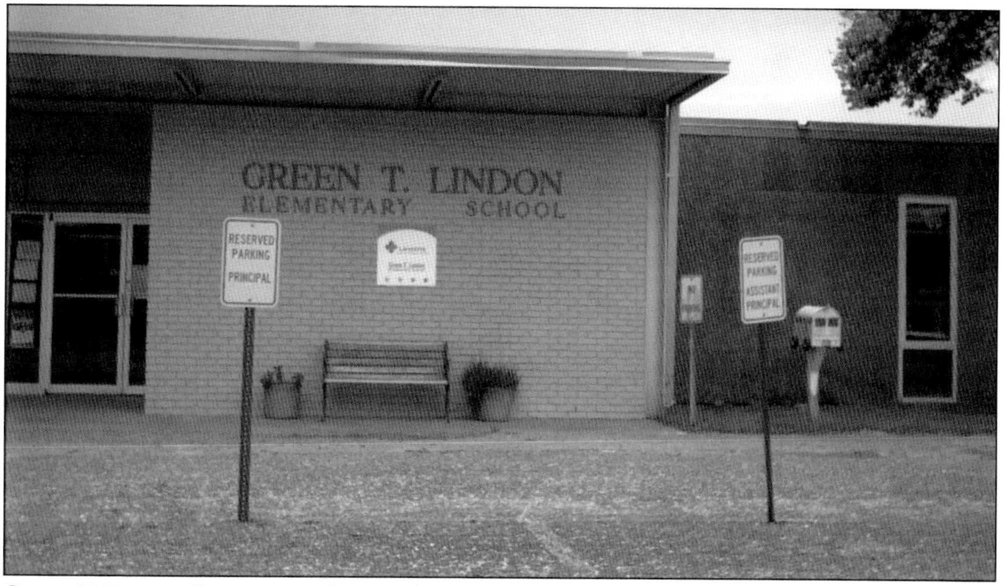

Green T. Lindon Elementary School (Lafayette Parish). The school is located in Youngsville, Louisiana, and named in honor of three African American men who built rural schools on their land to educate black children. Romain Green, Ovide Thibeaux, and John Lindon realized the need for a bigger and more modern school and approached the Lafayette Parish School Board about building one. The school board constructed the school at its present site, and it serves students from pre-kindergarten through the fourth grade. (Author's collection.)

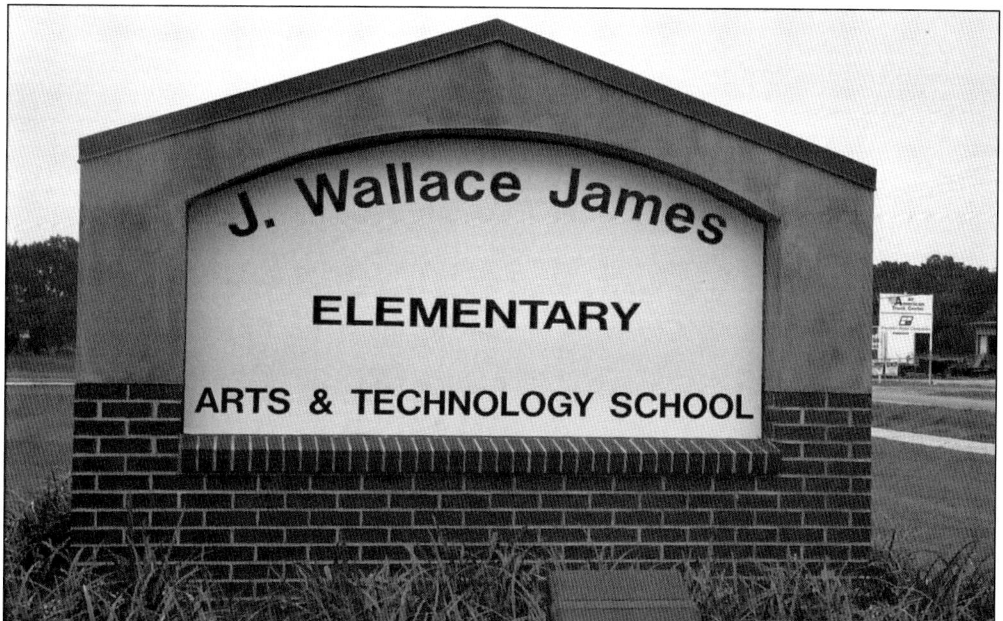

Joseph Wallace James Elementary Arts and Technology School (Lafayette Parish). The original school was closed, and a new school was built on Willow Street and was named J.W. James Elementary Arts and Technology School. Students combine an academic learning program that includes exploring various art forms, such as dance, music, visual arts, and band. (Courtesy of Lafayette Parish School System.)

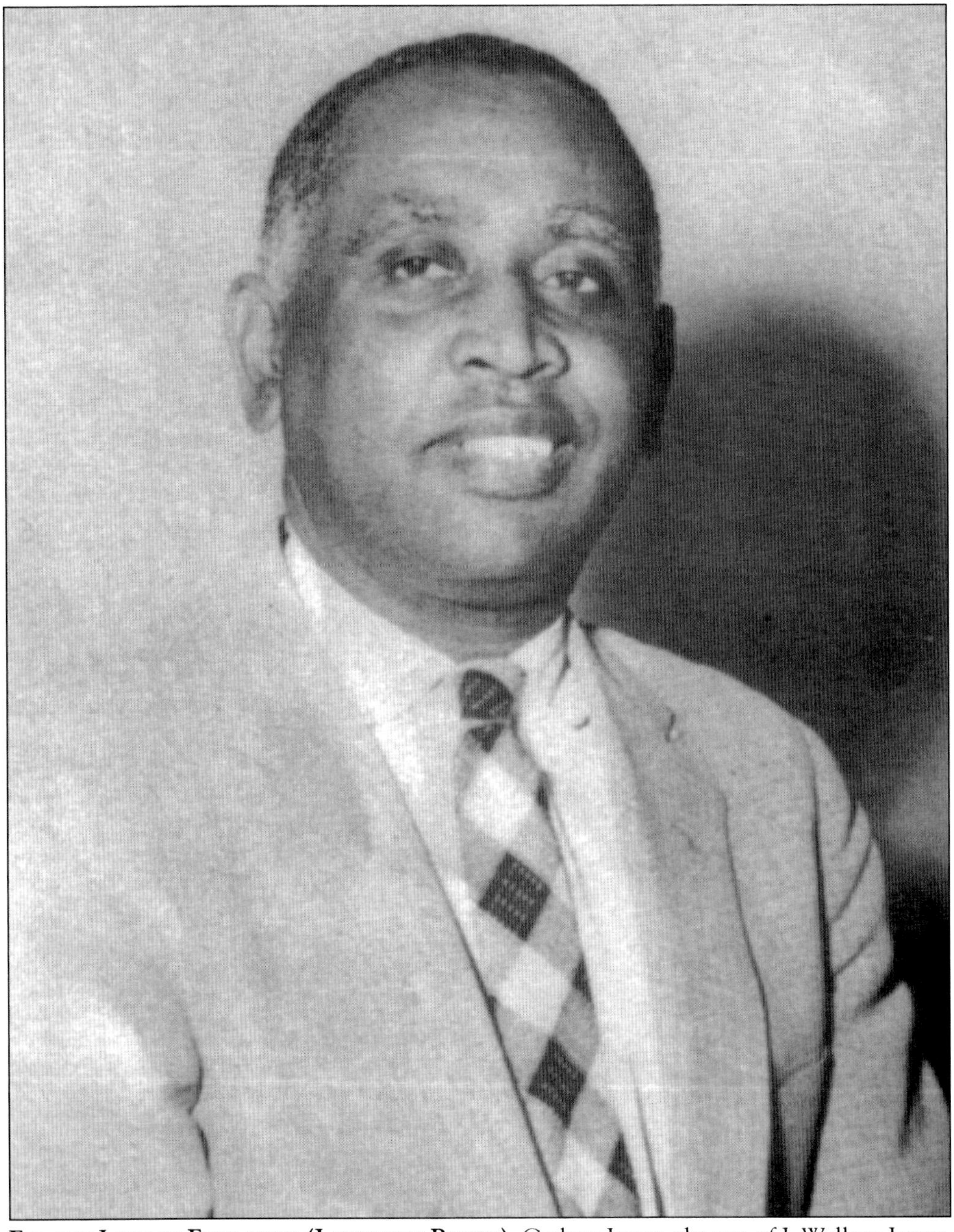

FOR THE LOVE OF EDUCATION (LAFAYETTE PARISH). Carlton James, the son of J. Wallace James, was a pioneer in the education of black students in Lafayette. He led the historical road to the naming of the J. Wallace James School in honor of his father. J.W. James was a community truant officer who made sure that all children attended school. He would pick children up and bring them to school if need be, as no child was allowed to roam around town on a school day. J.W. was the first black citizen to own a gas station in Lafayette, located on Cameron Street. Carlton was a longtime educator, serving as a teacher, a principal at some schools, and later as assistant principal at Paul Breaux High School. He remained an educator until his eyesight began to fail, which led to his retirement. (Author's collection.)

FEMALE PRINCIPALS (LAFAYETTE PARISH). Augustine L. Ventroy (pictured) was one of only two African American female principals who served in Lafayette Parish in the early decades of public school education. The first black female principal was Rita Thibodeaux, who served in the rural areas of Lafayette Parish. Ventroy's educational career spanned 50 years. (Courtesy of Edith G. Dupré Library Archives and Special Collections.)

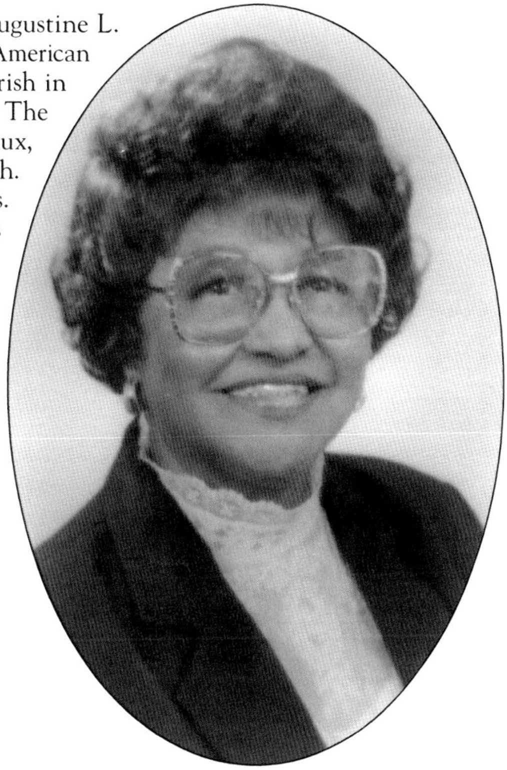

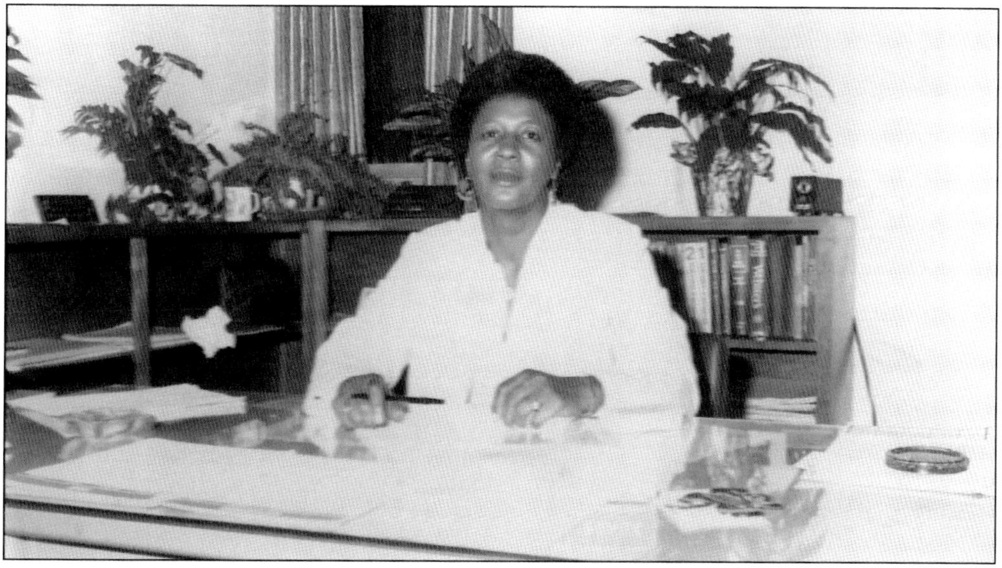

EMPHASIS ON EDUCATION (LAFAYETTE PARISH). Juanita Jackson Thibeaux was a dedicated educator. She is one of the earliest graduates of the University of Southwestern Louisiana, where she still harbors memories of unpleasant experiences because of segregation. Despite the hardships, she is a renowned educator. She was an English teacher, an assistant principal, and an elementary and high school principal at both public and Catholic schools. She taught for more than 50 years and was always was willing to help children at the various schools to achieve all that they could to become the best possible citizens. (Courtesy of Edith G. Dupré Library Archives and Special Collections.)

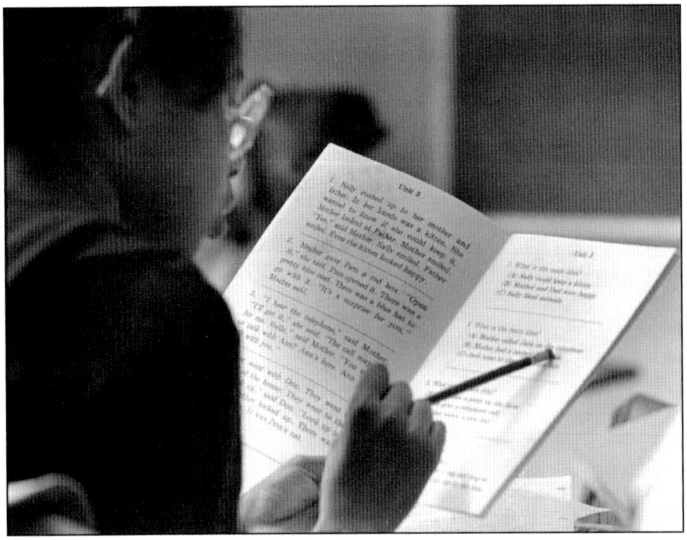

READING (LAFAYETTE PARISH). African American students excel in many areas of the curriculum, and most work hard to succeed in school. A large group will complete high school and further course work at community colleges, colleges, and universities, with some graduating and receiving advanced degrees in their career choices. (Courtesy of Edith G. Dupré Library Archives and Special Collections.)

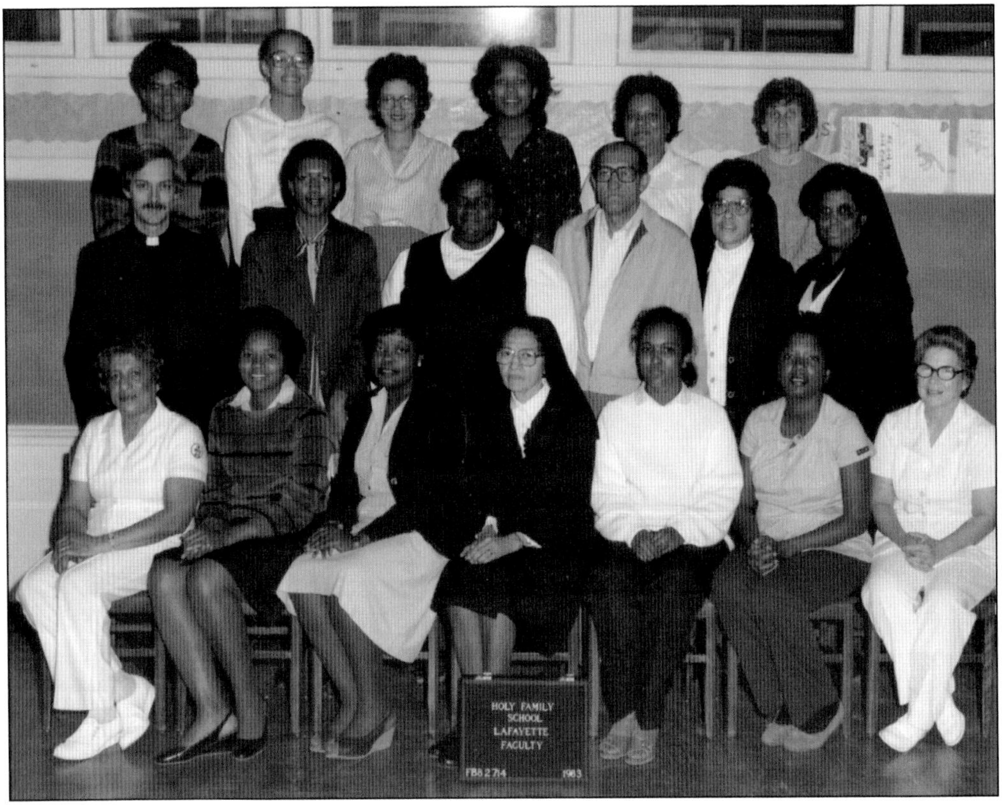

HOLY FAMILY SCHOOL FACULTY AND STAFF, 1983 (LAFAYETTE PARISH). Many parents send their children to parochial schools to learn in a Christian environment. Both Catholic and lay teachers teach classes at the schools, but religion classes are taught only by religious educators and practicing Catholics. (Author's collection.)

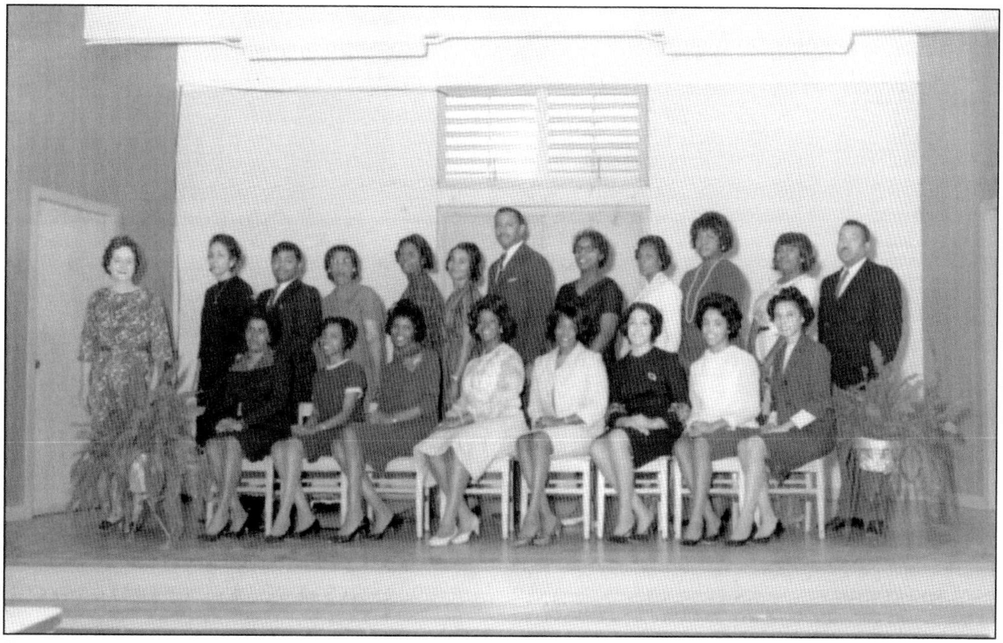

Scott Negro Elementary School (Lafayette Parish). Rita Thibodeaux (standing, behind the plant on the far left) was the first black female principal and is pictured with faculty at the school. Wilma R. Bowles (seated, far left) taught eighth grade at the school. Thibodeaux had a good working relationship with her faculty and staff. The children and parents admired her and the school. She even helped several parents with some personal financial problems. The school, renamed Westside Elementary, is located in Scott, Louisiana. (Courtesy of Wilma R. Bowles.)

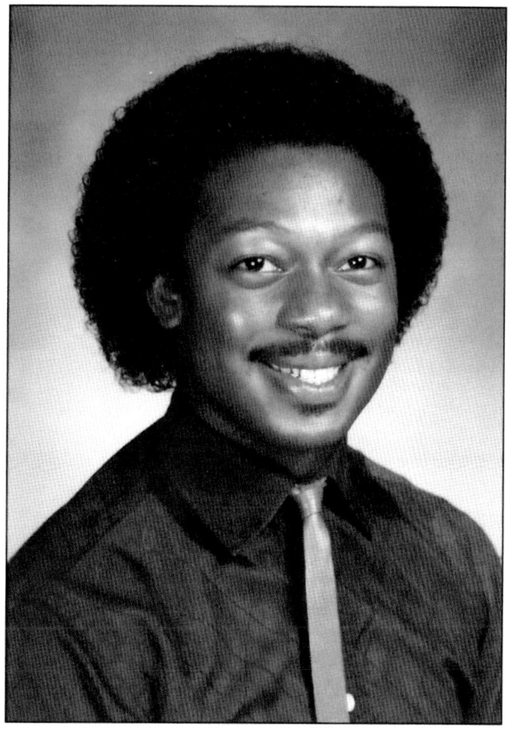

Many Talents (Lafayette Parish). Dorsey Forman is a music educator, choir director, and an assistant principal. He has played music in the Lafayette area for more than 30 years. He teaches piano lessons and voice lessons. He also attends and participates in music workshops. Forman graduated from the University of Southwestern Louisiana (now UL-Lafayette) and achieved advanced educational degrees as well. He is the director of music at Immaculate Heart of Mary (IHM) School and is the minister of music at IHM Church. He is the director of four choirs. Forman's passion and love of music is contagious and has touched the lives of children and adults who have performed under his direction. (Courtesy of Edith G. Dupré Library Archives and Special Collections.)

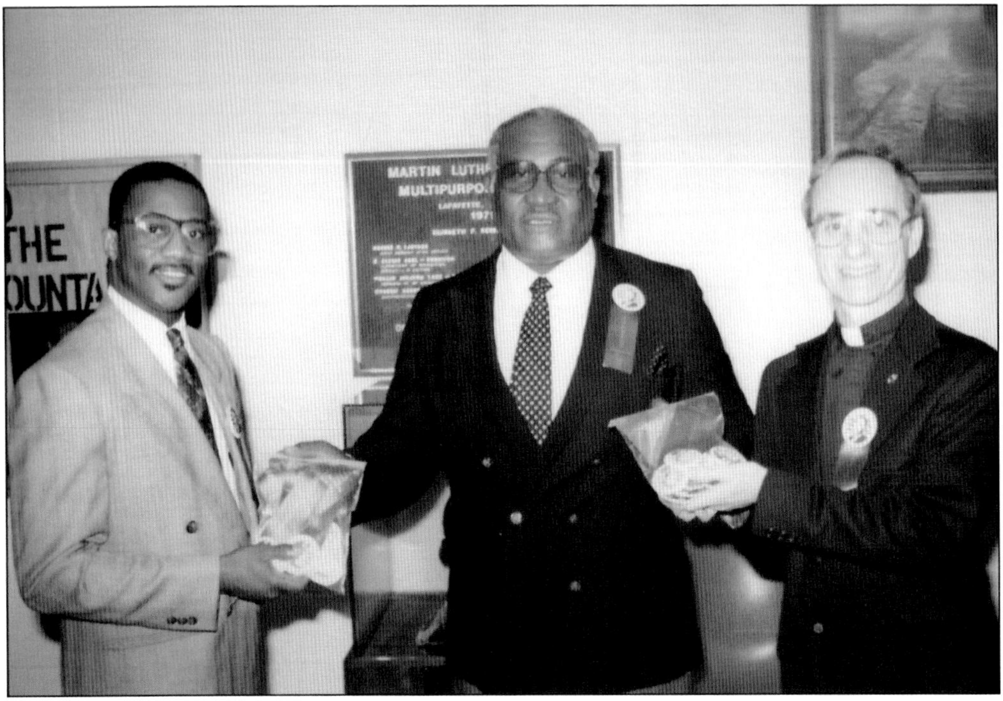

PRINCIPAL (LAFAYETTE PARISH). Ernest Nabors (center) was the first African American principal of Northside High School. He is pictured here with Rev. E. Henderson (left) and Fr. John Gonshar at a Martin Luther King Jr. Day celebration at the MLK Center. (Courtesy of Edith G. Dupré Library Archives and Special Collections.)

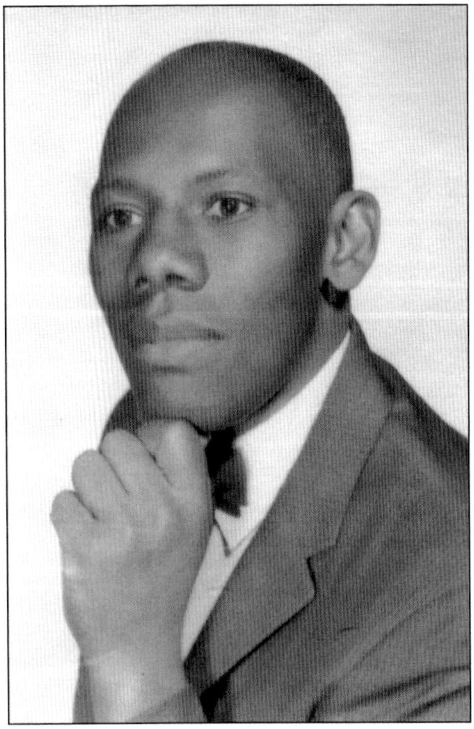

MOVING FORWARD (LAFAYETTE PARISH). George R. Bowles (pictured) and David Dunbar were the first African American teachers to integrate Lafayette Parish's high schools. Bowles taught science classes at Paul Breaux High School and physics classes at Lafayette High School beginning in 1968. (Courtesy of Wilma R. Bowles.)

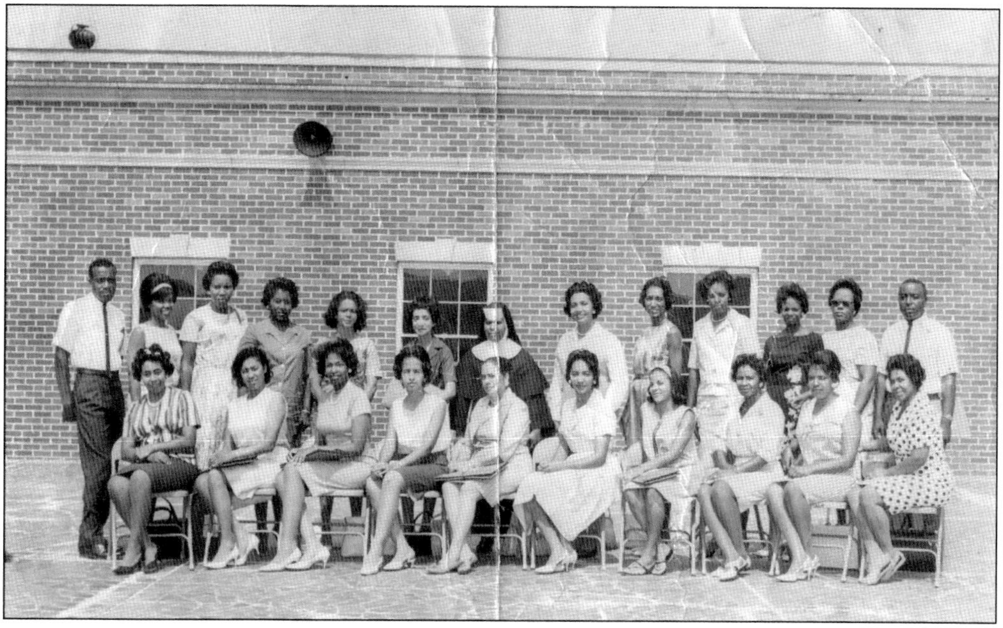

HEAD START (LAFAYETTE PARISH). Southern Consumers started the first Head Start Program in Lafayette Parish. Pictured are the first teachers who worked in the program. Head Start, an early childhood program, is a vital part of Lafayette and other southwest parishes. Head Start classes are located in elementary schools with various community organizations and centers. (Courtesy of Adele Minnard.)

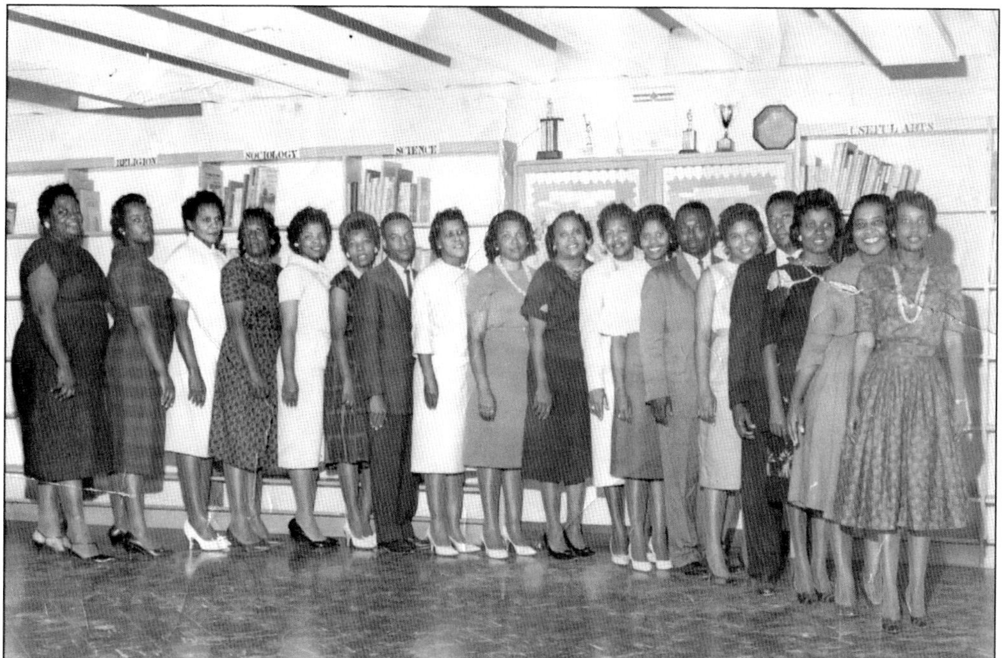

TRUMAN ELEMENTARY SCHOOL (LAFAYETTE PARISH). Pictured here is an all-black faculty of Truman Elementary in the 1950s. Students completed the eighth grade and enrolled in Holy Rosary Institute or Paul Breaux High School to complete their education. (Courtesy of Adele Minnard.)

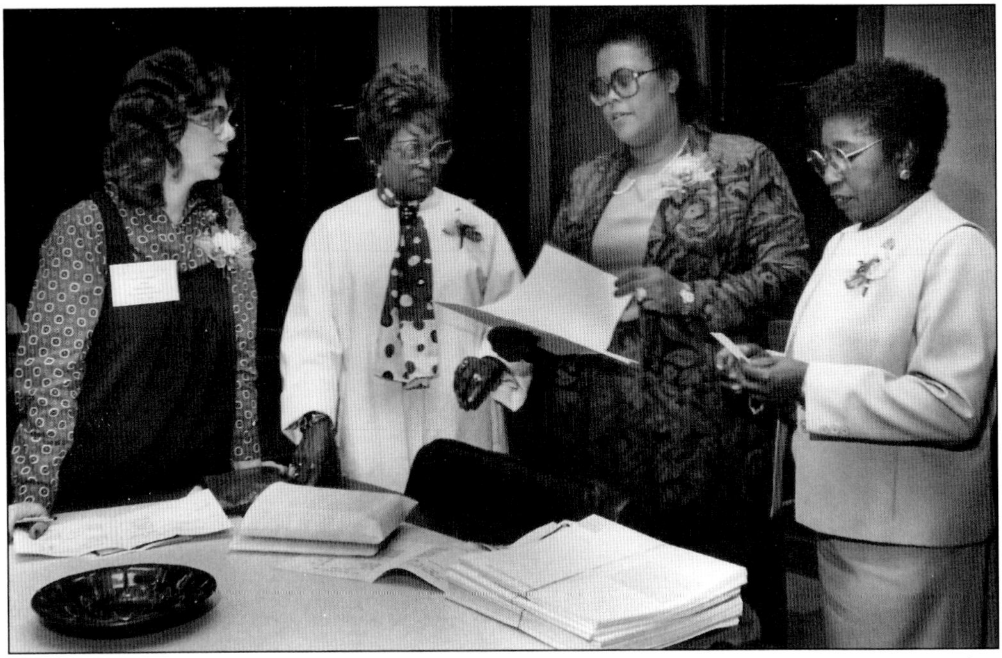

MEETING OF MINDS (LAFAYETTE PARISH). Educators and community leaders are working together to plan for an upcoming event. Pictured from left to right are an unidentified woman, Augustine Ventroy, Nelda Broussard, and Jessie Taylor, the first African American librarian in Lafayette Parish. (Courtesy of Edith G. Dupré Library Archives and Special Collections.)

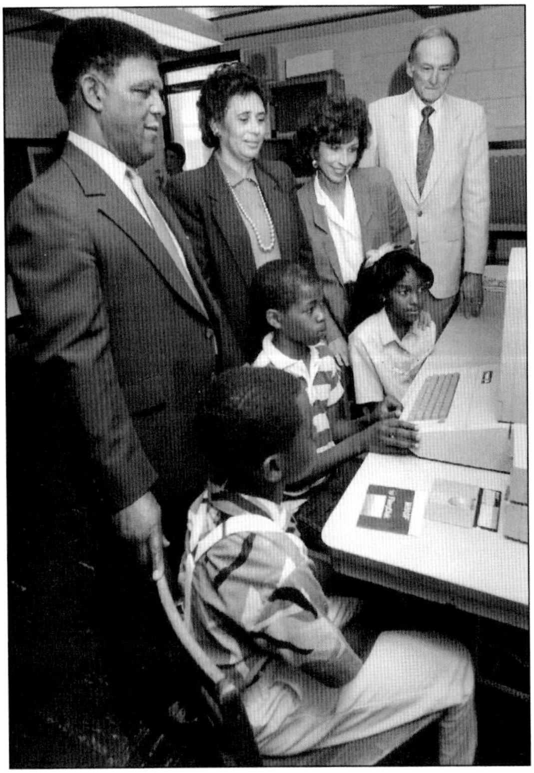

WATCHING CHILDREN LEARN (LAFAYETTE PARISH). Retired Lafayette Parish School Board member and principal Edward Sam (standing, at left) and others watch as students use a computer. Sam served on the school board for 21 years. A total of seven African American men have served on the board, but no black women have served; some black males have served as president and vice president of the school board. Tehmi Chaisson and Shelton Cobb are current members of the board, representing Districts 3 and 4. (Courtesy of Edith G. Dupré Library Archives and Special Collections.)

Three

Then and Now

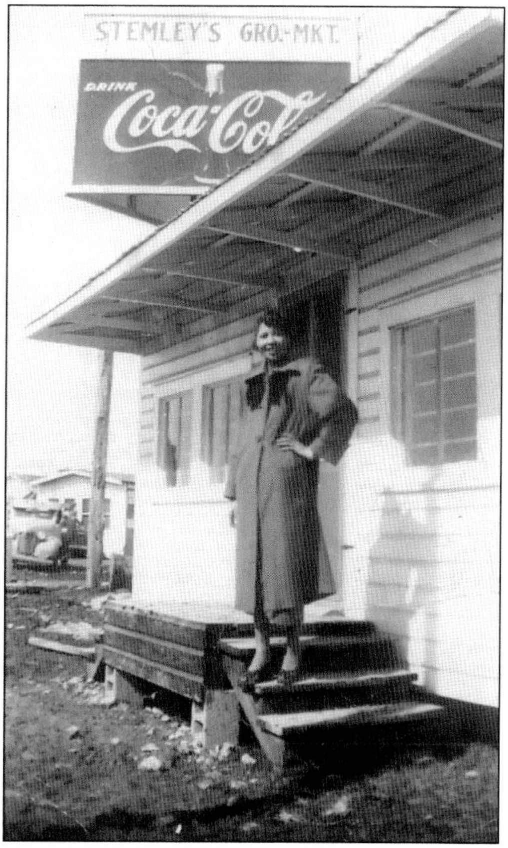

Stemley's Grocery and Market (Lafayette Parish). Leroy and Rita Stemley owned Stemley's Grocery and Market Store, and it was the first black grocery store in the Lafayette area, opening in the 1950s. The store sold food items such as meat, eggs, canned foods, candy, milk, juice, bread, and other perishables. The store also sold nonfood items like soap and detergent. Families struggling to raise their children frequently purchased needed items on credit. The store operated for several years as a neighborhood grocery store. Hazel St. Julien is the lady pictured here in front of the store. (Courtesy of Amater Traylor.)

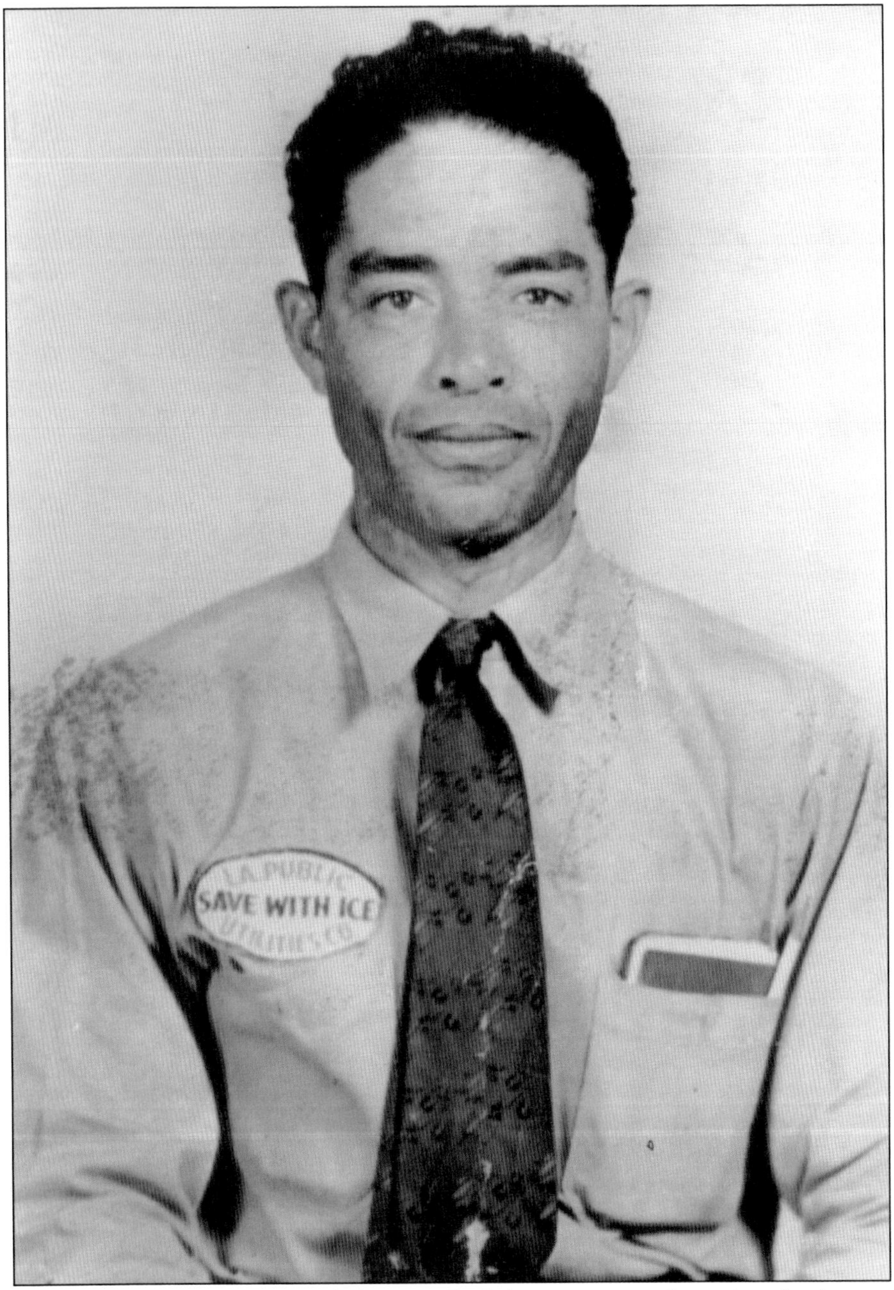

Keeping Cool (Lafayette Parish). Loomis St. Julien was an independent businessman in Lafayette for 46 years. He delivered ice to residential customers and to local restaurants in his truck. He insisted on looking and being professional. Every day he wore a starched and ironed khaki shirt and pants to work. Every summer, St. Julien would provide summer jobs for family members or a young people in the community to help with delivery of the ice. His son Lumis worked with him in the business. There were no icemakers at the time, and the community depended on the iceman to deliver ice for their iceboxes. St. Julien's last delivery was a much-needed one to Lafayette General Hospital when their modern ice machine failed. (Courtesy of Marlene St. Julien Broussard.)

BEST FARMERS IN LOUISIANA, 1957 (LAFAYETTE PARISH). The family of Clarence J. (back row) and Mathilda Green Broussard (receiving trophy) were recipients of the Best Farmer of the Year Award in 1957. The award was presented by Dr. Felton G. Clark, president of Southern University Agricultural and Mechanical College in Baton Rouge, Louisiana. The Broussard children pictured here are, from left to right, Ida Mae, John, Ophelia, Monica, Paul, Earl, and Madelon; Eruadell is not shown. (Courtesy of John A. Broussard.)

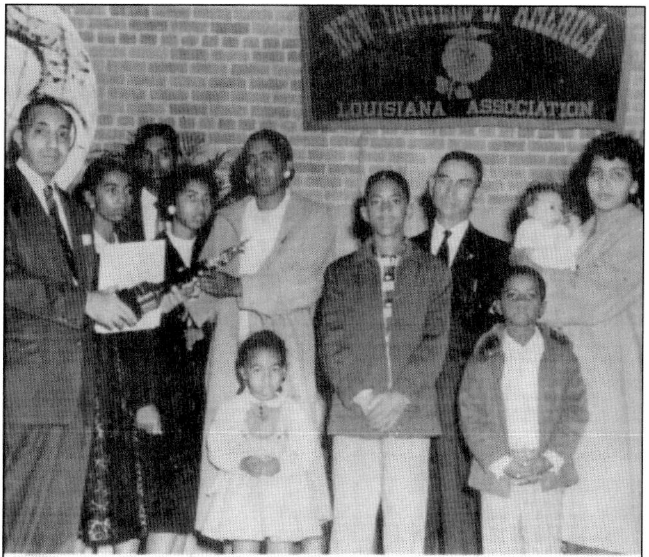

They were the best in Louisiana . . .

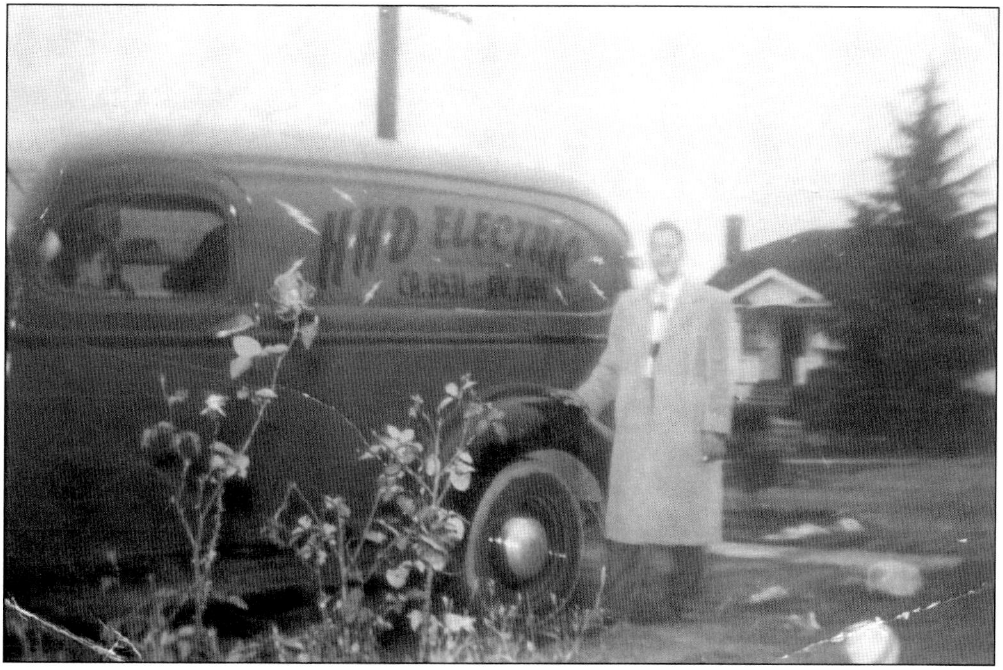

FIRST AFRICAN AMERICAN ELECTRICIAN (LAFAYETTE PARISH). Herman Decuir was the first licensed African American electrician in Lafayette. He was a student at Tuskegee Institute, where he received training as an electrician. After the death of his mother, he did not return to Tuskegee. He married Annabelle Gordon and later took the examination for electrical contracting. He was successful in passing the test given by the Local 46 Electrical Union. He established the first black electrical contracting business in Lafayette and called it HHD Electric Company. (Courtesy of Rita Stemley.)

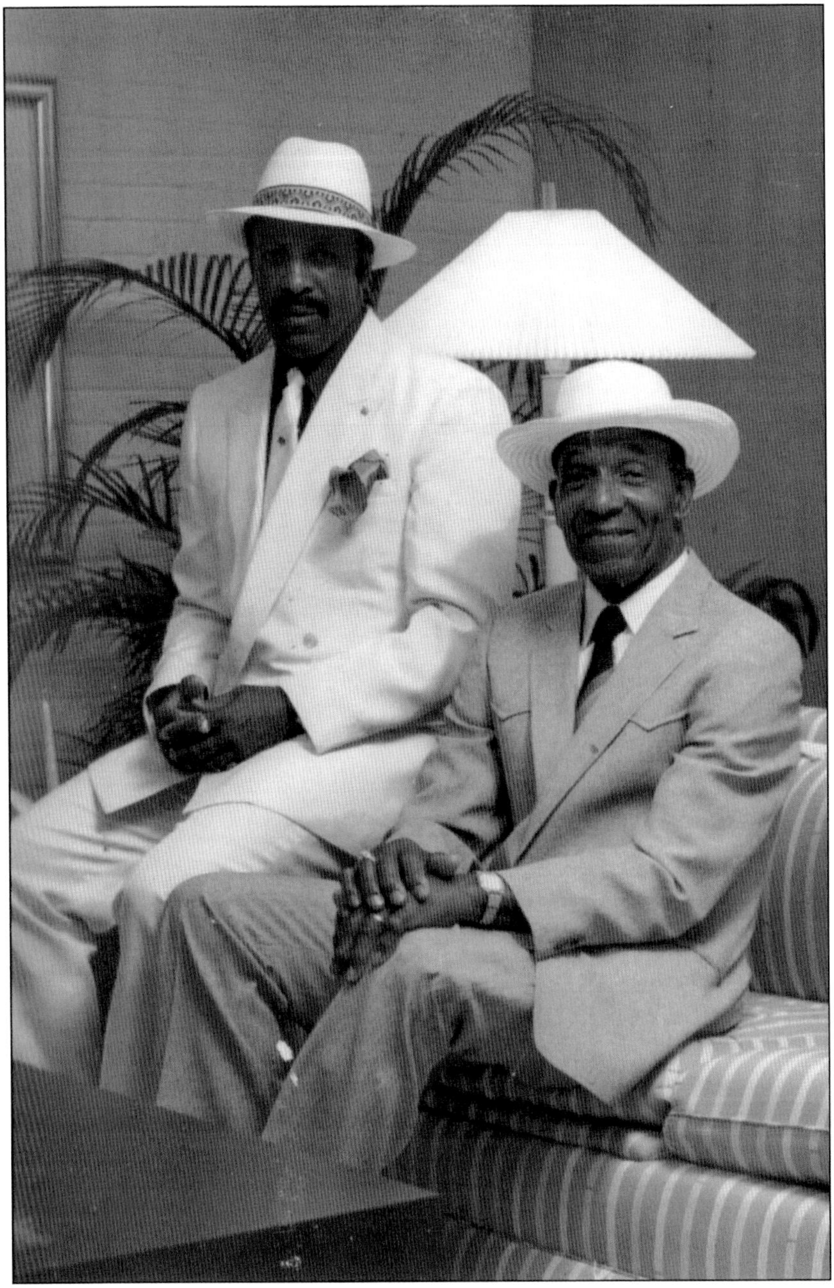

On the Move (Lafayette Parish). Alex Louis Sr. (right) was the owner of the first African American moving-furniture company in Lafayette, Louisiana. His first business of hauling trash led to his most successful business of moving furniture for local residents. He actually used the truck for both the trash and the moving business in the beginning. Alex's daughter stated that whenever he had a moving job, he would scrub and clean the truck to prepare it. Alex Louis Jr. (left) managed the business with his father. Walter Louis, another son, also worked and helped to manage the business. Mary E. LaFontaine, daughter of Alex Louis Sr., and her husband, Herman, also own a furniture-moving company called LaFontaine's Furniture Moving Company, which is located in Lafayette. (Courtesy of Merline Herbert.)

CIRCLE M OILFIELD SUPPLY COMPANY (LAFAYETTE PARISH). Lyle Mouton Sr. and Phyllis C. Mouton were owners and operators of Circle M Oil Field Supply Company. The company operated for 15 years and served as a beacon for people interested in starting a successful business. Mouton assisted other men interested in working for oil companies, such as American Oil Company (now Amoco), to secure jobs. Lyle graduated from Southern University with a degree in business. Phyllis graduated from the University of Southwestern Louisiana (now UL-Lafayette) with a degree in computer science management and a master's degree in rehabilitative psychology from USL and business administration at Louisiana State University. The Moutons have three children: Lyle Jr., Lynn, and Leah. (Courtesy of Lyle and Phyllis Mouton.)

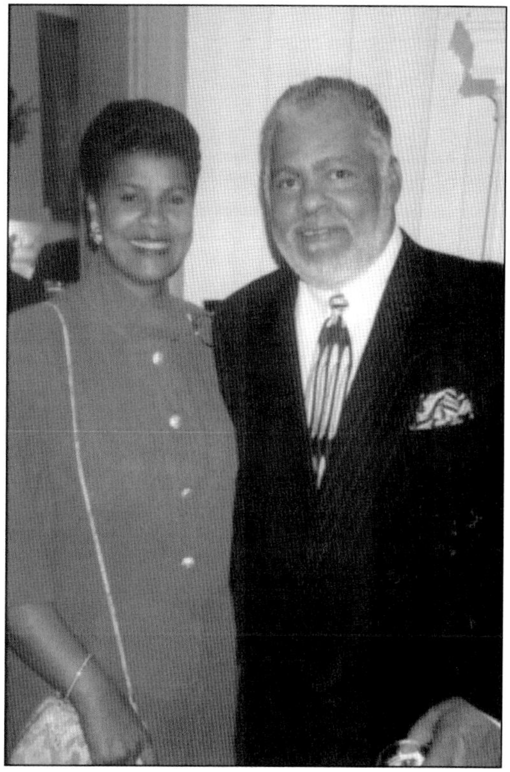

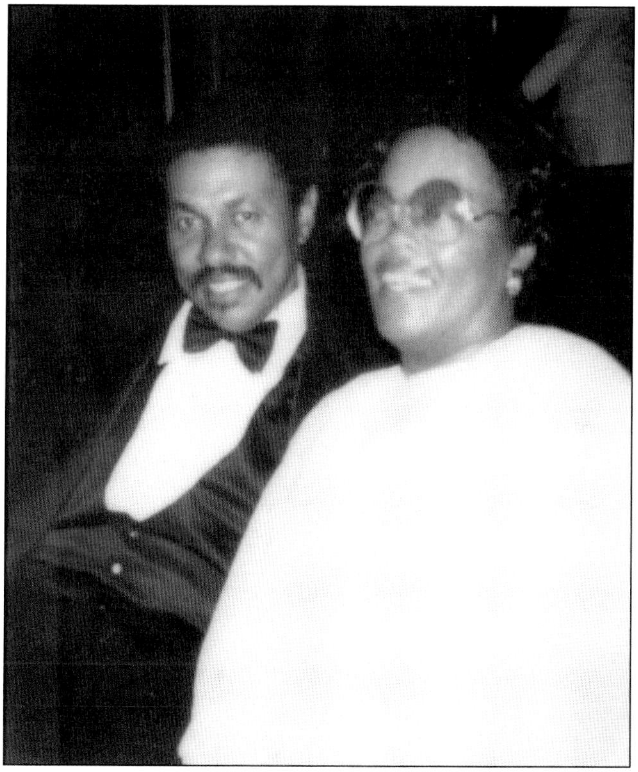

OILFIELD BUSINESS (LAFAYETTE PARISH). Ophilas W. Minnard (pictured with his wife, Adele) was the first African American to own and operate an oil-field rental business in Lafayette. He started Big O Construction Company in the 1970s. Prior to starting his business, he worked as a merchant seaman and for the sheriff and police departments. (Courtesy of Adele Minnard.)

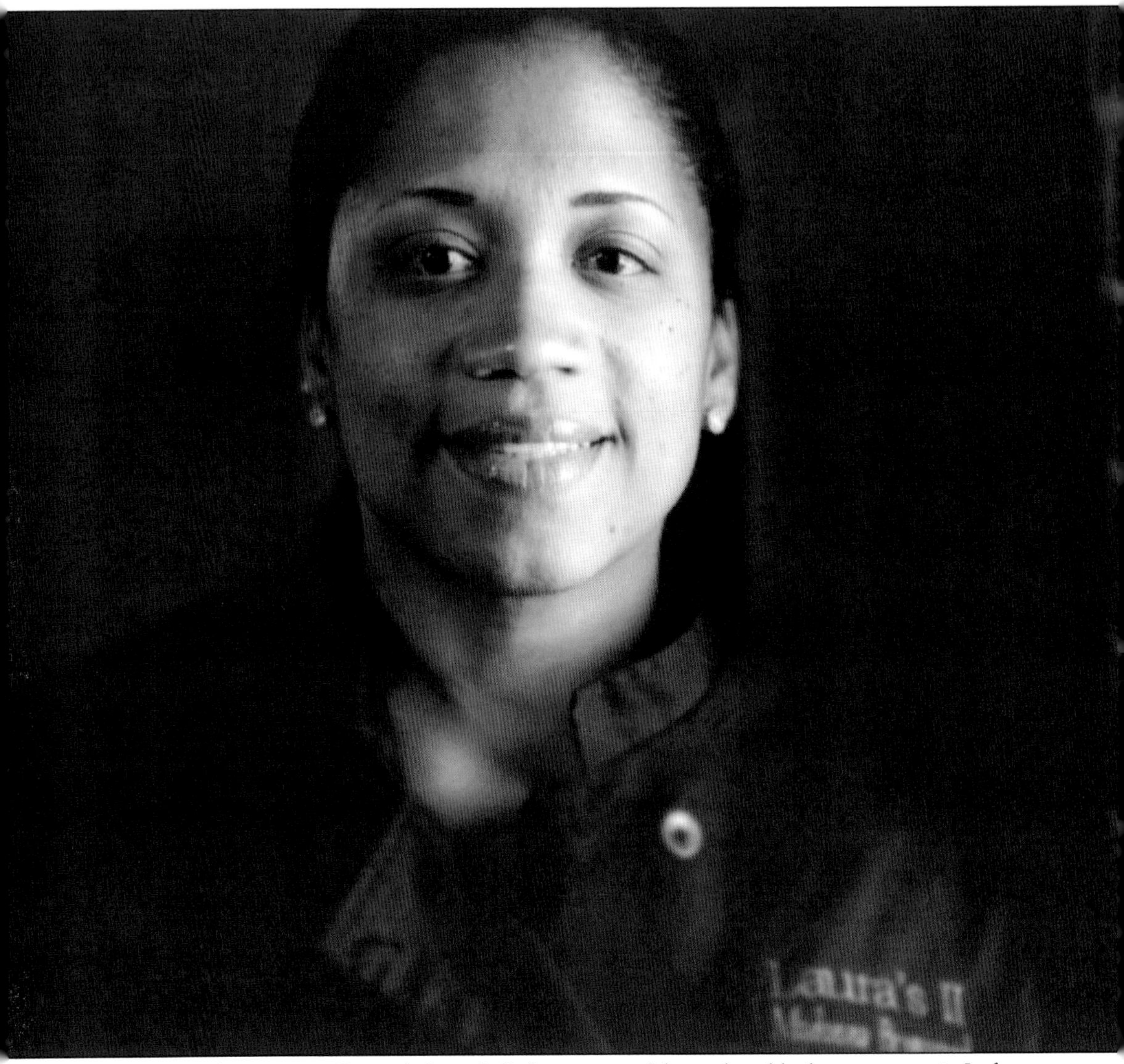

LAURA'S II (LAFAYETTE PARISH). Laura's Café was one of the earliest black restaurants in Lafayette, which was owned operated by Laura W. Broussard. She started the business in the back of her home and served home-cooked plate lunches for several years until 1984. Broussard's son and his wife managed the restaurant for 15 years. Laura's II is owned and operated by Madonna (granddaughter of Laura) and Olies Broussard. The restaurant also has a catering service and continues to serve delicious Creole food for citizens of Lafayette. (Courtesy of Madonna Broussard.)

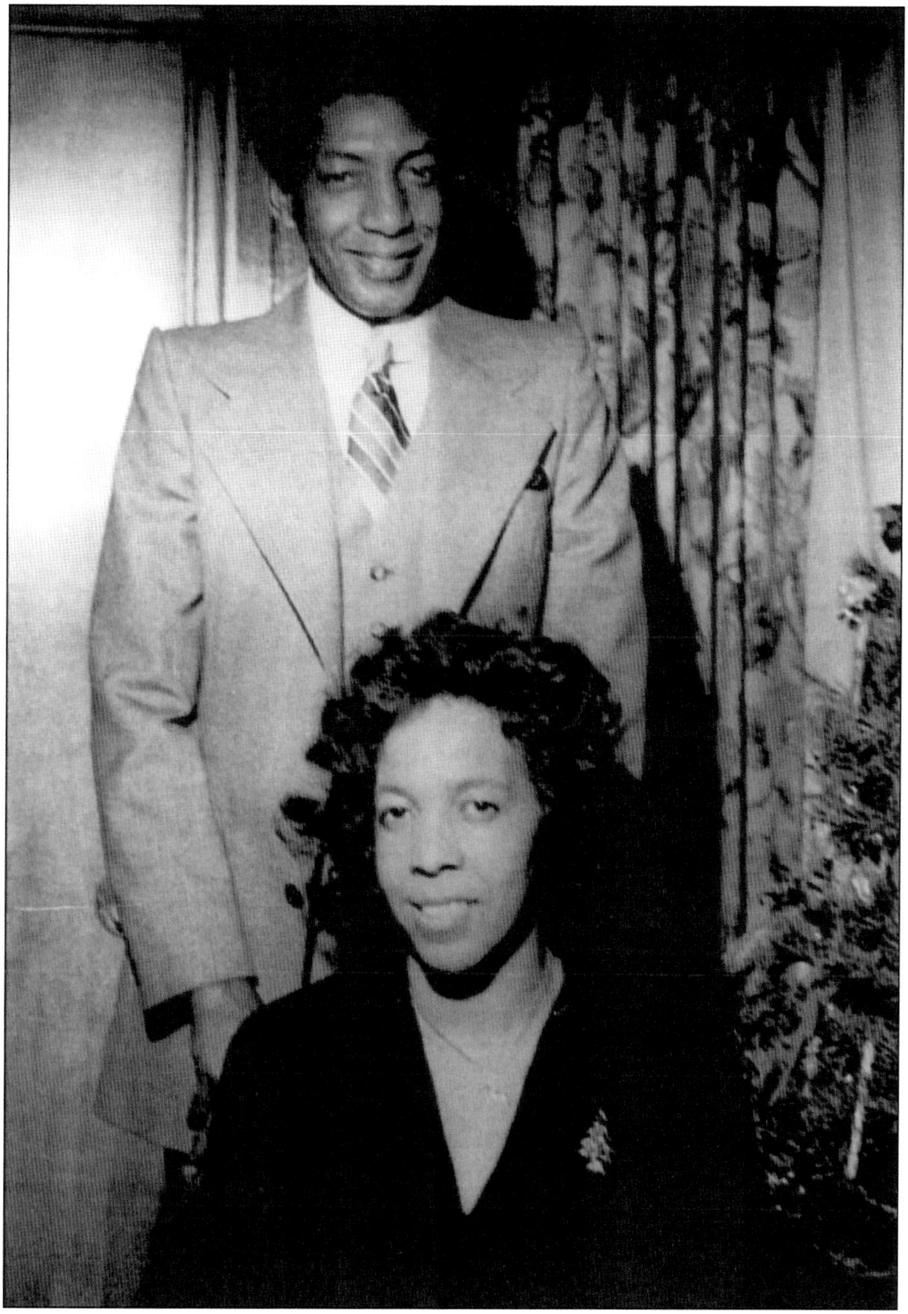

CREOLE LUNCH HOUSE (LAFAYETTE PARISH). Merline Louis Herbert, the owner of Creole Lunch House and M&R Creole Enterprises Inc., started the business with her late husband, Raymond Herbert. She and her sons Raymond Jr. and Jason Herbert work together to run the successful businesses. The Creole Lunch House restaurant, a local favorite, serves old-fashioned plate lunches and Creole stuffed bread, the specialty of the house. M&R Creole Enterprises, a USDA food processing plant, produces the Creole stuffed bread for wholesaling. Merline, a former educator for 22 years, comes from a family of entrepreneurs. The businesses are providing incomes for future generations. (Courtesy of Merline Herbert.)

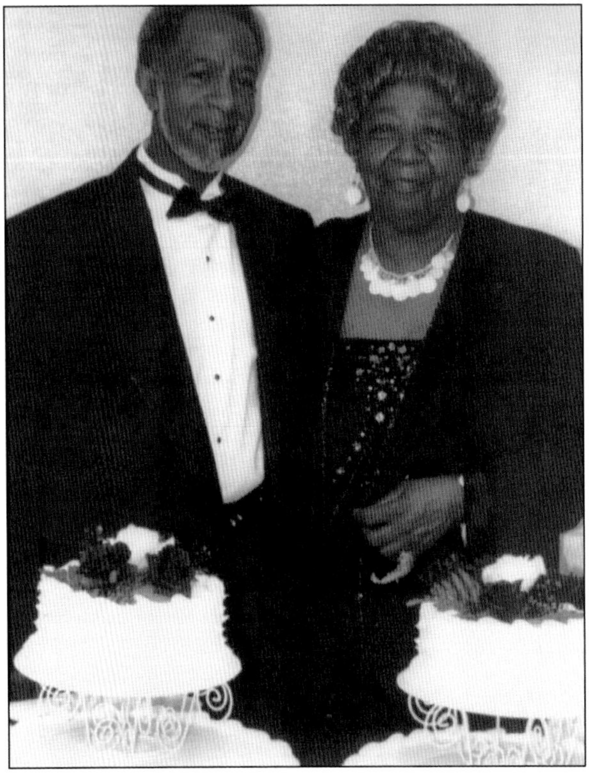

The Cake Lady (Lafayette Parish). Mary Williams (pictured here with her husband, Gabriel Williams) bakes some of the best homemade cakes in Lafayette. Williams's offerings have been centerpieces for weddings, christenings, graduations, grand openings, and many other occasions. Williams is known in Lafayette and the surrounding areas as the "Cake Lady." Whether her cakes are round, square, or sheet-cake sized with various pictures, flavors, and colors, each one is baked with love and care. Williams is an entrepreneur who bakes cakes for many residents and businesses in Lafayette and the southwest areas. (Courtesy of Mary Williams.)

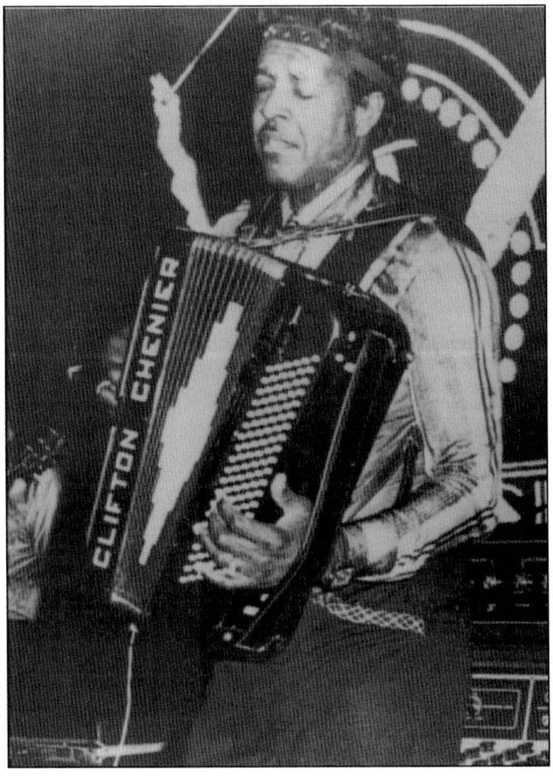

Honored (St. Landry Parish). Born in Opelousas, Louisiana, in 1925, Clifton Chenier was dubbed the "King of Zydeco." He won a Grammy in 1983 for his album *I'm Here* and was inducted into the Blues Hall of Fame in 1989. (Courtesy of Louis J. Perret, clerk of court, Lafayette Parish.)

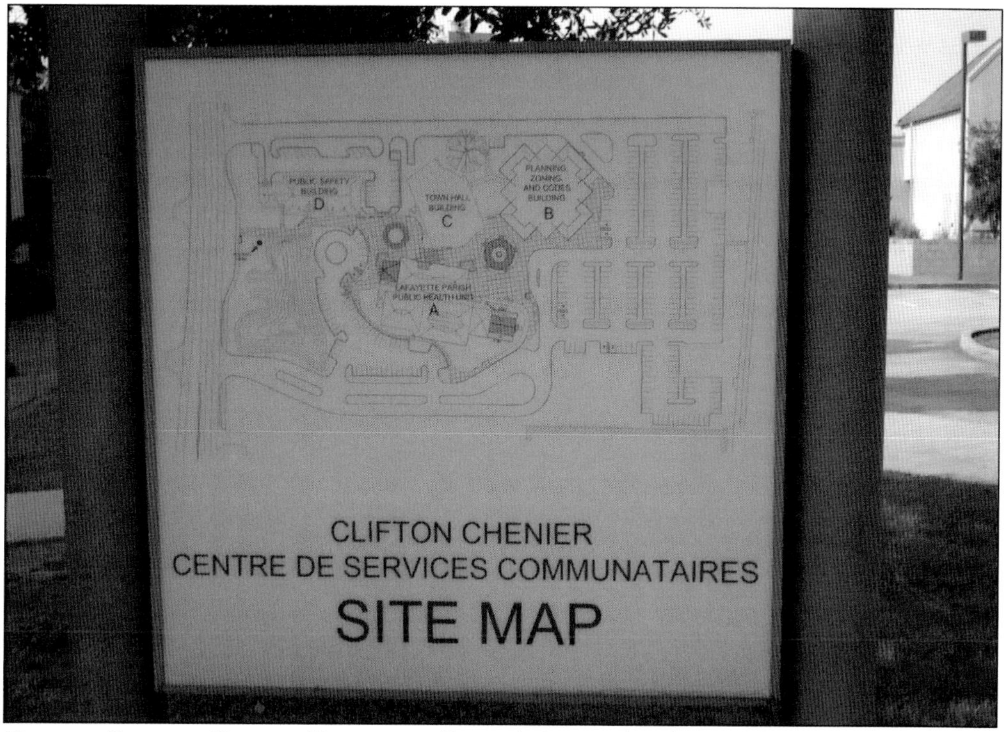

CLIFTON CHENIER CENTER (LAFAYETTE PARISH). Located in beautiful North Lafayette, the Clifton Chenier Center is in the heart of the community and is a productive and essential cluster of government buildings that houses an auditorium, library, health unit, police station, ambulance station, and planning and zoning commission. The building was named in honor of Clifton Chenier, the "King of Zydeco," for creating popularity for this style of music played with an accordion. Many musicians followed in Chenier's footsteps and play and perform zydeco music. (Both courtesy of S. Taylor.)

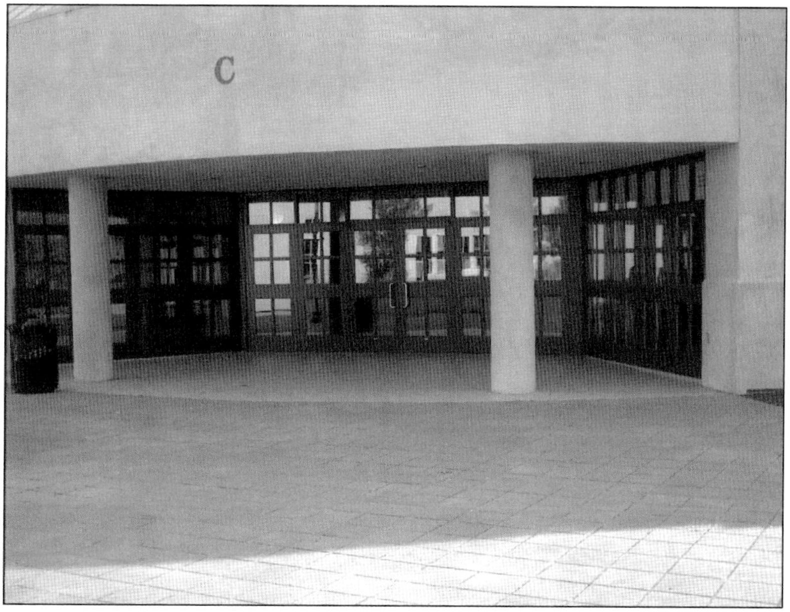

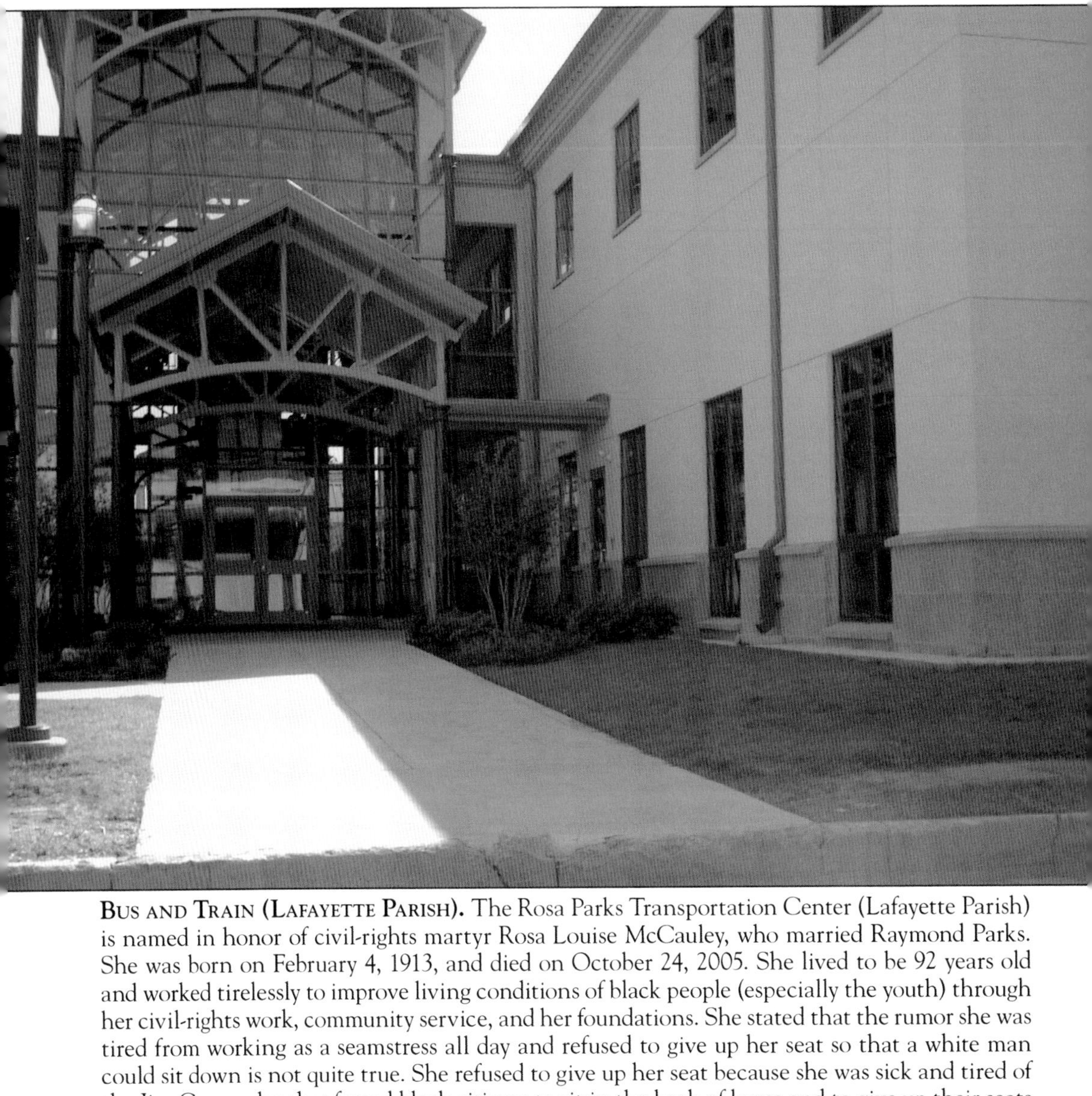

Bus and Train (Lafayette Parish). The Rosa Parks Transportation Center (Lafayette Parish) is named in honor of civil-rights martyr Rosa Louise McCauley, who married Raymond Parks. She was born on February 4, 1913, and died on October 24, 2005. She lived to be 92 years old and worked tirelessly to improve living conditions of black people (especially the youth) through her civil-rights work, community service, and her foundations. She stated that the rumor she was tired from working as a seamstress all day and refused to give up her seat so that a white man could sit down is not quite true. She refused to give up her seat because she was sick and tired of the Jim Crow rules that forced black citizens to sit in the back of buses and to give up their seats to white citizens as needed. Parks is called the "mother of the freedom movement." The Rosa Parks Transportation Center houses a train depot, city-bus terminal, a post office, a community television station, and may house the Greyhound bus terminal. It is located in downtown Lafayette on Cypress and Jefferson Streets. (Courtesy of S. Taylor.)

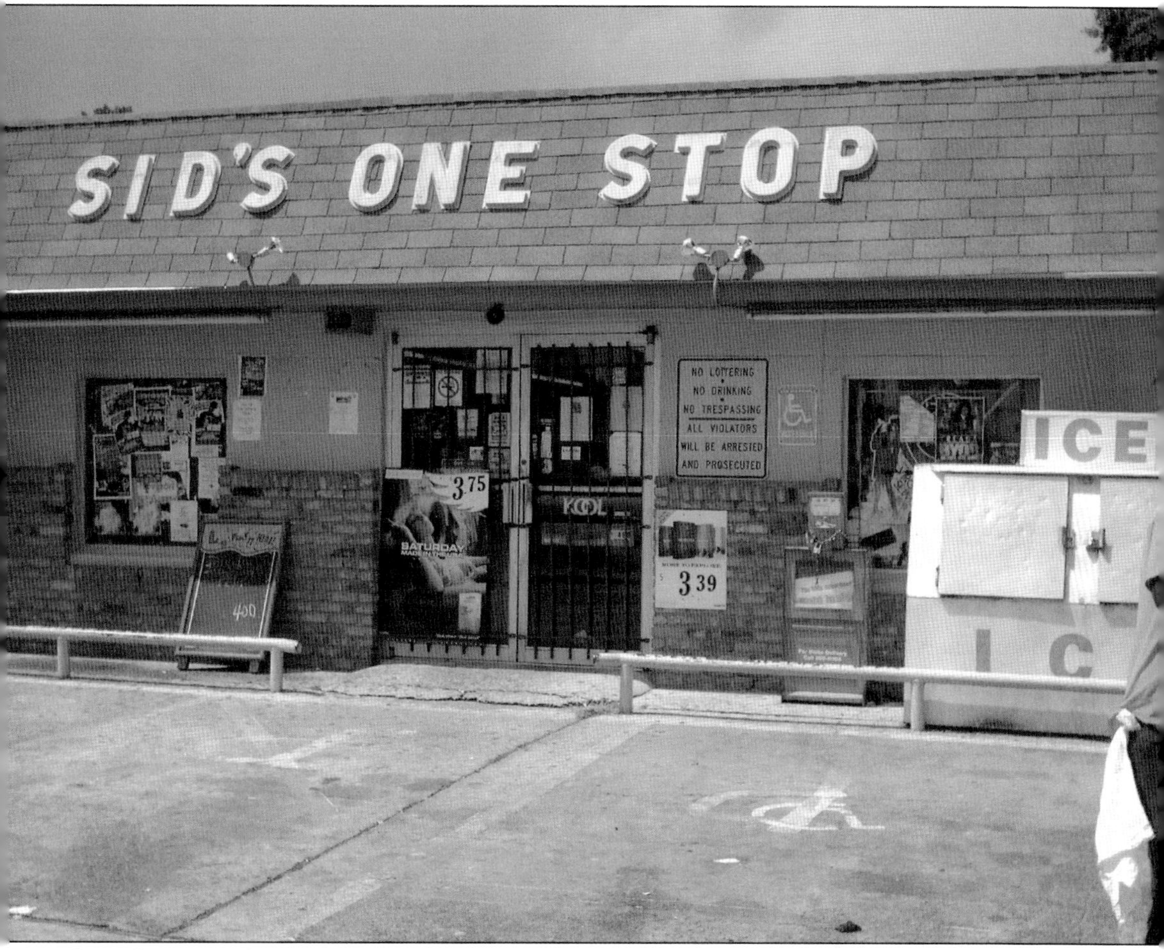

Sid's One Stop (Lafayette Parish). Sidney and Susanna Williams and family are the owners of a local community grocery store, Sid's One Stop. The store opened in 1977 and is located on Martin Luther King Jr. Drive. Sidney was born and raised in St. Martinville, Louisiana. Sidney and Susanna are the parents of three daughters: Jodi Williams Gonzalez, Rhonda Williams Brown, and Shelly Williams. The couple also has seven grandchildren. Each year the family donates Thanksgiving baskets to needy families in Lafayette. (Author's collection.)

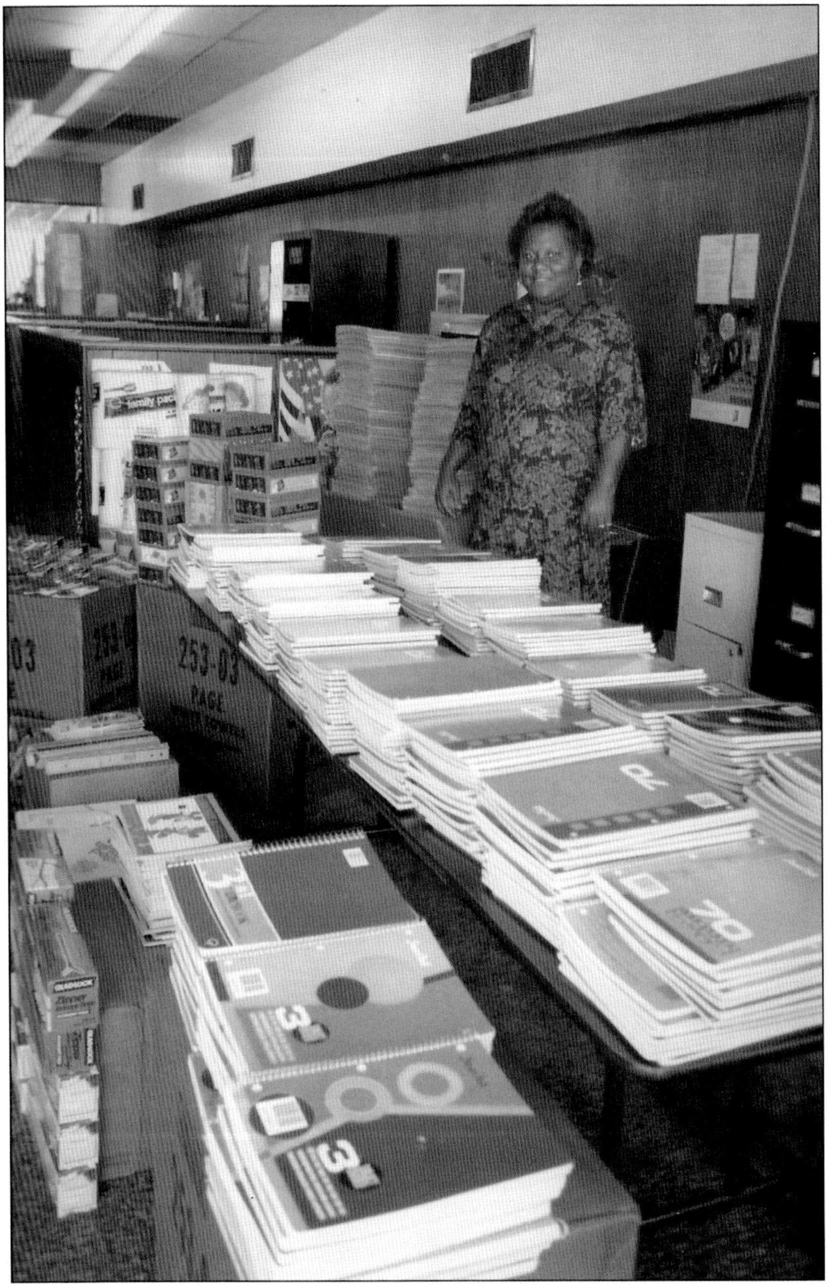

SERVING THE COMMUNITY (LAFAYETTE PARISH). Je'nelle Chargois is innovative and creative. She served as station manager of the first and only black-owned radio station in Lafayette, KJCB. Some of Chargois's innovative ideas included the school-supply drive, the Black Heritage Band, and outdoor concerts at KJCB. She helped organized the Black Chamber of Commerce, the Black History Month Parade, and most recently the Freedom Banquet for the presidents of NAACP chapters and was also president of the NAACP (Lafayette chapter). Chargois worked with various groups, community partners, and local citizens with these projects, which also included television station Channel 10, a co-sponsor of the school-supply drive. (Courtesy of Edith G. Dupré Library Archives and Special Collections.)

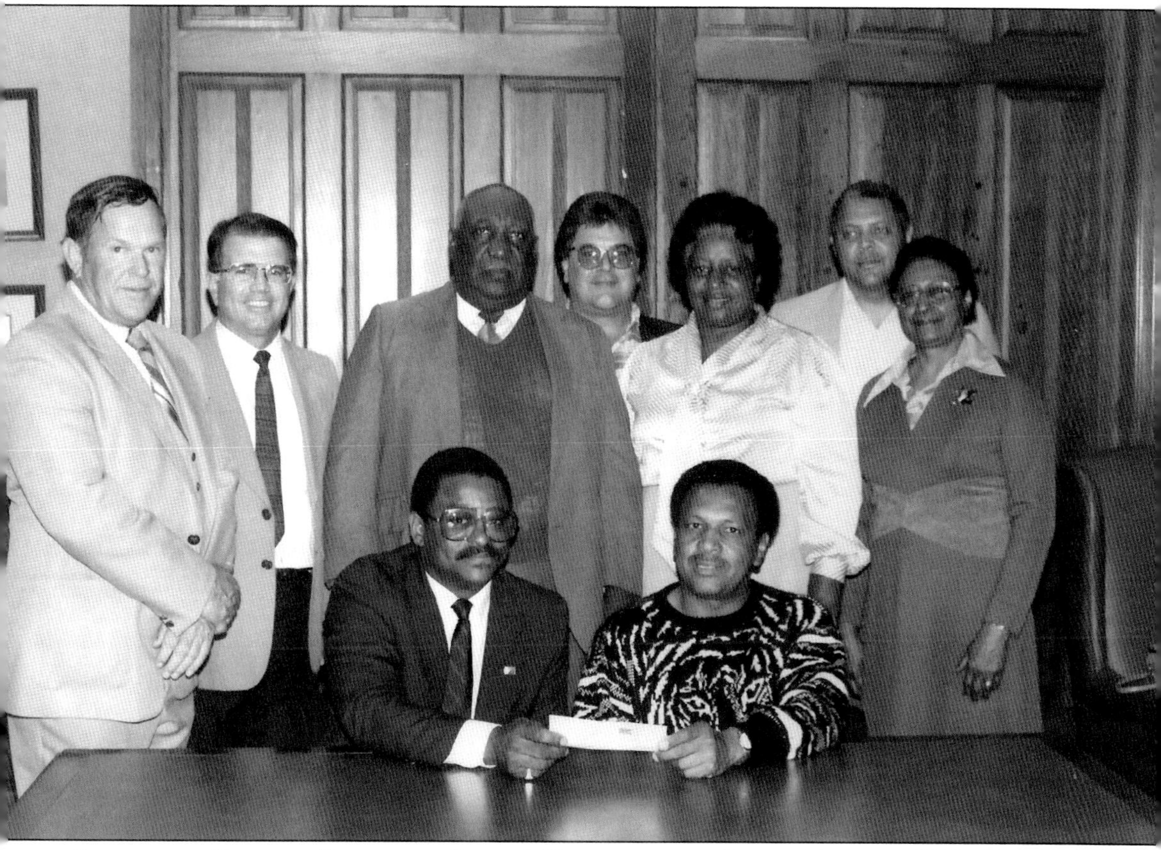

Service for Citizens (Lafayette Parish) Organization. Pictured here are Wilfred Pierre (seated, left) and Alvin Wiltz (seated, right) with other group members at a meeting. Pierre was the first elected city councilman and the first elected state representative. Wiltz is a former teacher, assistant principal, principal, and director of SMILE Community Action Agency, which provides various kinds of assistance to citizens in Lafayette and other southwest parishes. (Courtesy of Edith G. Dupré Library Archives and Special Collections.)

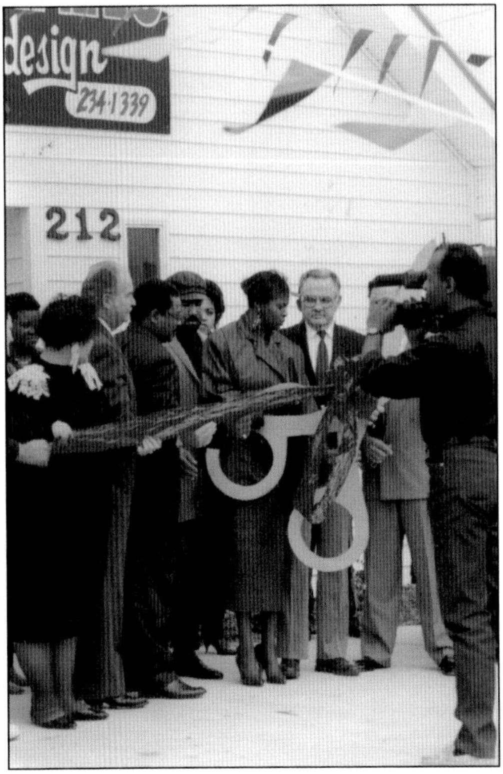

SPARKLES (LAFAYETTE PARISH). Sandra S. Broussard is pictured at left at the opening of her hair salon, Sparkles Hair Design, as well as below. Broussard, a licensed professional hair stylist, has been in the business for 33 years. The shop has one barber, three hairstylists, and a nail technician. She is married to Ronald Broussard, and together they have a son, Jamal. Today, several men and women own barber and beauty salons in Lafayette and southwest Louisiana, and today the option exists to be trained in any cosmetology field. In earlier times, the only beauty school in Lafayette for African Americans, LaBelle's Beauty School, was owned by the Gant family from New Orleans. The school was located on Eleventh Street, and many hair professionals from previous generations were trained there by Isabel Gant. (Both courtesy of Sandra Broussard.)

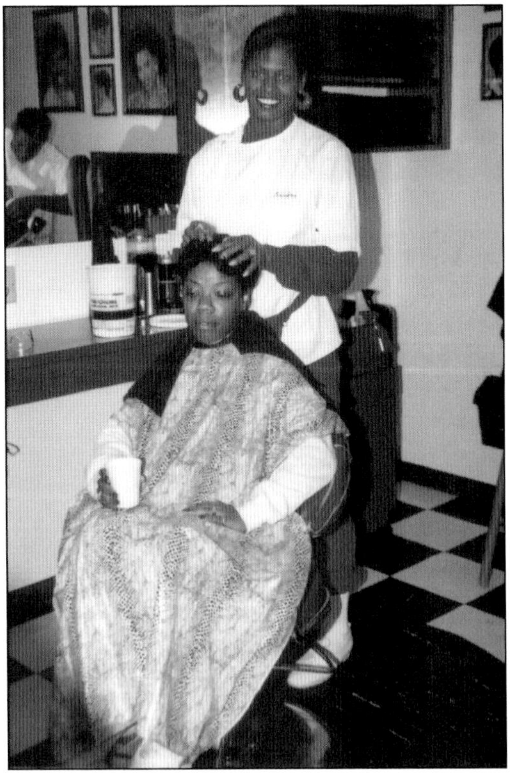

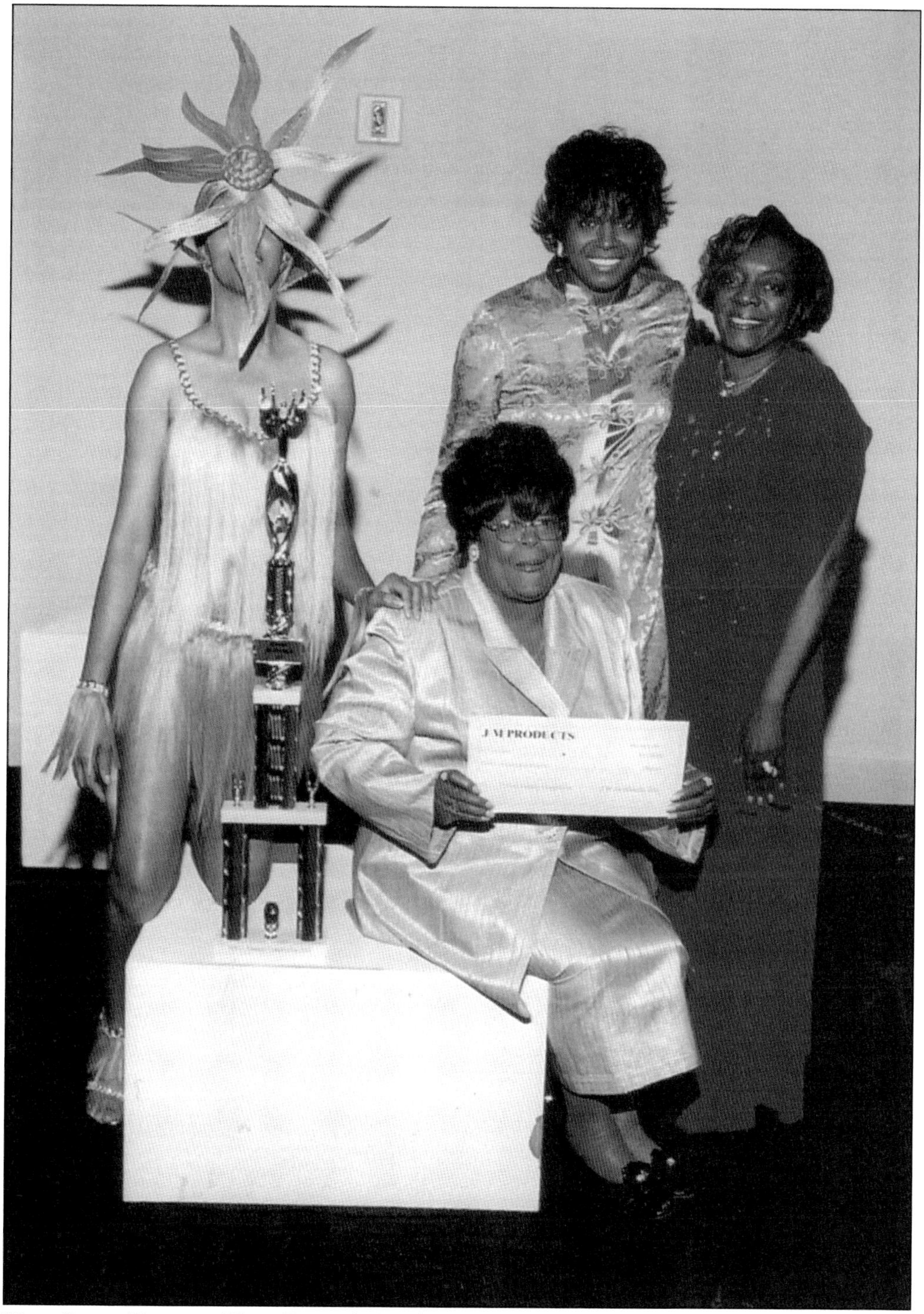

Hair Show (Sparkles Hair Design). Sandra Broussard (standing, center) is pictured here with a model from a hair show wearing an outfit of the sun, which is made completely from hair. Broussard created the model's entire outfit from head to toe. Also pictured are Broussard's mother (seated) and a sponsor from the hair show. (Courtesy of Sandra Broussard.)

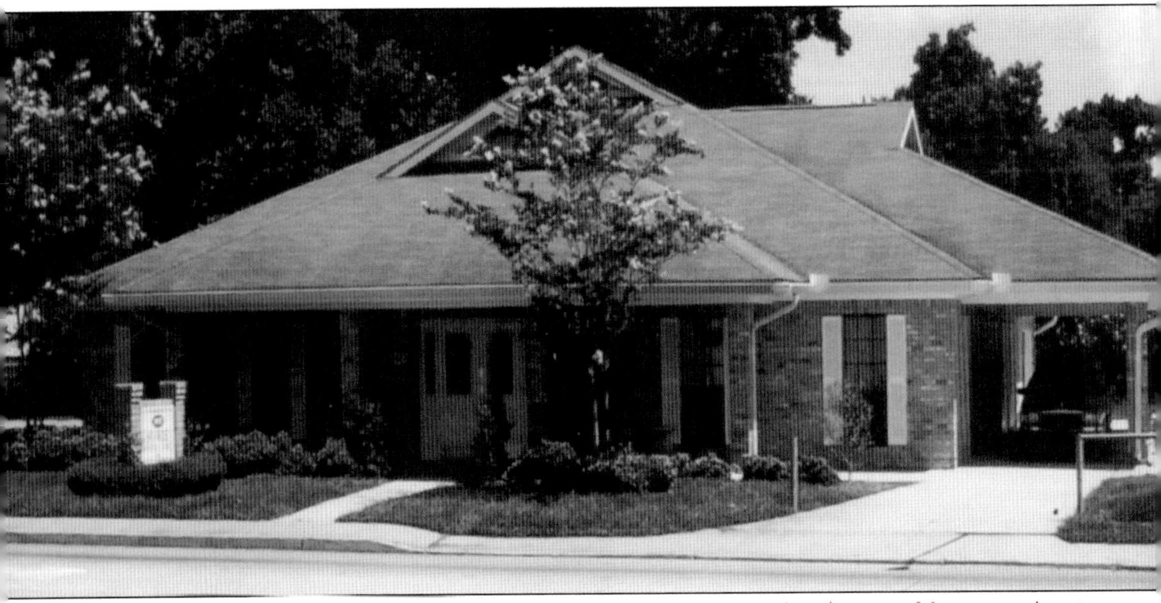

FUNERAL HOME (LAFAYETTE PARISH). Syrie Funeral Home is a family-owned business that is managed by the children and family members of founders Carol and Sedonia G. Syrie. The people involved with the business are Evelyn E. Syrie, corporate secretary/funeral director; Wesley Syrie, manager and mortician; Sedonia V. Syrie, secretary/receptionist; Clifton Syrie, funeral director/corporate president; Willie Syrie, funeral assistant/board of directors member; Virgie Syrie Cotton, Joseph Cotton Sr., and Earl Broussard, funeral assistants; and Brien Syrie (son of Wesley) and Eugene Sonnier II, assistant morticians of the successful community establishment. (Courtesy of Evelyn E. Syrie.)

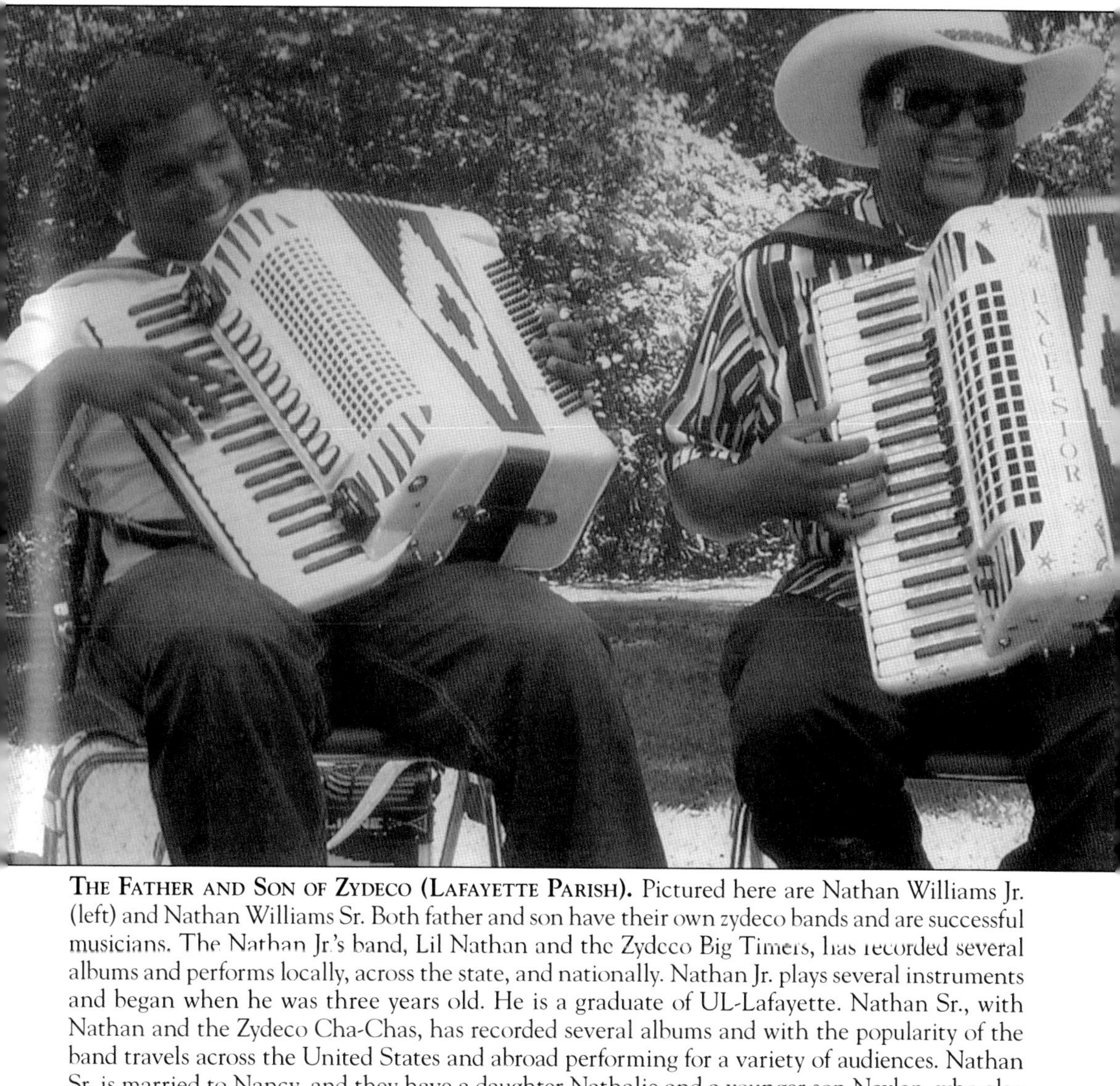

The Father and Son of Zydeco (Lafayette Parish). Pictured here are Nathan Williams Jr. (left) and Nathan Williams Sr. Both father and son have their own zydeco bands and are successful musicians. The Nathan Jr.'s band, Lil Nathan and the Zydeco Big Timers, has recorded several albums and performs locally, across the state, and nationally. Nathan Jr. plays several instruments and began when he was three years old. He is a graduate of UL-Lafayette. Nathan Sr., with Nathan and the Zydeco Cha-Chas, has recorded several albums and with the popularity of the band travels across the United States and abroad performing for a variety of audiences. Nathan Sr. is married to Nancy, and they have a daughter Nathalie and a younger son Naylan, who also plays zydeco music. (Courtesy of Nathan Williams Sr.)

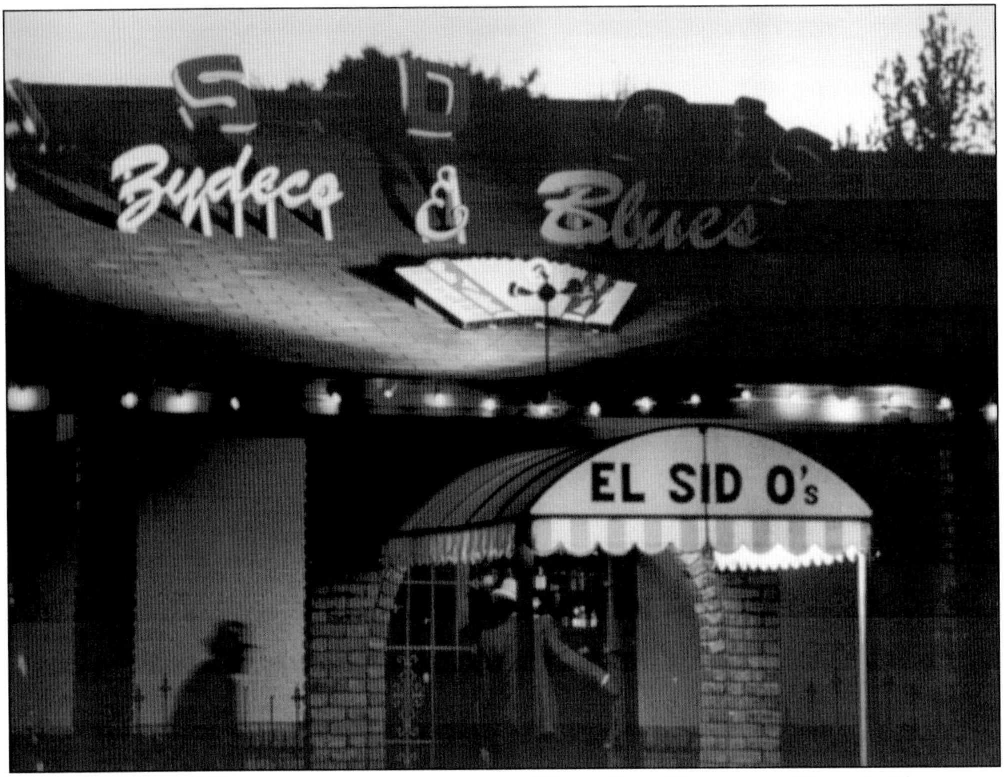

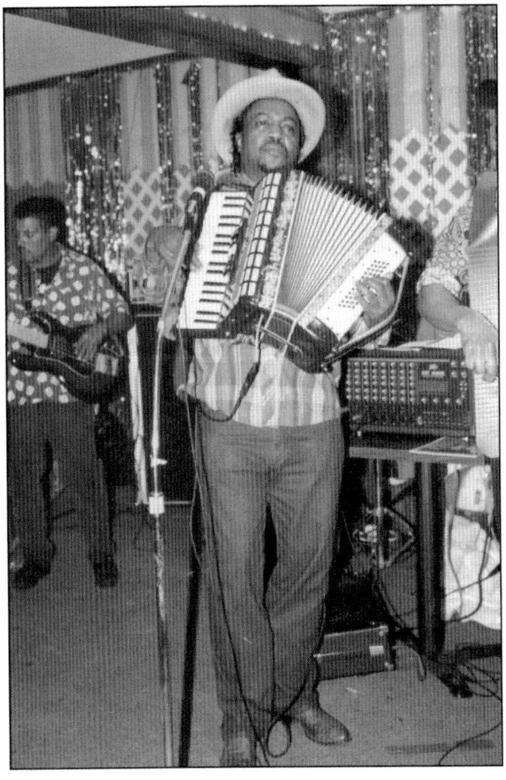

Night Life (Lafayette Parish). El Sido's Zydeco and Blues Club is a popular nightclub owned by Sidney and Susanna Williams. Many prominent citizens attend dances and other social events at the club. From the "King of Zydeco" Clifton Chenier to Nathan Williams and the Zydeco Cha-Chas, all sorts of performers and dignitaries have made appearances at the club. The club was opened in 1984 and continues to thrive as a successful business in Lafayette. (Courtesy of Sidney Williams Jr.)

Entertainment (Lafayette Parish). Sidney Williams Jr. is the oldest of eight children born to Sidney Williams Sr. and Florita H. Williams in St. Martinville, Louisiana. He has six brothers and one sister. Sidney and his siblings are musically and artistically talented. Williams was the 2010 recipient of the Jefferson Award that honors volunteer service in the community; the award is given annually in Washington, DC. (Courtesy of Sidney Williams Jr.)

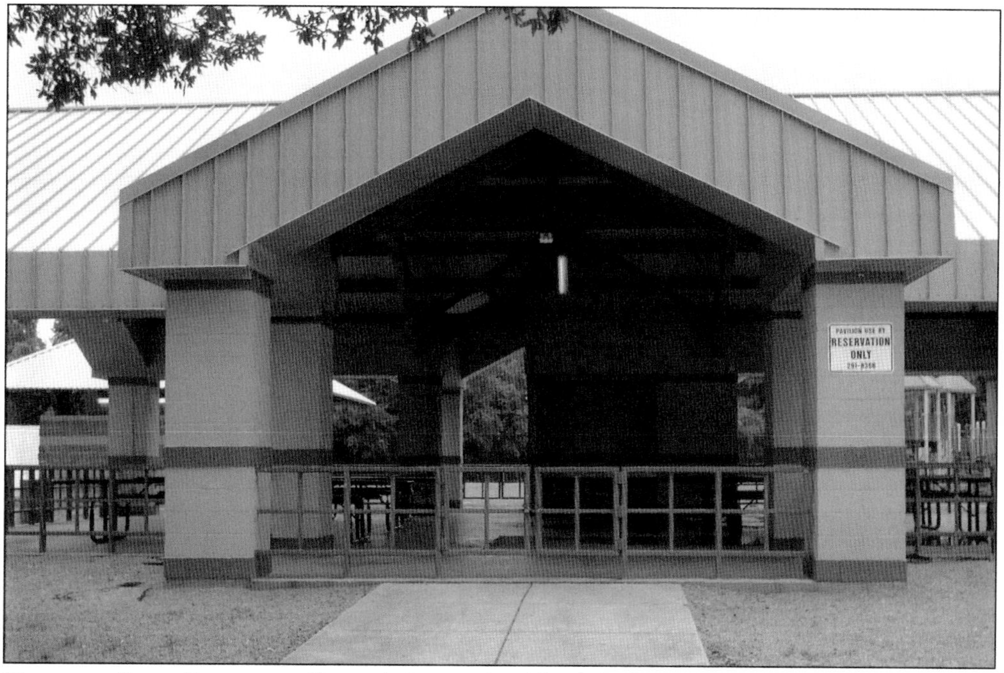

HEYMANN PARK (LAFAYETTE PARISH). Located in North Lafayette, Heymann Park is named in honor of Herbert H. Heymann, who supported many African American public facilities, such as schools, parks, and recreation. Heymann was born in Lafayette in 1925 and followed his father's leadership as a businessman, philanthropist, and civic leader. (Both courtesy of S. Taylor.)

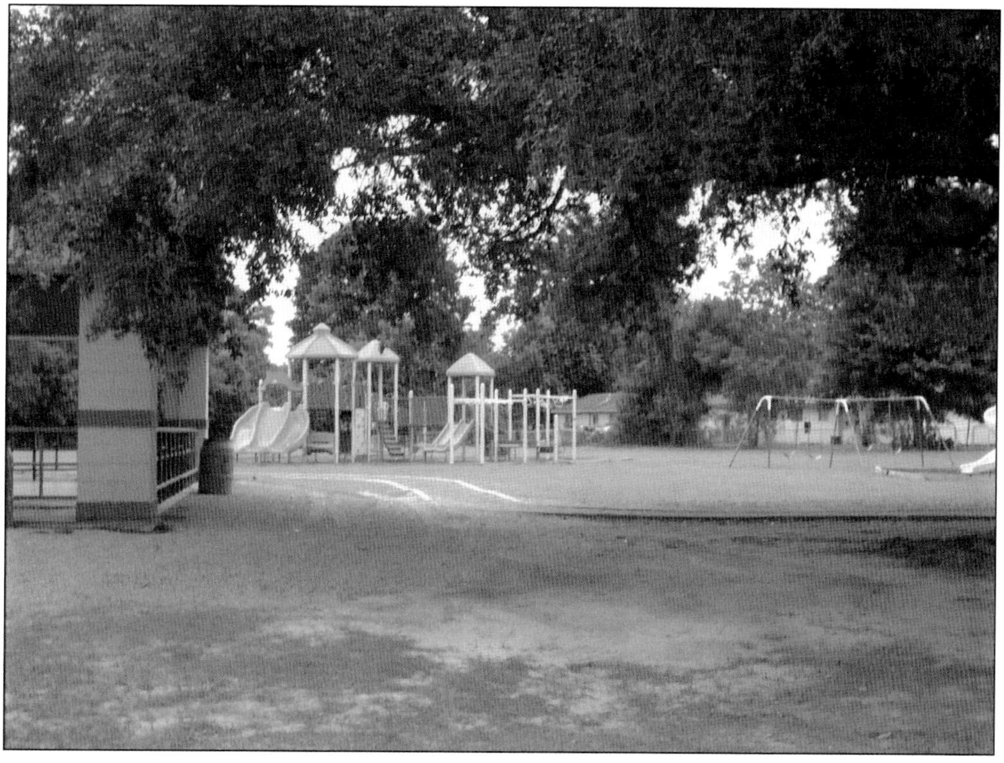

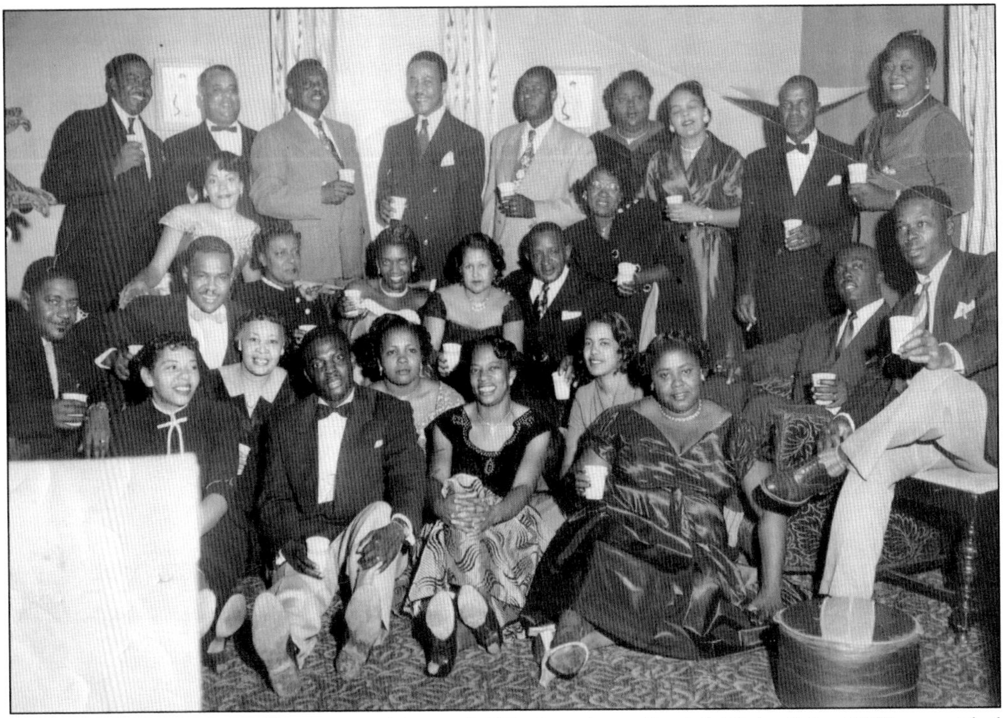

Les Amis Social Club (Lafayette Parish). The Les Amis Social Club of the 1950s provided an opportunity for social events for African Americans. The club members were married couples who held such social activities as Christmas balls, dances, and Pokeno card games. This photograph depicts a scene from a Christmas ball for club officers, members, and guests. (Courtesy of Rita Stemley.)

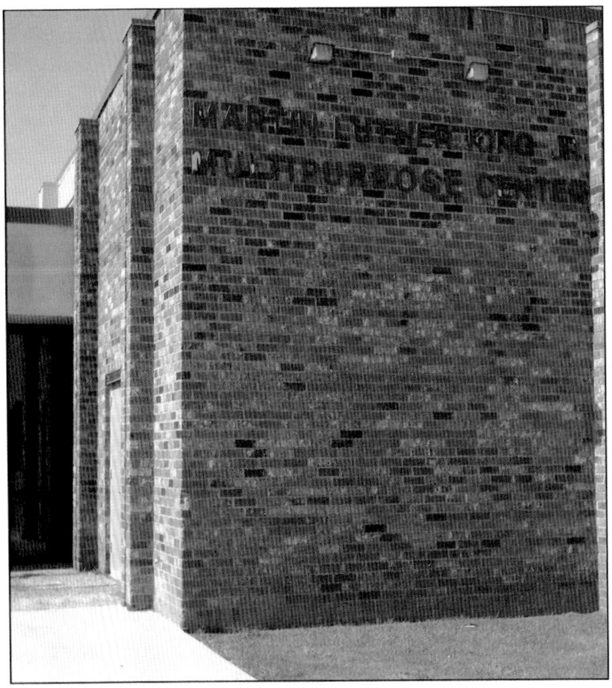

Community Center (Lafayette Parish). The MLK Multipurpose Center is located on Martin Luther King Jr. Drive in the Truman Addition neighborhood. The center is used for recreational purposes, meetings, receptions, and many other social events. The center has a gym, Butler Branch Library (a branch of the Lafayette Parish Public Library), and a park located on the grounds. An annual celebration occurs every year to commemorate the life and contributions that Dr. Martin Luther King Jr. gave to America and to the world. A celebration of his life is held each year at the MLK center, with the primary focus on health care, business and economics, voter registration, and other community needs. (Author's collection.)

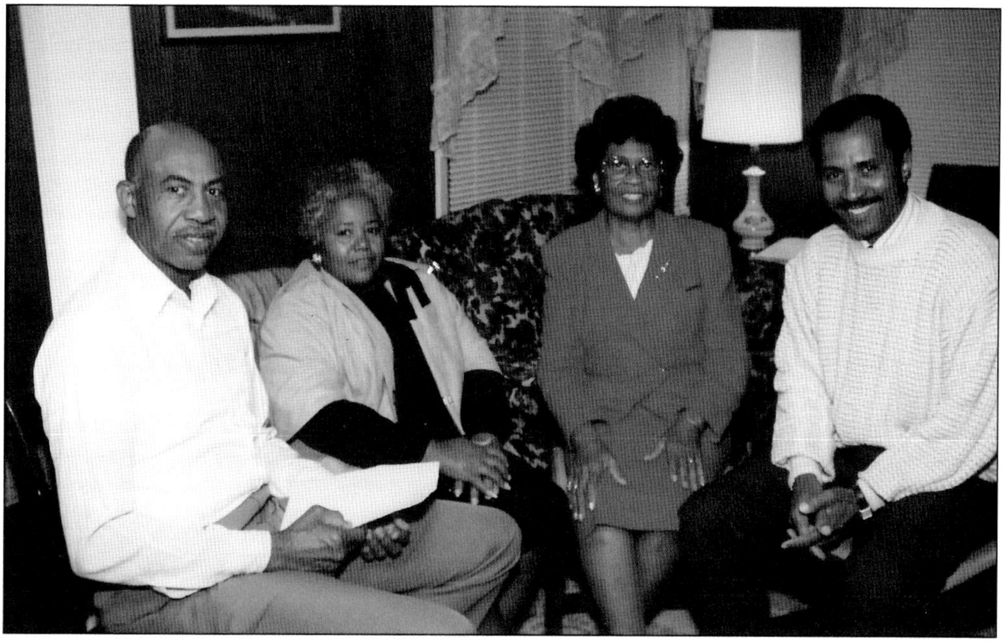

Discussing Community Issues (Lafayette Parish). Joseph Dennis (left) and John Broussard are at a meeting with two ladies to discuss issues concerning the community. Dennis is a member of the Black Alliance for Progress. Broussard is a member of Creole Inc. and is also a radio personality for KRVS at UL-Lafayette; every Saturday morning, he plays zydeco music until noon. (Courtesy of Edith G. Dupré Library Archives and Special Collections.)

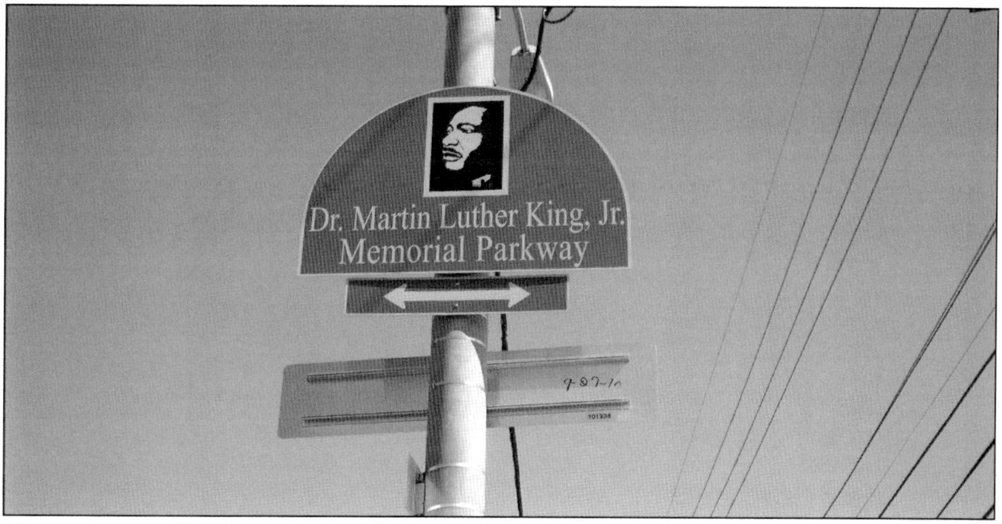

Martin Luther King Jr. Memorial Parkway (Lafayette Parish). Willow Street from Ambassador Caffery to Teurlings Drive is named Martin Luther King Jr. Memorial Parkway. It is the desire of many citizens that Dr. King, one of the world's greatest humanitarians, is given a place of honor in Lafayette, Louisiana, as he is honored in progressive cities throughout America. He was a member of Alpha Phi Alpha, whose colors are black and gold. There are purple signs along the light poles for a few miles, and the MLK Multipurpose Center is located on a small community street. Both are the only reminders of the influential Baptist minister in Lafayette, as no other major streets, highways, or thoroughfares are officially named in King's honor. (Courtesy of S. Taylor.)

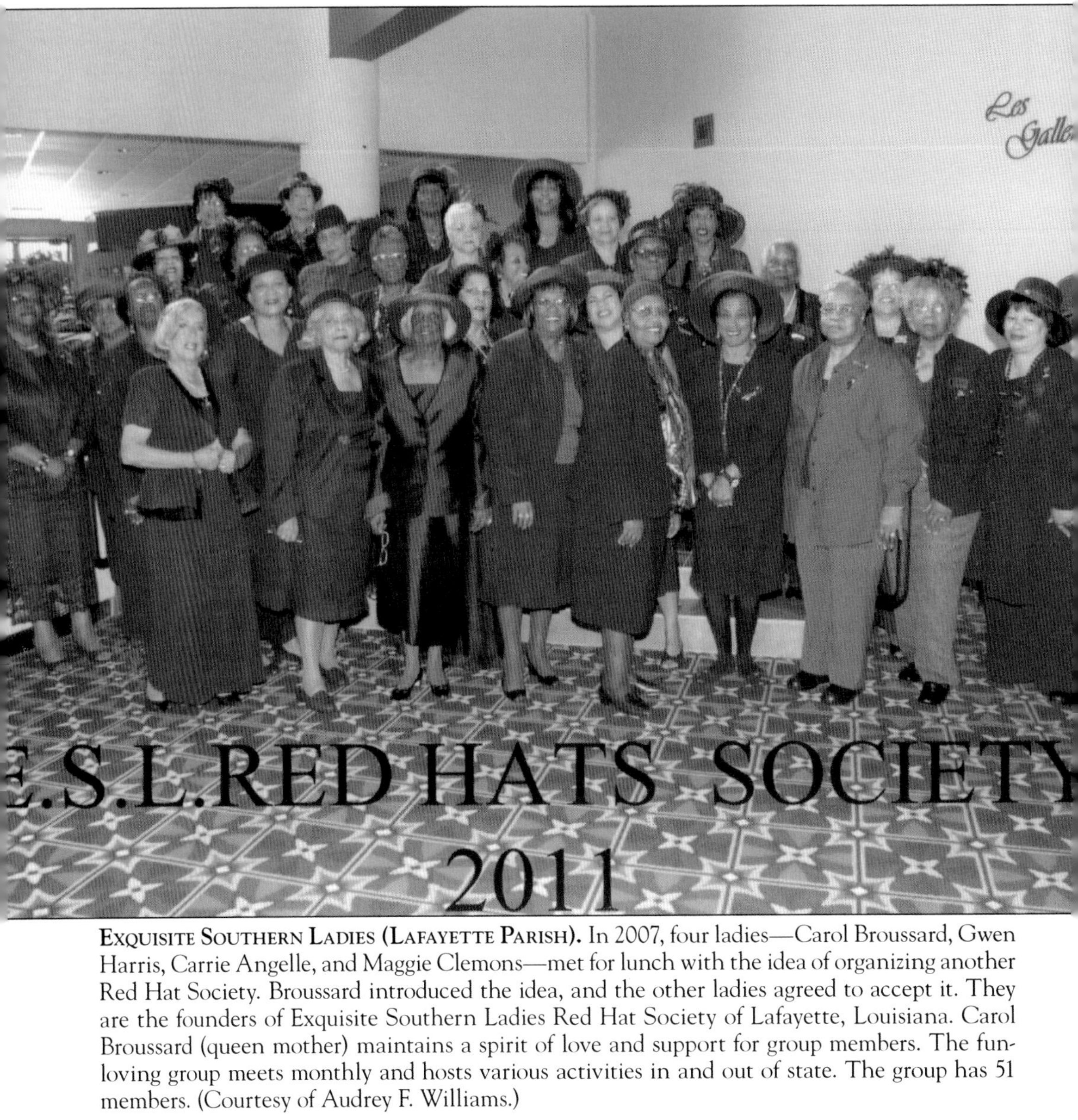

Exquisite Southern Ladies (Lafayette Parish). In 2007, four ladies—Carol Broussard, Gwen Harris, Carrie Angelle, and Maggie Clemons—met for lunch with the idea of organizing another Red Hat Society. Broussard introduced the idea, and the other ladies agreed to accept it. They are the founders of Exquisite Southern Ladies Red Hat Society of Lafayette, Louisiana. Carol Broussard (queen mother) maintains a spirit of love and support for group members. The fun-loving group meets monthly and hosts various activities in and out of state. The group has 51 members. (Courtesy of Audrey F. Williams.)

Four

Community Action

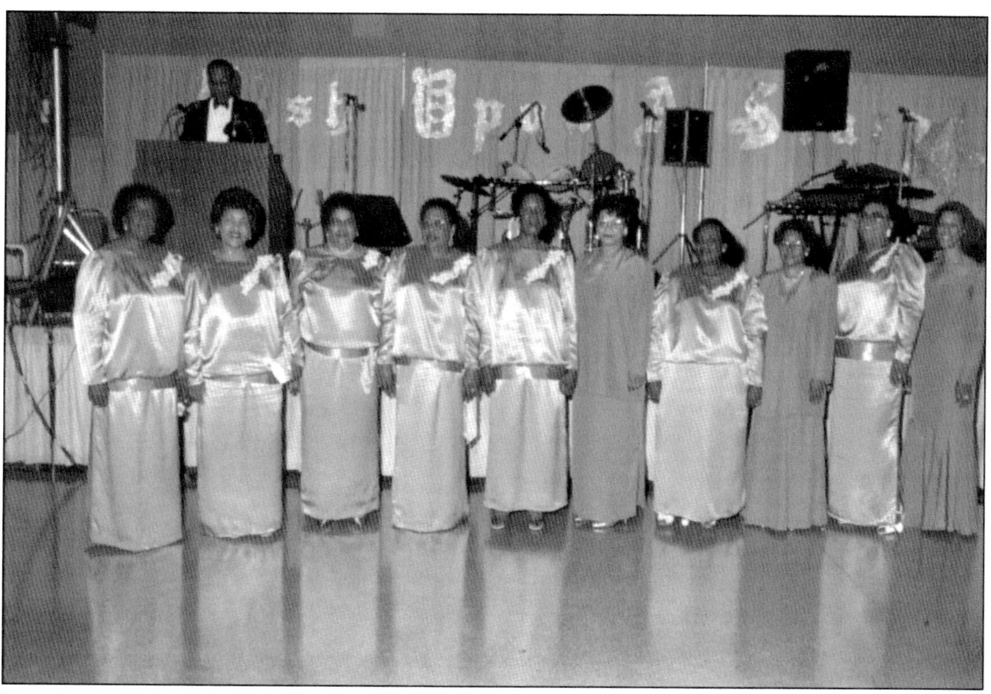

Les Femme de Mode Social and Civic Club (Lafayette Parish). The ladies in this image are the founders of Les Femme de Mode Social and Civic Club. From left to right they are G. Mack, M. Bastite, A. Perrot, O. Gallien, D. Johnson, E. Brown, S. Sam, G. Andrews, A. Minnard, and B. Ratliffe. The group was founded in 1959 and continues to present young ladies to society. A spectacular annual Debutante Ball is held each year. (Courtesy of Adele Minnard.)

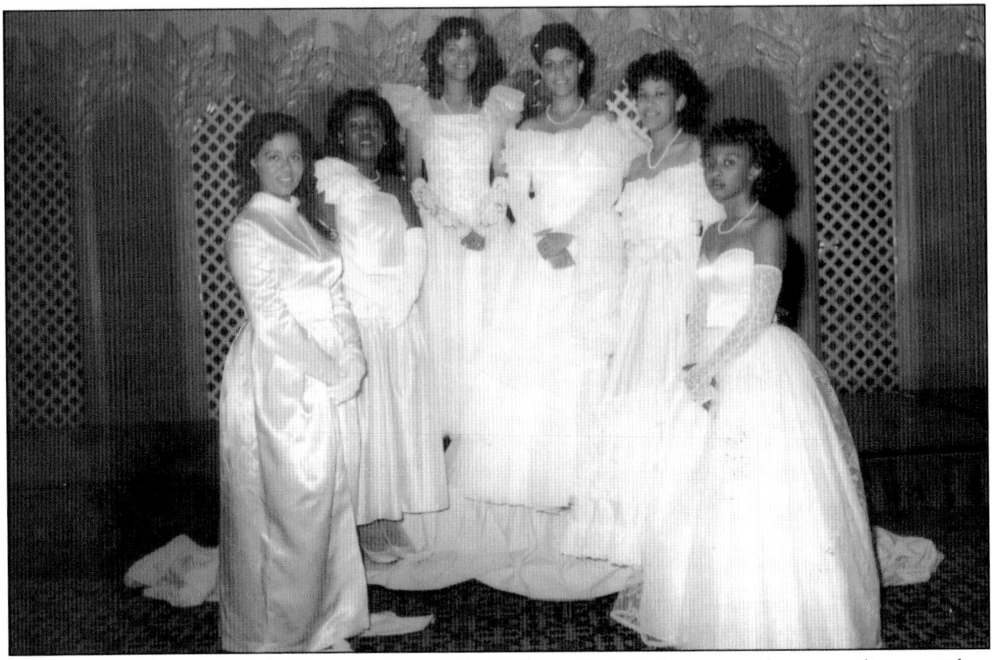

Debutantes (Lafayette). Young ladies in the 12th grade in Lafayette and surrounding parishes participate in activities such as the mother-daughter banquet, a community service project, and a beauty clinic. Young women, who participate as debutantes, must attend all activities and adhere to a specific schedule. (Courtesy of Adele Minnard.)

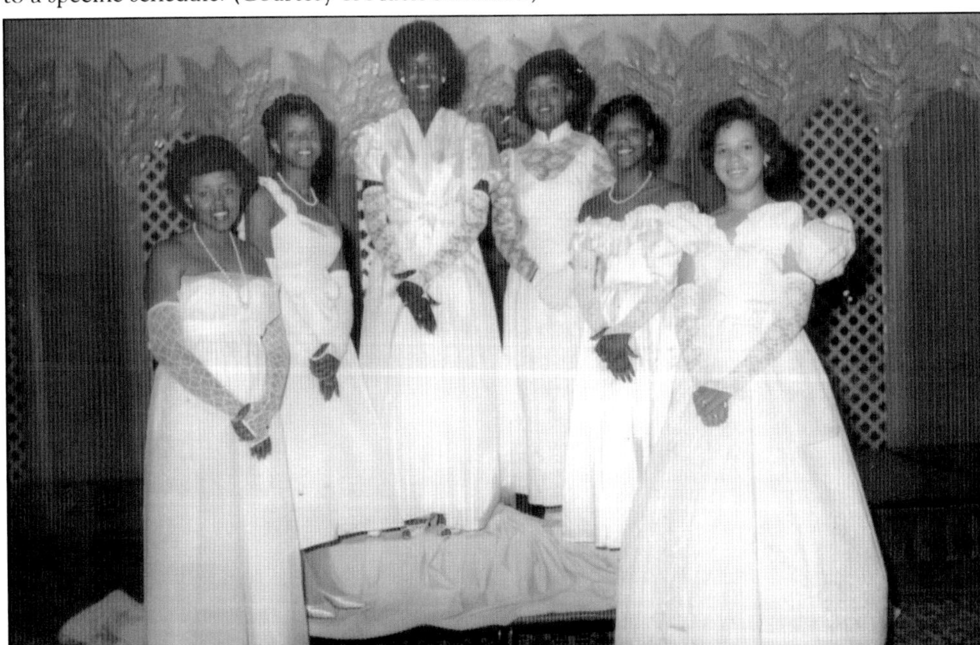

Love Day. Debutantes participate in a love activity where they attend a family dinner at a local church. A different church is chosen each year to sponsor Love Day where debutantes enjoy eating a delicious catered meal and spend time with their families. The wholesome activity of Love Day is a favorite among debutantes. (Courtesy of Adele Minnard.)

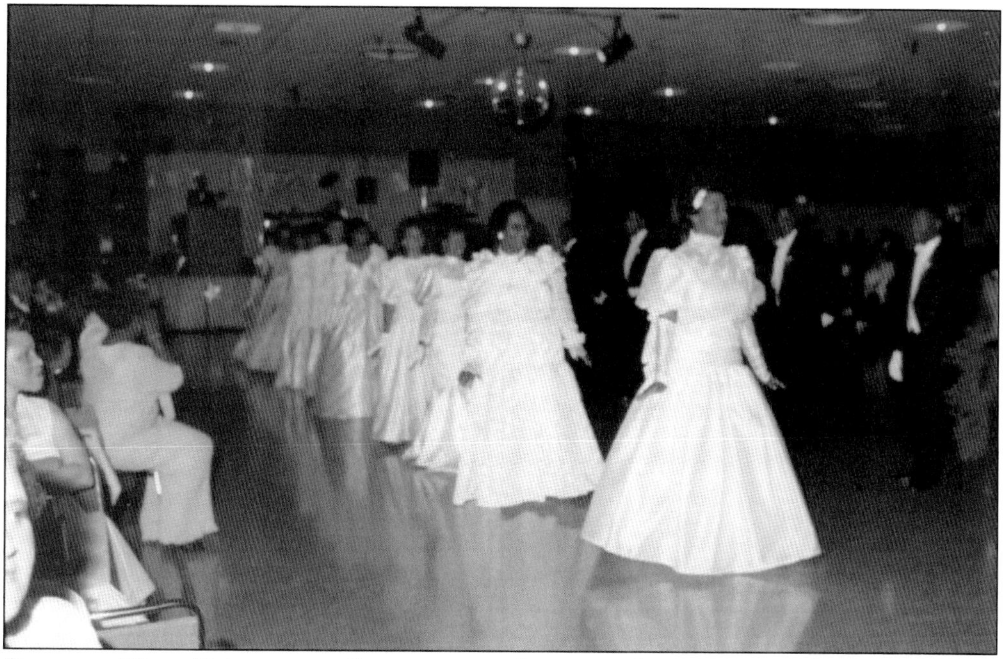

GRACEFUL WALK. Debutantes walk among invited guests as they are presented to society. These young ladies adorned in beautiful white dresses look like princesses as they walk among the guests. Each debutante will have a select amount of family members and friends attend the ball, seated at reserved tables. (Courtesy of Adele Minnard.)

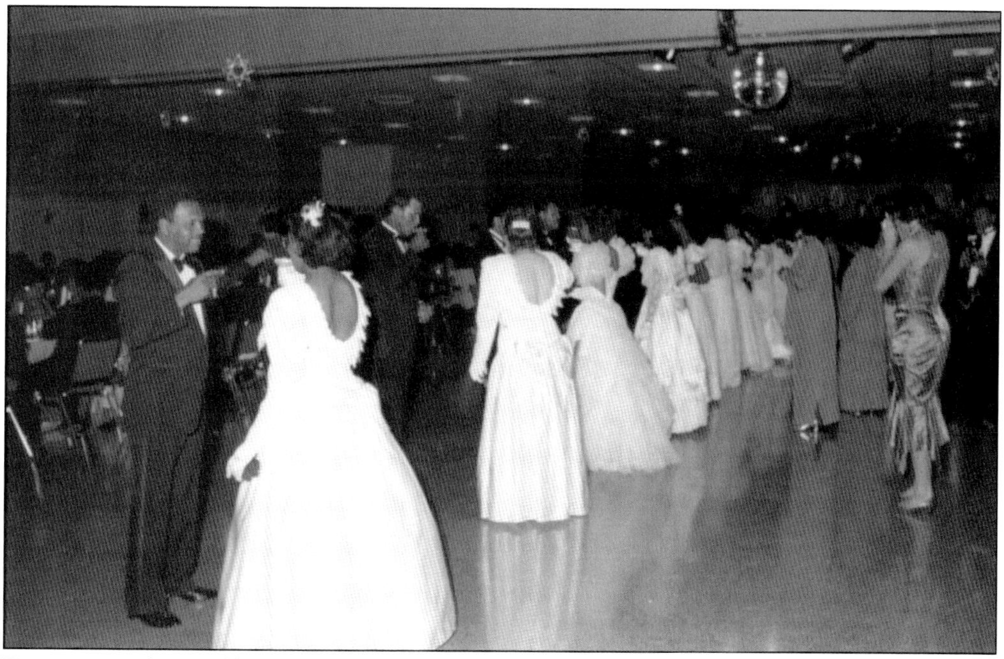

DANCING. A featured highlight of the debutante ball is the father-daughter dance. Alvin Wiltz (far left) is dancing with one of his daughters at the ball. The father-daughter dance requires practice or a rehearsal prior to the actual event. It is one of the most memorable experiences for both father and daughter. (Courtesy of Adele Minnard.)

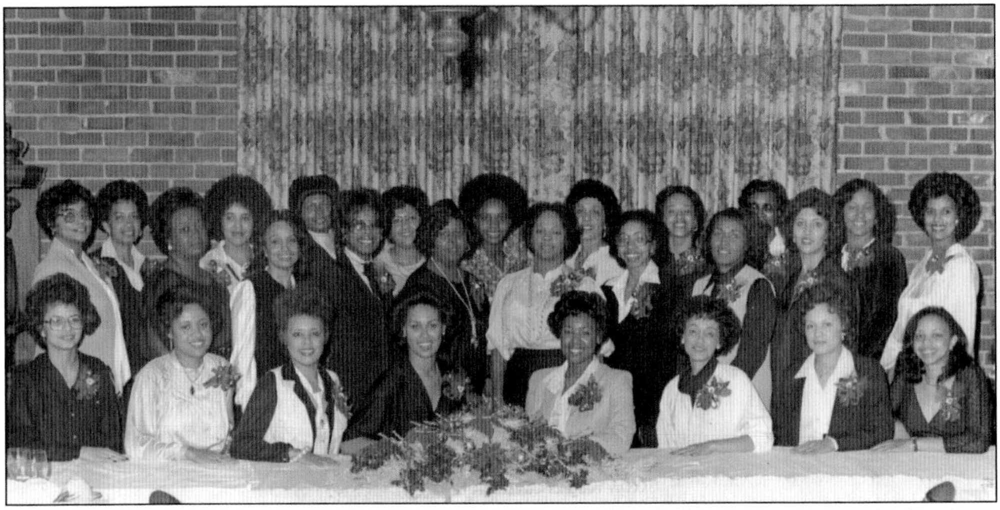

Onyx Women (Lafayette Parish). Founded in the 1970s by Phyllis Mouton and Ruby Rochon, the Acadiana Society of Onyx Women sponsors positive programs and activities that promote community involvement. (Courtesy of Phyllis Mouton.)

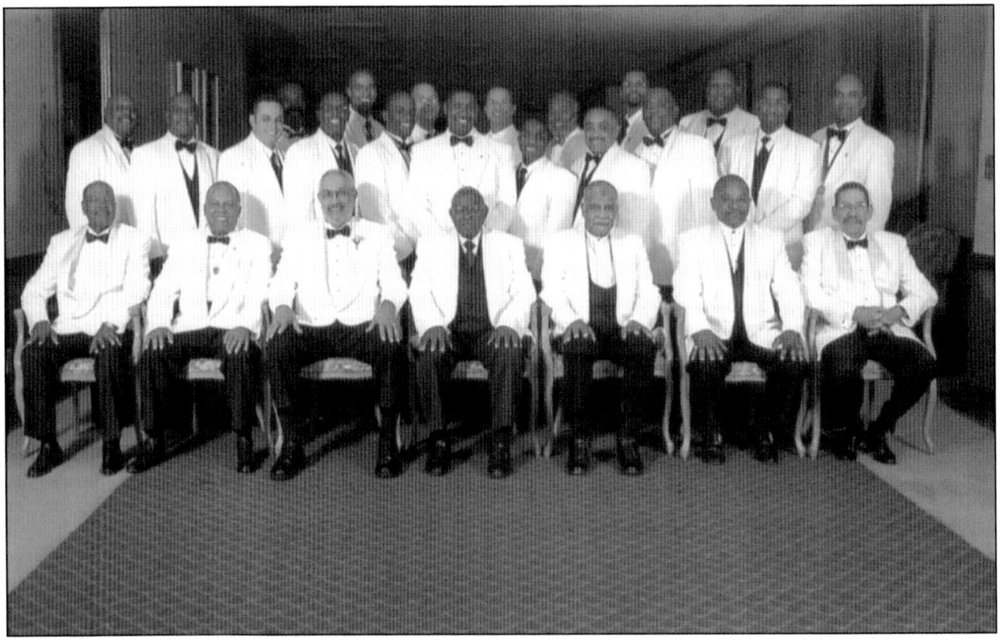

Brotherhood (Lafayette Parish). The Eta Gamma Lambda chapter of Alpha Phi Alpha celebrated its 100-year anniversary of the founding of the fraternity. Seated from left to right in the first row are F. Johnson, G. Brown, R. Baranco, D. Pipkin, E. Terrell, W. Pierre, and C. Arceneaux. (Courtesy of Richard Travers.)

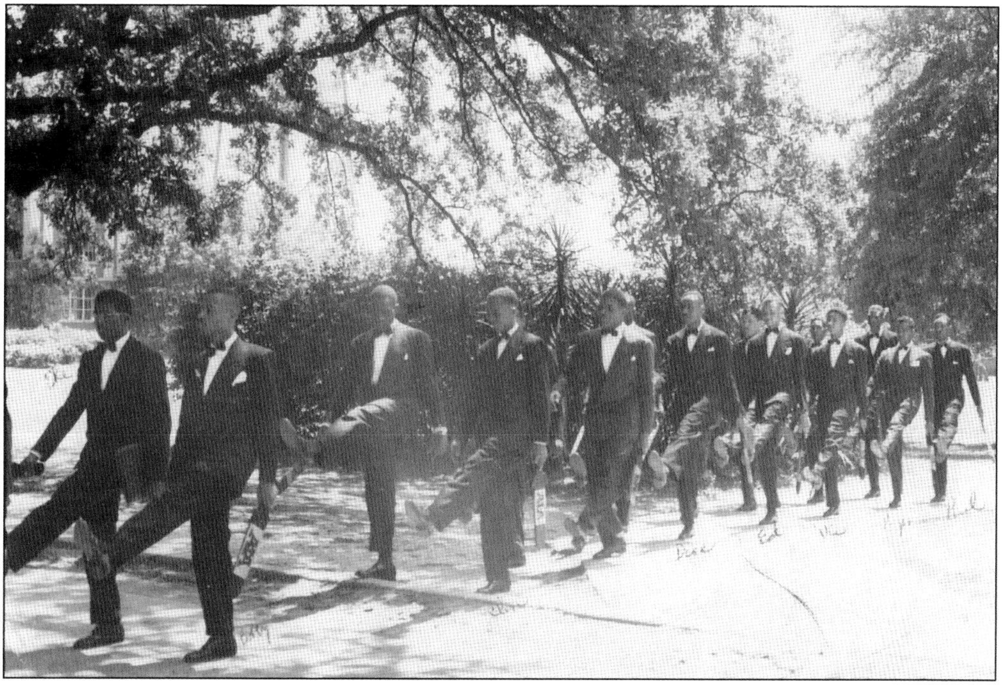

Bowles at Tuskegee (Lafayette Parish). Pictured here is George R. Bowles (third in line) during Hell Week activities with the Alpha Phi Alpha fraternity at the Tuskegee Institute in Alabama. (Courtesy of Wilma R. Bowles.)

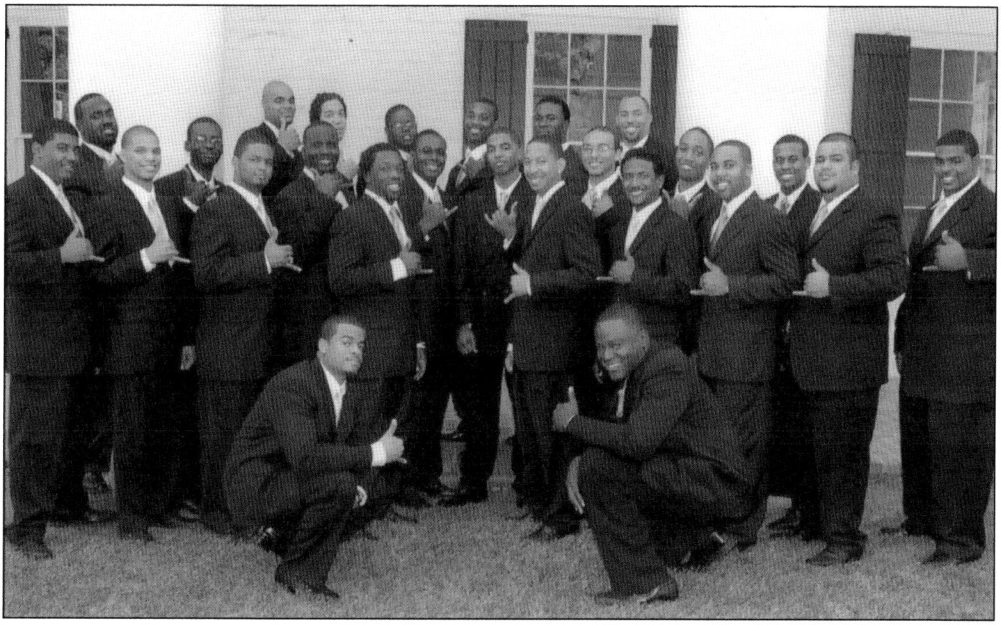

Fraternity (Lafayette Parish). The Zeta Xi chapter of Alpha Phi Alpha at UL-Lafayette is celebrating the initiation of new brothers. The chapter sponsors several events during the year, and members participate in activities such as those offered by the March of Dimes and Big Brothers/ Big Sisters, as well as the Miss Black and Gold Scholarship Pageant. Richard Travers, who holds a doctoral degree, is the chapter advisor. (Courtesy of Richard Travers.)

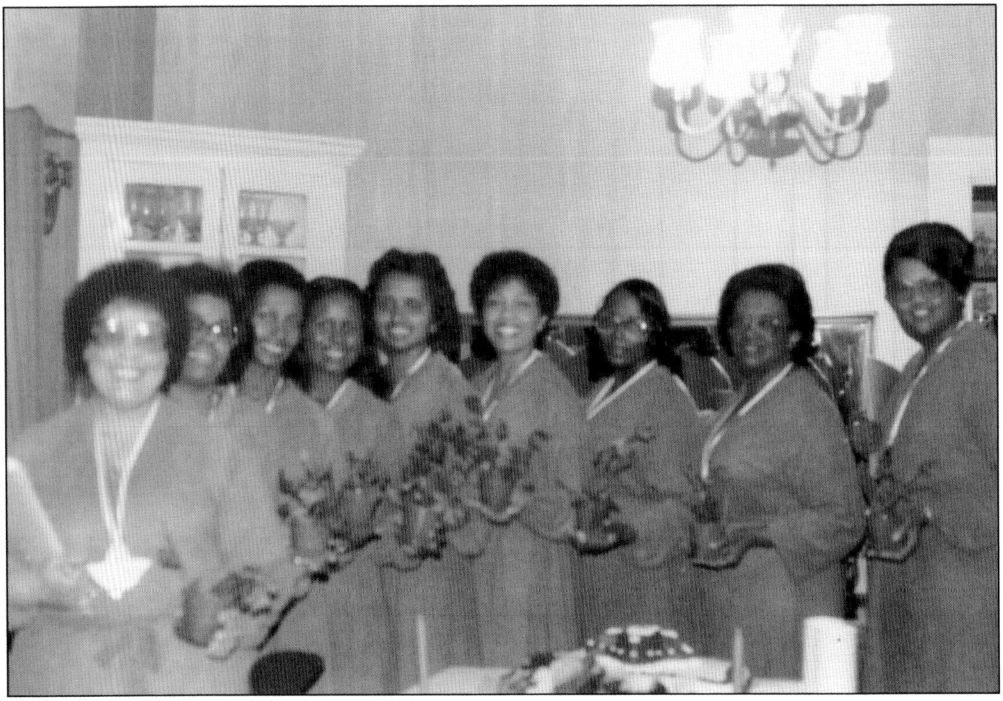

Alpha Kappa Alpha (Lafayette). The Eta Chi Omega chapter of the AKA sorority celebrated 100 years in 2008. Featured are members of the Lafayette chapter. Its colors are salmon pink and apple green. It sponsors several community activities. (Courtesy of Wilma R. Bowles.)

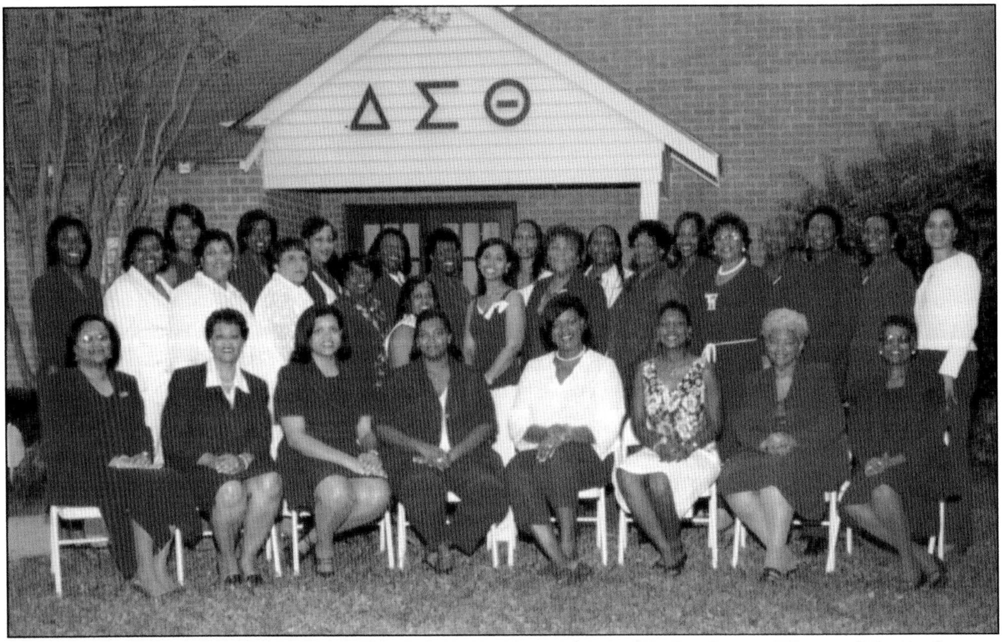

Sisterhood (Lafayette Parish). The officers and members of Delta Sigma Theta of the Lafayette chapter (founded in 1913) proudly wear their colors of crimson and cream. The sorority sponsors the annual Beautillion, an event that introduces young men into society, and offers scholarships to participants with the highest grade-point averages. (Courtesy of Adele Minnard.)

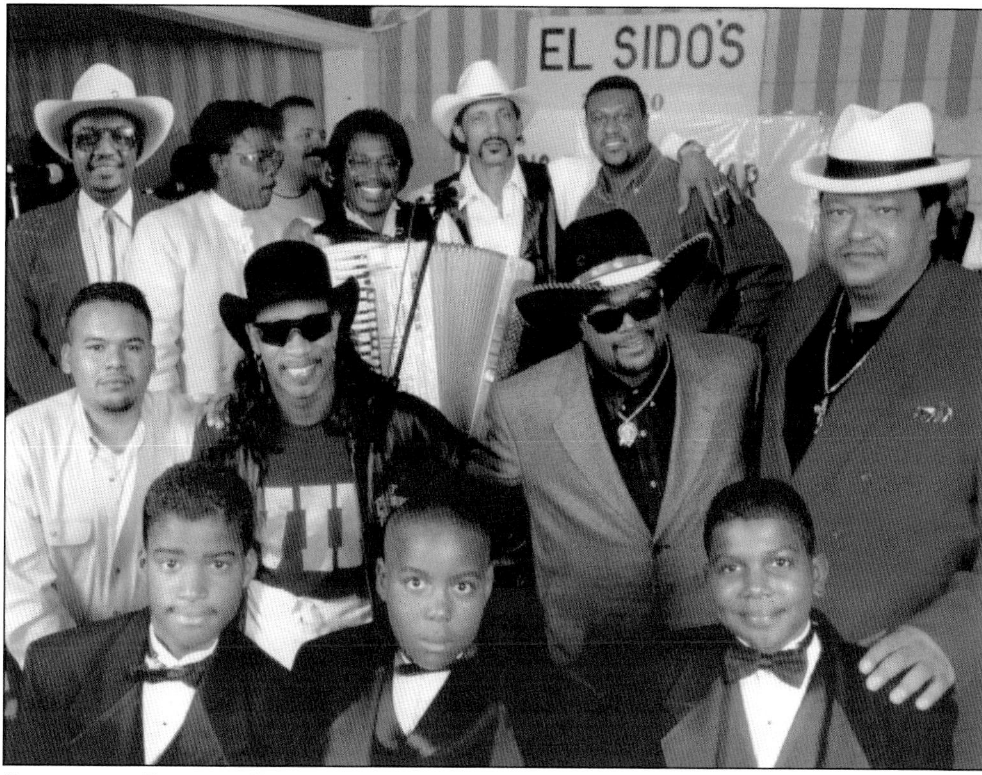

SINGING AND DANCING ZYDECO. From one generation to the next, zydeco music is an absolute favorite in Lafayette and southwest Louisiana. Nathan Williams, Rockin' Dopsie Jr., Corey (of Corey and the Hot Peppers), Beau Jocque (deceased), Zydeco Joe (deceased), Chubby Carrier, Sidney Williams, Terrance Simien, Buckwheat Senegal, and Lil Nathan (front right), as well as others in the image, are some of the most talented musicians in America. (Courtesy of Sidney Williams.)

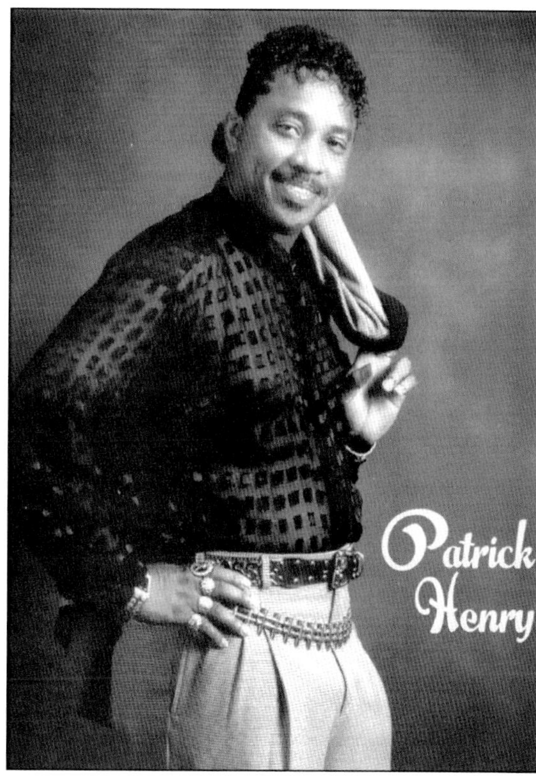

SUNSET, LOUISIANA, NATIVE (ST. LANDRY PARISH). Patrick Henry was born in Sunset and began singing at a young age. He is a member of the Liberation Band, and they have performed with many professional groups and recorded hit songs. Henry and the Liberation Band are marvelous entertainers who play blues, R&B, and soul music. (Courtesy of Edith G. Dupré Library Archives and Special Collections.)

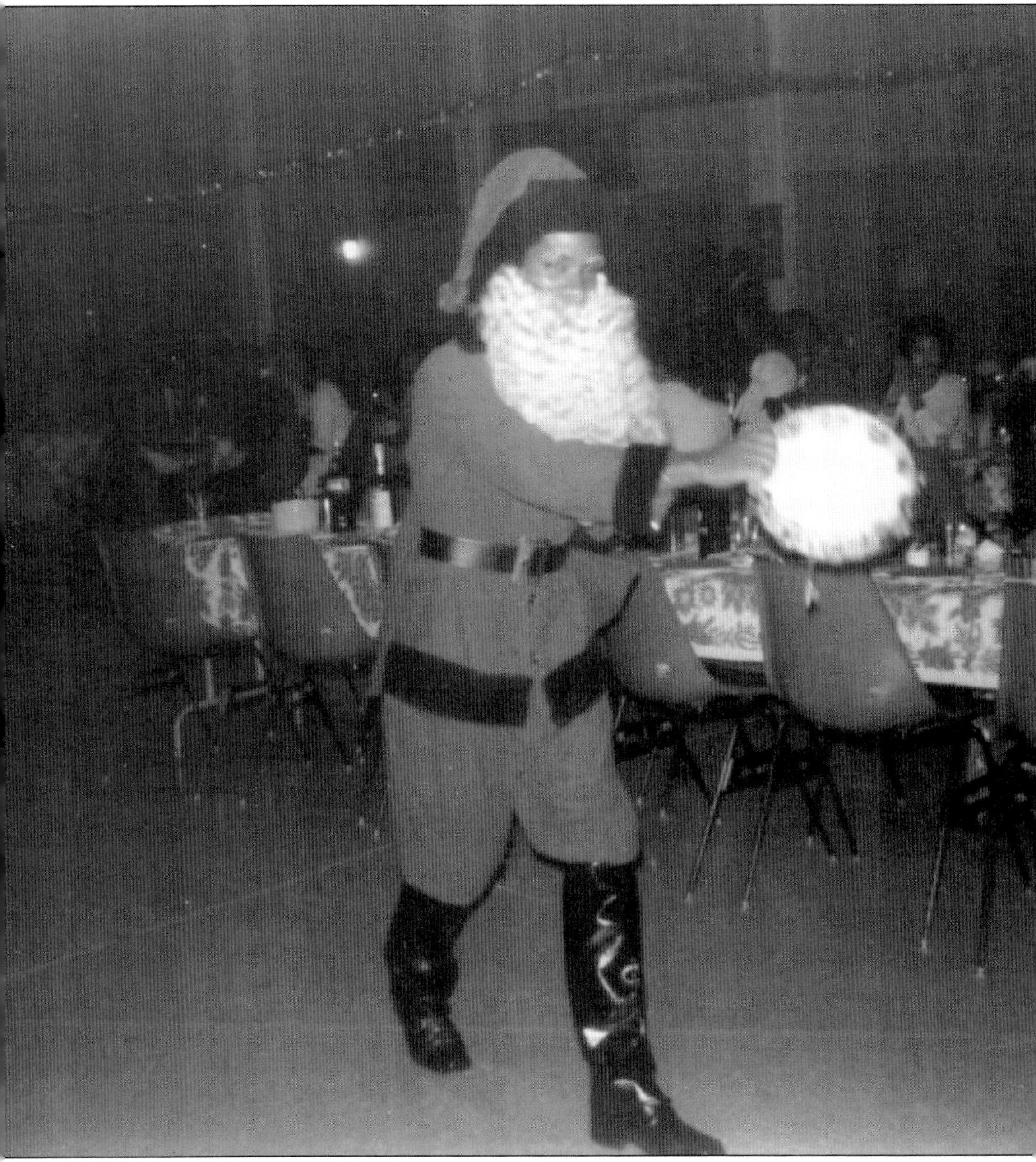

THE BLACK SANTA PROJECT (LAFAYETTE PARISH). The Black Santa Project spanned 10 years and provided education about healthy eating, information on the history of Africa, heritage songs and stories, and a dancing black Santa who dressed in red, black, and green. Santa's helpers (mostly family members and close friends of Adofo and Jaha Harmon) educated and entertained audiences and gave gift bags with healthy food items. The Black Santa entertained at schools and parties and visited hospitals, spreading joy and cheer. Members of the Black Santa Project often dressed in African-style clothing, demonstrated how to celebrate Kwanzaa, and presented cultural skits. The performers with the Black Santa Project mesmerized audiences as they sang, danced, and shared cultural history with the audience. (Courtesy of Adofo Harmon.)

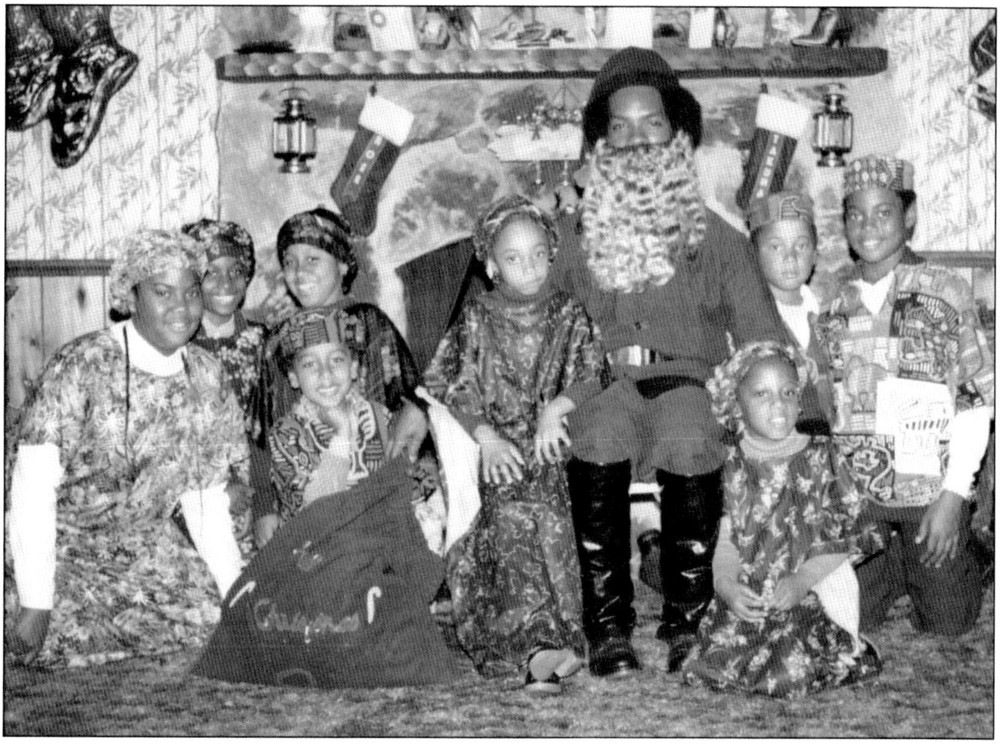

YOUNG PERFORMERS WITH BLACK SANTA ADOFO HARMON (LAFAYETTE PARISH). It was a family-and-friends affair when it came to the performers. Adofo and Jaha Harmon delighted audiences while sharing valuable information about healthy eating, cultural history, dancing, and singing. They wore beautiful African clothing complete with head wraps and hats that were often handmade. They performed in Lafayette and other southwest parishes. (Courtesy of Adofo and Jaha Harmon.)

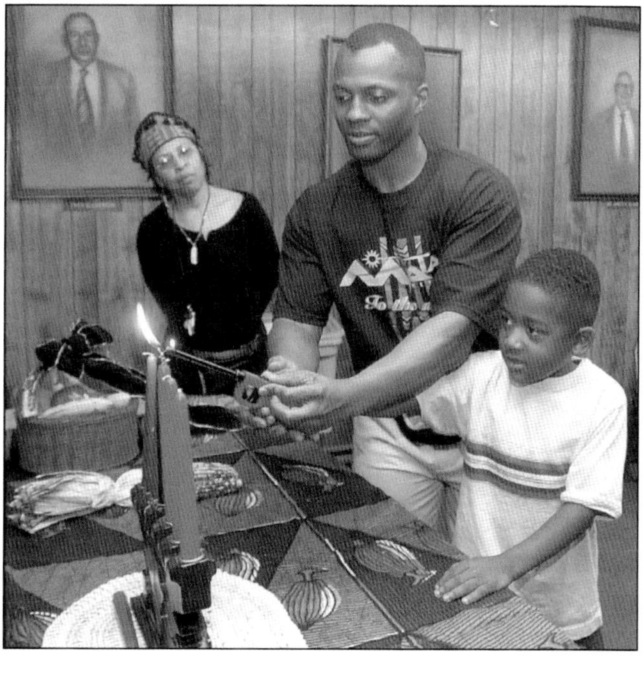

CELEBRATING KWANZAA (LAFAYETTE PARISH). Pictured here are Jahmilah Sekhmet (back), who is the local videographer of community events, and Uuka Thandiwe, standing with a young boy who is earning the importance of celebrating Kwanzaa. Kwanzaa teaches family values and focuses on the seven principles of the Nguzo Saba. Kwanzaa was founded by Dr. Maulana Karenga in 1966. It is celebrated annually by five million people for seven days from December 26 to January 1. (Courtesy of the *Daily Advertiser*.)

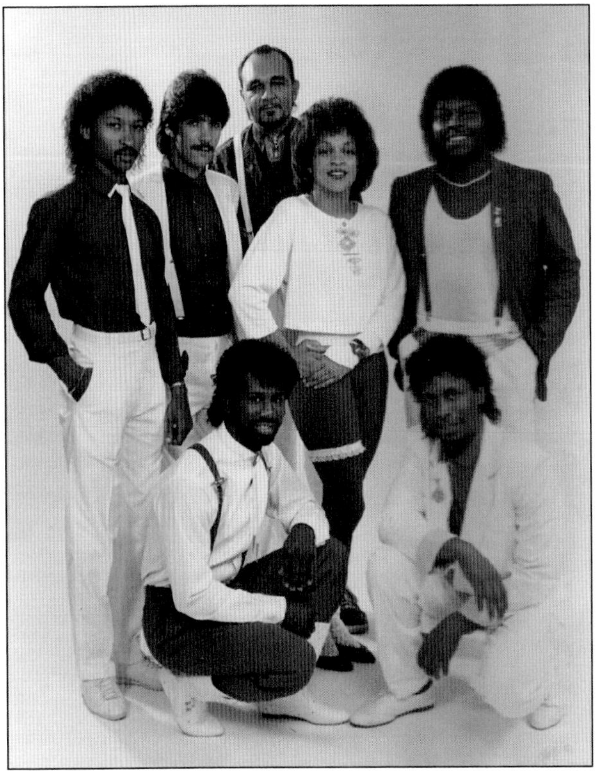

Popular Band (Lafayette Parish). Krossfyre is a sensational Louisiana party band that has entertained people for over 30 years. The talented group plays, sings, and performs locally as well in and out of Louisiana. Matt Noel (front left) is the founder of the group. Some other members pictured here are Connie Alexander and Emmitt Wiltz. (Courtesy of Edith G. Dupré Library Archives and Special Collections.)

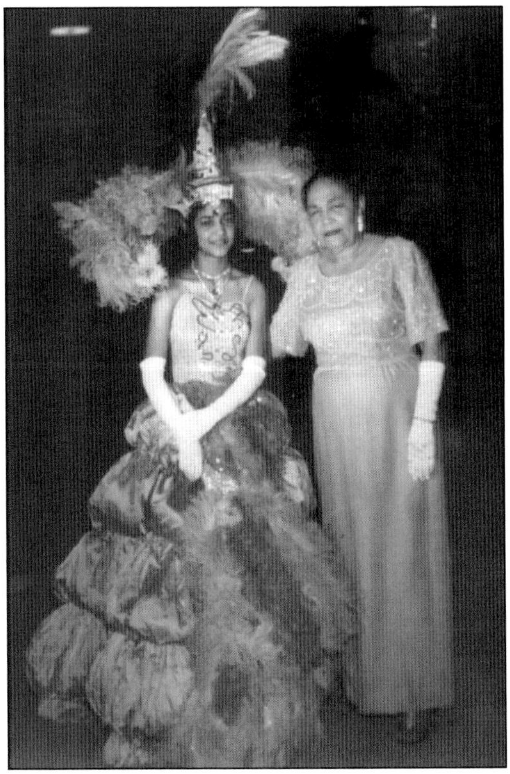

Mardi Gras Grandeur (Lafayette Parish). Thelma Fleming (right) is one of the original founders of the Lafayette Mardi Gras Festival, Inc. She is seen here with an unidentified princess. Fleming served as Queen Suzanne Simonne of the 1972 Mardi Gras Ball and Festival. (Courtesy of Louis J. Perret, clerk of court, Lafayette, Parish.)

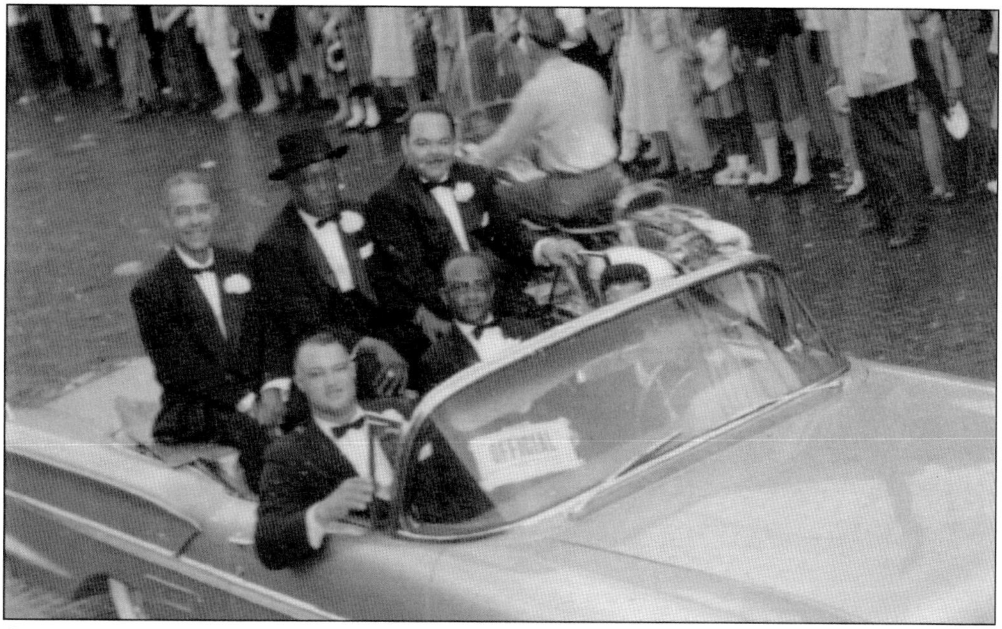

Celebrating Mardi Gras (Lafayette Parish). Officers, members, and dignitaries of a 1950s Lafayette Mardi Gras Festival are riding in the parade. The group had its own floats, bands, and sponsors for the black Mardi Gras celebration. The parade rolled down Lafayette streets in the afternoon on "Fat Tuesday," beginning on Simcoe Street. This car depicts L. Broussard, Doremus Dorsey, and others. (Courtesy of Lyle Mouton Sr.)

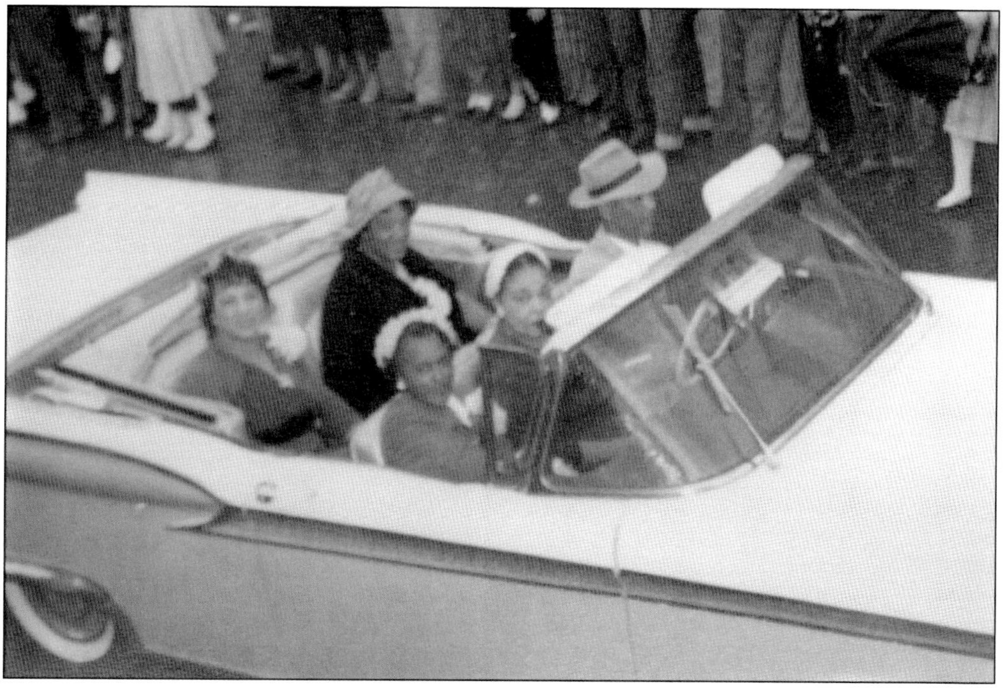

The Car. This second car shows Ruth Hayes, Thelma Fleming, and others riding in the parade. Citizens filled the streets to enjoy the celebration. Early black parades had a separate parade route from white parades, but the festivities were fun for all who attended. (Courtesy of Lyle Mouton Sr.)

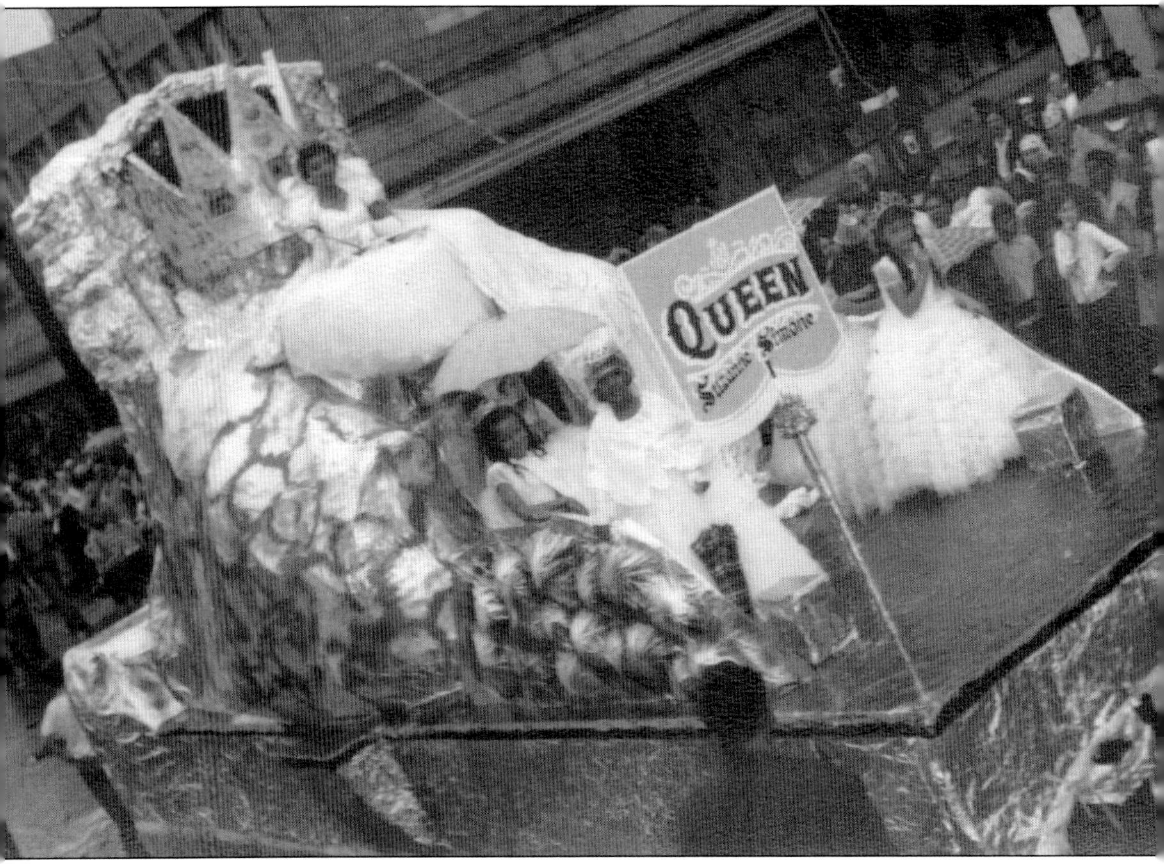

Queen Suzanne Simonne in Mardi Gras Parade, 1950s (Lafayette Parish). The queen is pictured here waving to the large crowd at the parade. Parade attendees line the streets to see the beautiful queen's float. Attendance for the parade grows each year. Some young ladies serve as princesses and later serve as Queen Suzanne Simonne. The seating of the royal families, presenting past royals, and the seating of dignitaries occurs at the pageant. (Courtesy of Lyle Mouton Sr.)

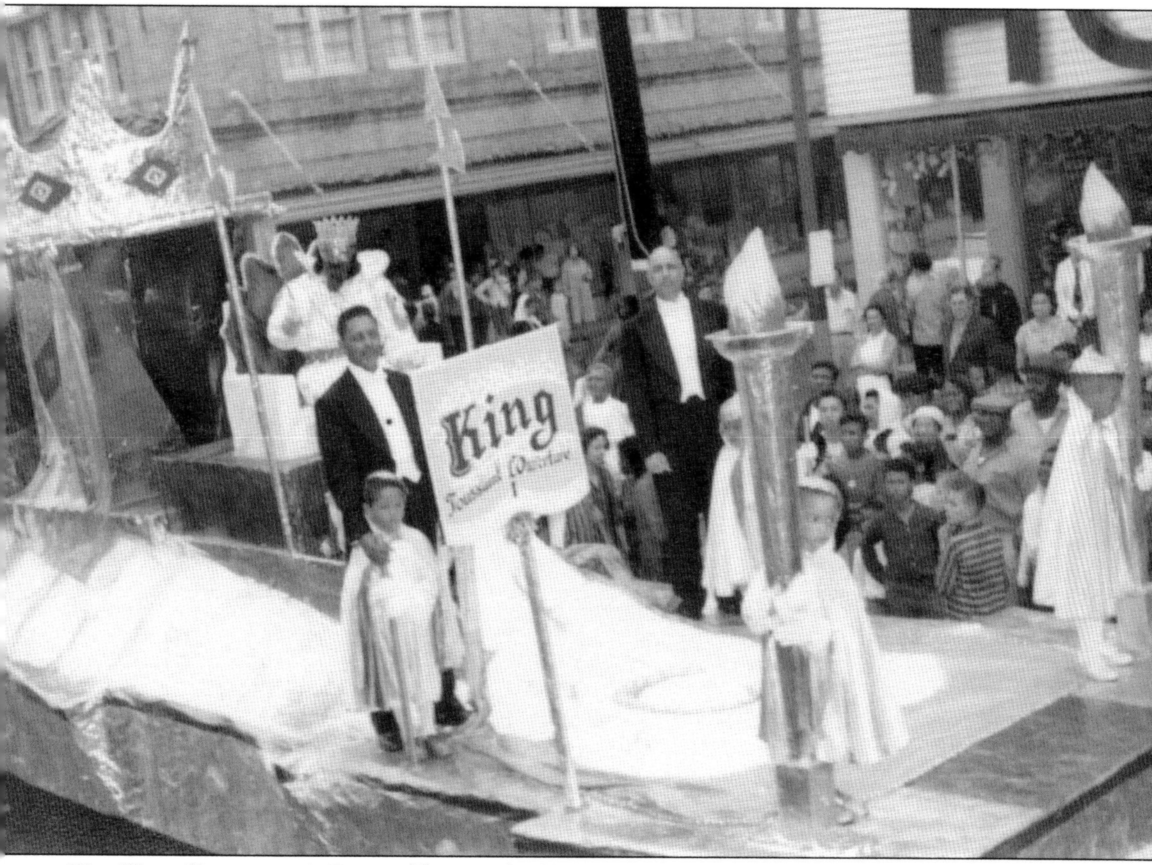

The King (Lafayette). Pictured here is the King Toussaint L'Ouverture float at a 1950s Mardi Gras parade. The king's float is the first one to roll down the street. Marching bands, theme floats, and colors of purple, green, and gold are present throughout the parade. Many beautiful colors fill this event, from the hair and skin of some individuals to the elaborate costumes of others. (Photograph by Wallace Mouton, courtesy of Lyle Mouton Sr.)

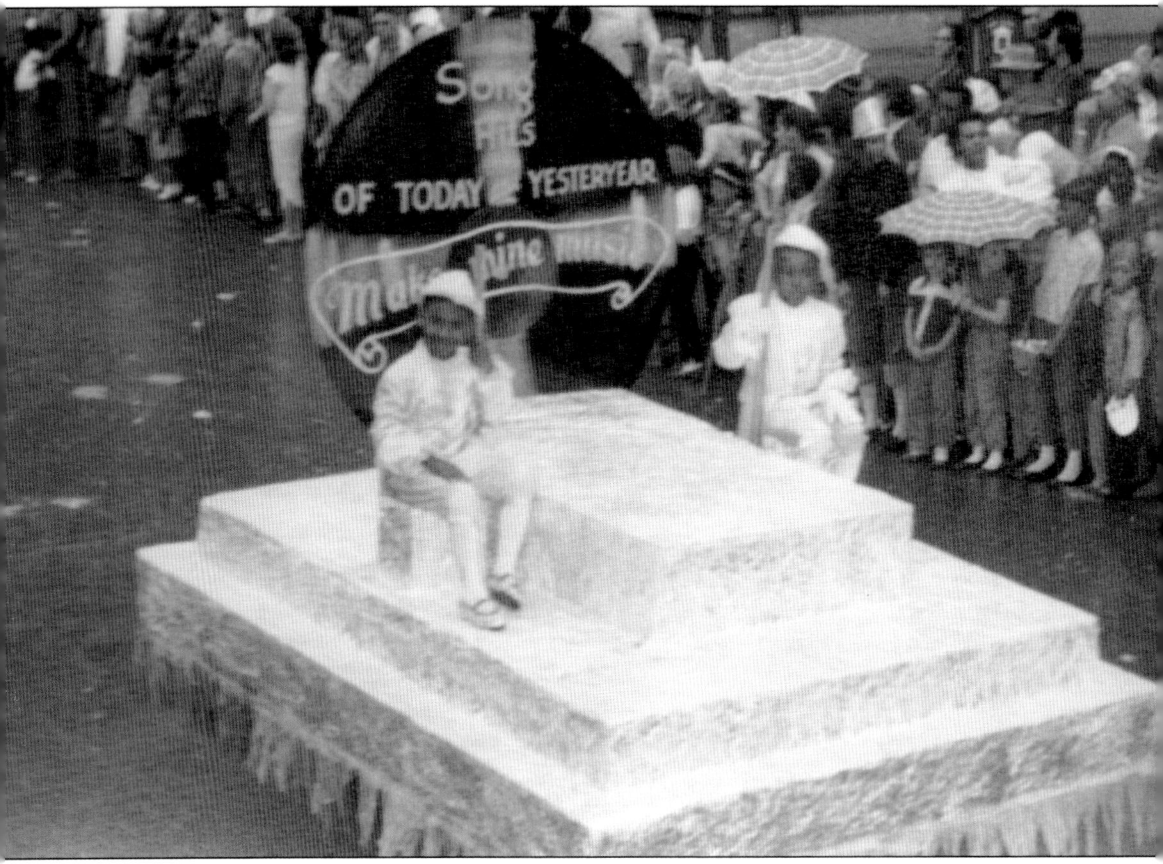

RIDING ON THE FLOATS. Children enjoyed the festivities of Mardi Gras, especially riding on the various floats in the parade. They throw candy, colorful beads, and other trinkets to people along the route. In early years, no barricades were used at the parades, but today they are placed along the route to keep people safe. (Courtesy of Lyle Mouton Sr.)

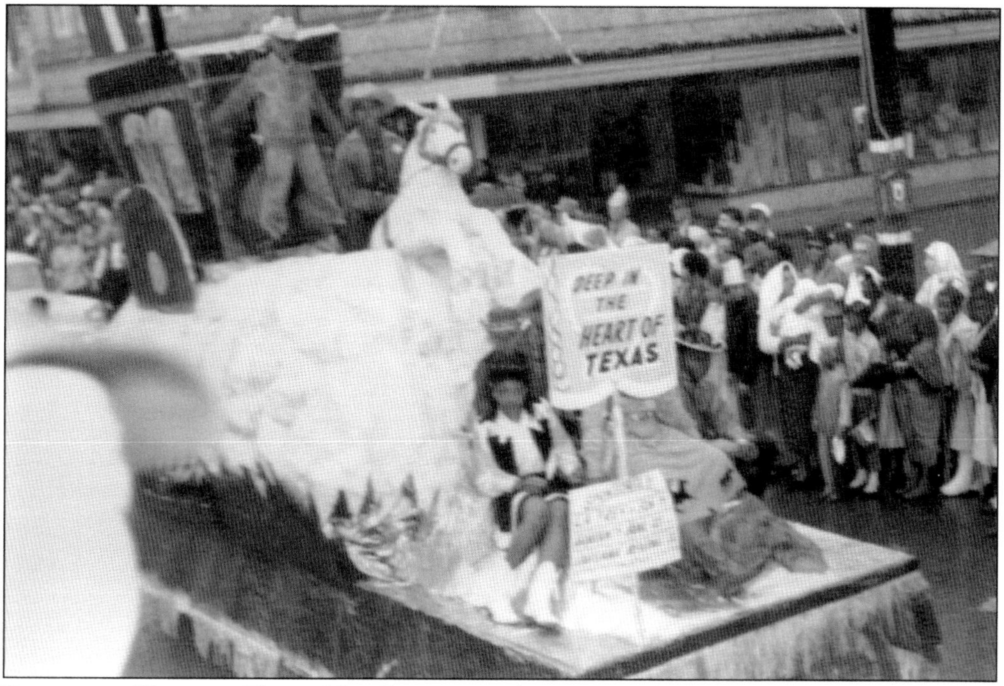

Deep in the Heart of Texas. This float is part of a 1950s Mardi Gras parade. It has a stagecoach on top, while cowgirls and cowboys ride on the float. All floats have a design that reflects the overall theme of the parade. Costumes were made by local seamstresses for the children and adults who participated in the Mardi Gras activities. (Courtesy of Lyle Mouton Sr.)

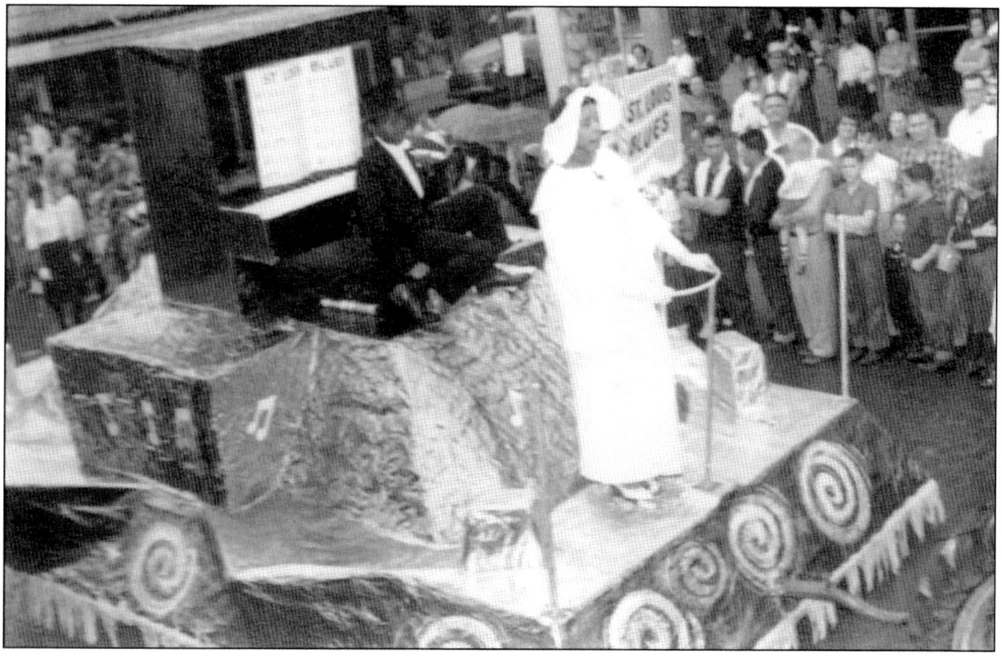

Keep on Floating. This float features a singer and piano player as part of a 1950s Mardi Gras celebration. Popular music is played and sung at the parades much to the delight of attendees. During modern times, some people on floats toss music CDs to the crowds. (Courtesy of Lyle Mouton Sr.)

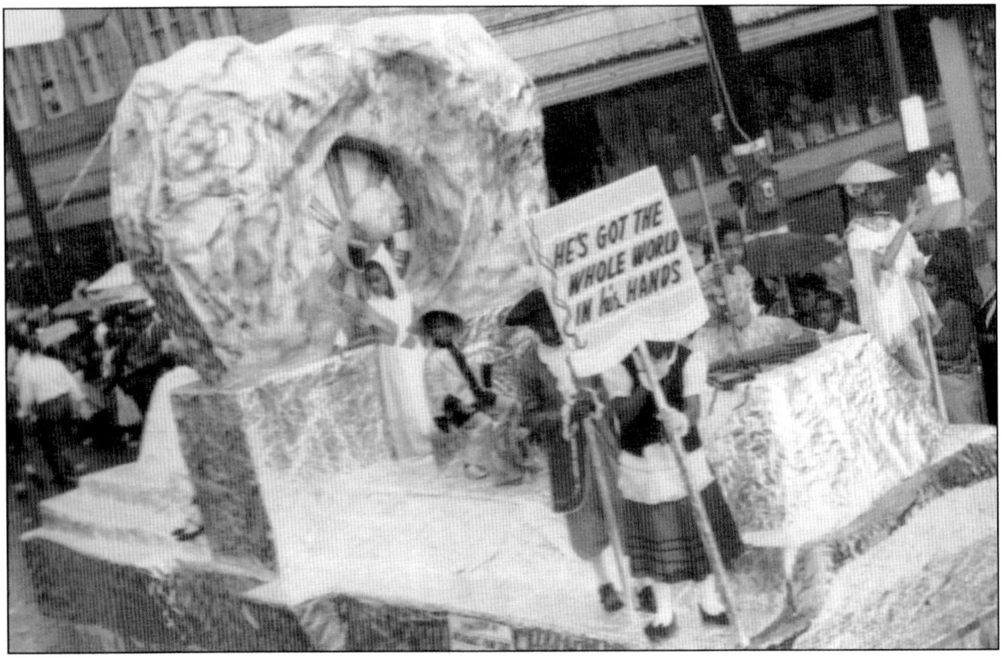

He's Got the Whole World (Lafayette Parish). This photograph shows enchanting and lively bands playing music to entertain and energize people at the parade. The popular song, "He's Got the Whole World in His Hands," is the highlight of the float. It features a piano, a piano player, and a singer in front of a microphone. (Courtesy of Lyle Mouton Sr.)

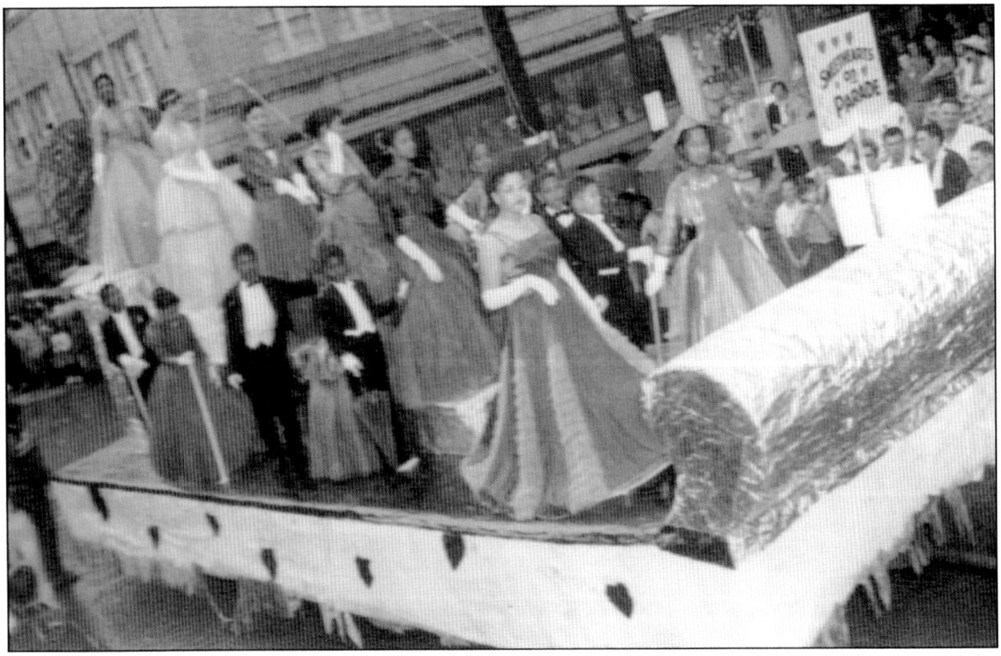

Princess Float, 1950s Mardi Gras Parade (Lafayette Parish). One of the princesses on the float may be the next Queen Suzanne Simonne. Princesses and their attendants wear elaborate handmade costumes that depict the theme of the float. They are presented at the pageant in the order of princess, duke, and attendants. (Courtesy of Lyle Mouton Sr.)

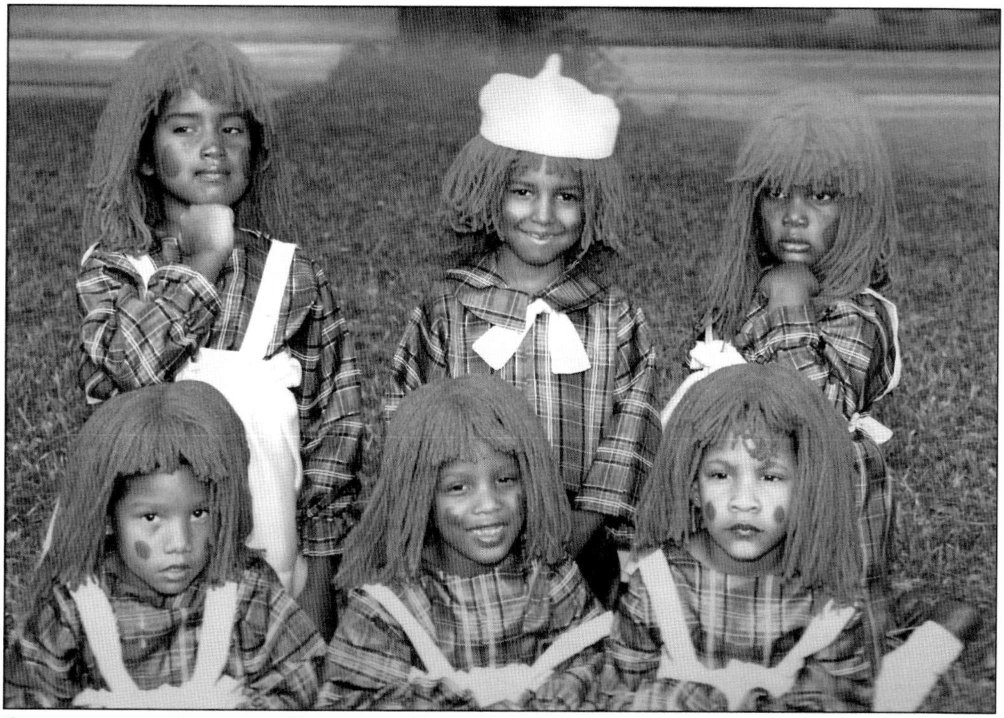

Children and Costumes (Lafayette Parish). These children wore colorful costumes, participating in the parade dressed like Raggedy Ann and Andy. Parents and sponsors walk along the parade route on either side of the float with the children as a precaution to keep them safe. (Courtesy of Edith G. Dupré Library Archives and Special Collections)

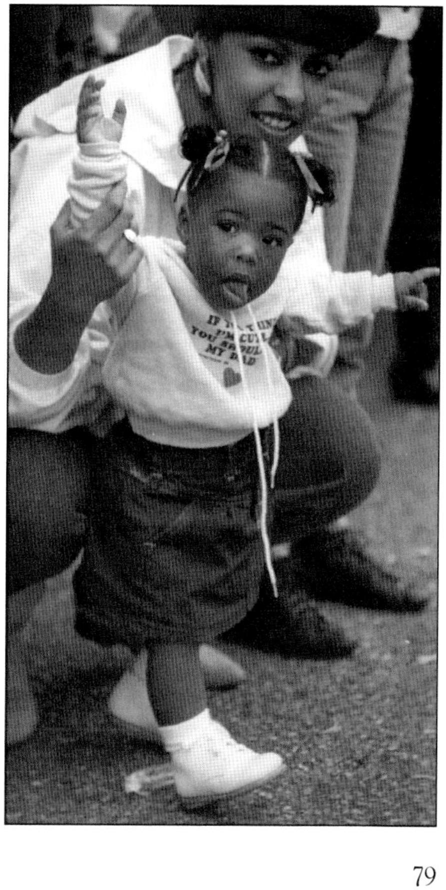

Mother and Child at Parade (Lafayette Parish). Citizens participate in and enjoy various parades, such as those for MLK Day, Mardi Gras, black history, and Christmas. Parade attendees receive items such as beads, CDs, cups, books, T-shirts, caps, candy, and other promotional items. They enjoy marching bands, creatively designed floats, and the waves and smiles of participants in the parades. (Courtesy of Edith G. Dupré Library Archives and Special Collections.)

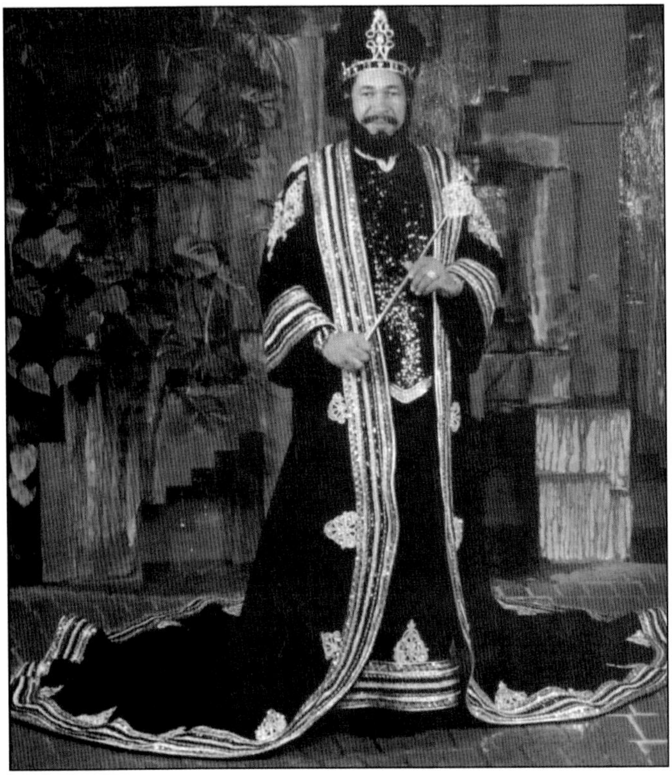

MARDI GRAS ROYALTY, KING (VERMILION PARISH). Charles Guidry was King Toussaint L'Ouverture of the 1992 Lafayette Mardi Gras Ball and Festival. Guidry is the owner of the Charles Guidry Sugar Cane Farm and employs 32 people. He is a member of St. Mary's Sugar Cane Cooperative. Guidry is a former middle school math and science teacher, a Vietnam veteran, and a graduate of Grambling State University. His elaborate king's robe and crown were made by Omega Costumes in New Orleans, Louisiana. (Courtesy of Nelda Broussard.)

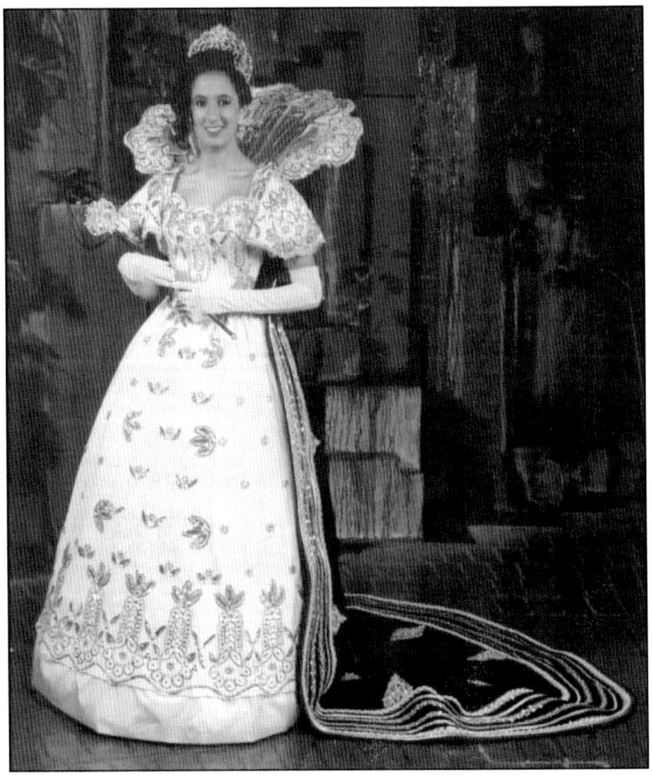

MARDI GRAS ROYALTY, QUEEN DEIDRE RENEE VALLOT. Deidre Renee Vallot from Abbeville, Louisiana, was the 1992 Queen Suzanne Simonne of the Mardi Gras celebration. The queens selected are usually much younger than the kings and dress in similar royal gowns and suits as seen here. The dresses are usually as elaborate as Vallot's beautifully designed gown. (Courtesy of Nelda Broussard.)

THE "ZYDECO BOSS" (ST. LANDRY PARISH). Keith Frank began playing professionally with his father when he was four years old. His band, Keith Frank and the Soileau Zydeco Band, includes his sister and brother. He has the leadership role in the family band, and his style of zydeco music is popular with audiences of all ages. (Courtesy of Edith G. Dupré Library University Archives and Special Collections.)

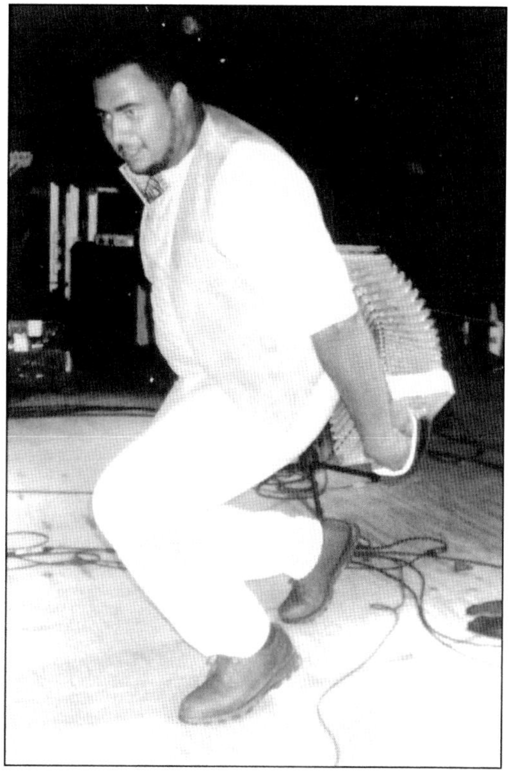

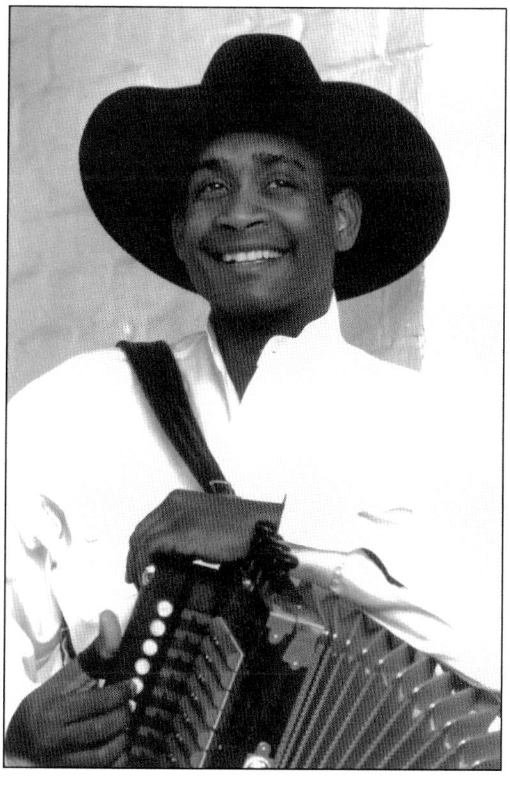

GENO DELAFOSE & FRENCH ROCKIN' BOOGIE (EVANGELINE PARISH). A native of Eunice, Louisiana, Geno Delafose grew up in a world surrounded by zydeco music played by his late father, John Delafose, an accordion player. Geno originally played the drums and the rub board in his father's band, the Eunice Playboys. (Courtesy Edith G. Dupré Library Archives and Special Collections.)

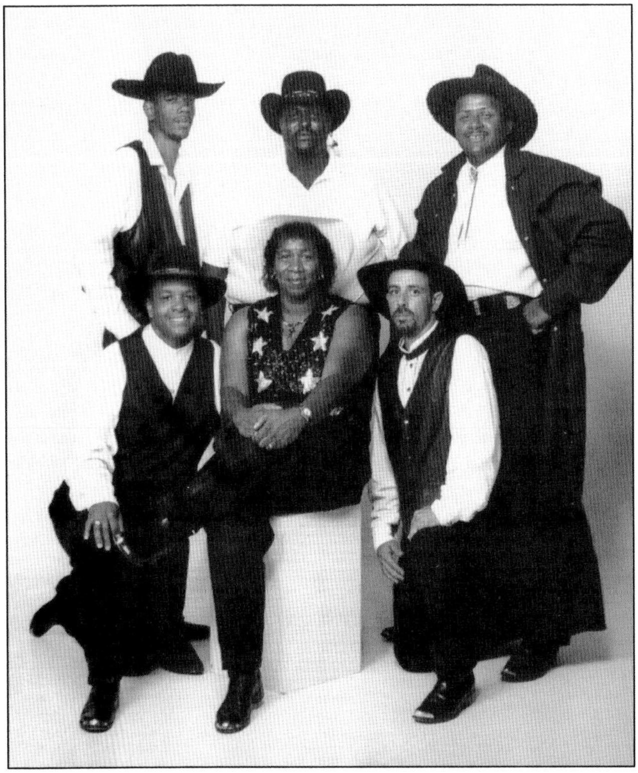

The Women of Zydeco (Lafayette Parish). Donna Angelle & the Zydeco Posse' performs rhythm and blues and zydeco music locally and in and out of the state. Donna sings and plays the bass and accordion and is the founder of two bands. She has won awards for her performances, and Donna Angelle & the Zydeco Posse' is a popular group that performs at festivals and many other events. (Courtesy Edith G. Dupré Library Archives and Special Collections.)

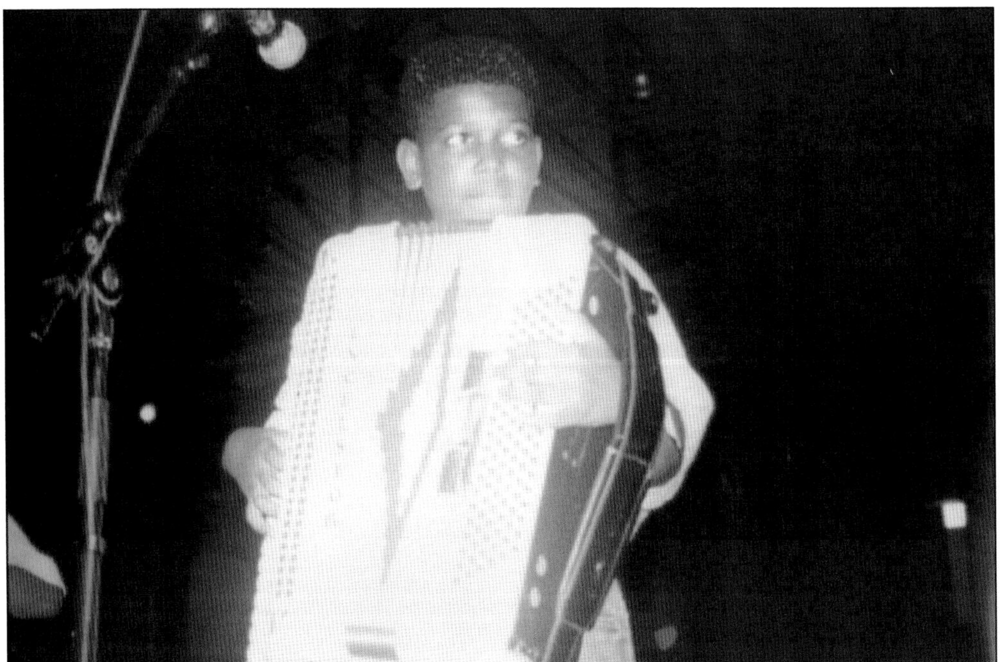

Growing Up With Zydeco (Lafayette Parish). Pictured here is Nathan Williams Jr. (Lil Nathan) at a young age playing the accordion at a local event. Most zydeco musicians learn to play their instruments early and are exceptional entertainers. (Courtesy of Sidney Williams Jr.)

Playing the Rub Board. Naylan Williams, son of Nathan Williams Sr., is three years old in this picture and playing the rub board. He is the younger brother of Lil Nathan. (Courtesy of Sidney Williams Jr.)

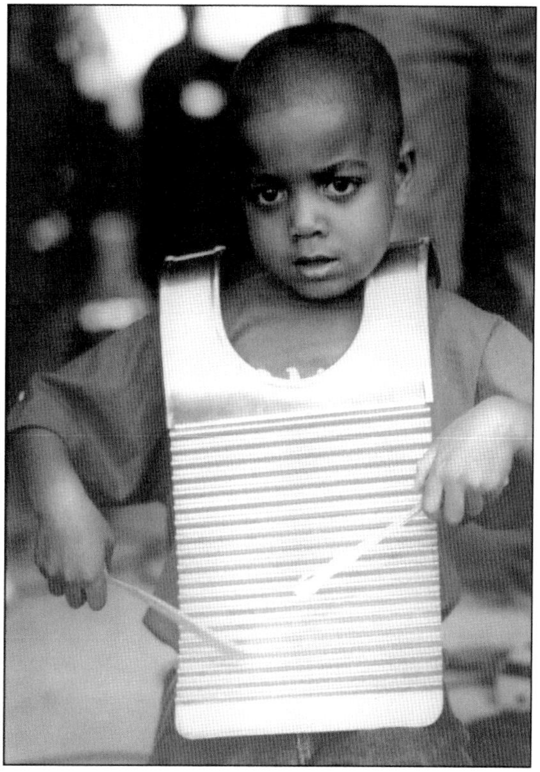

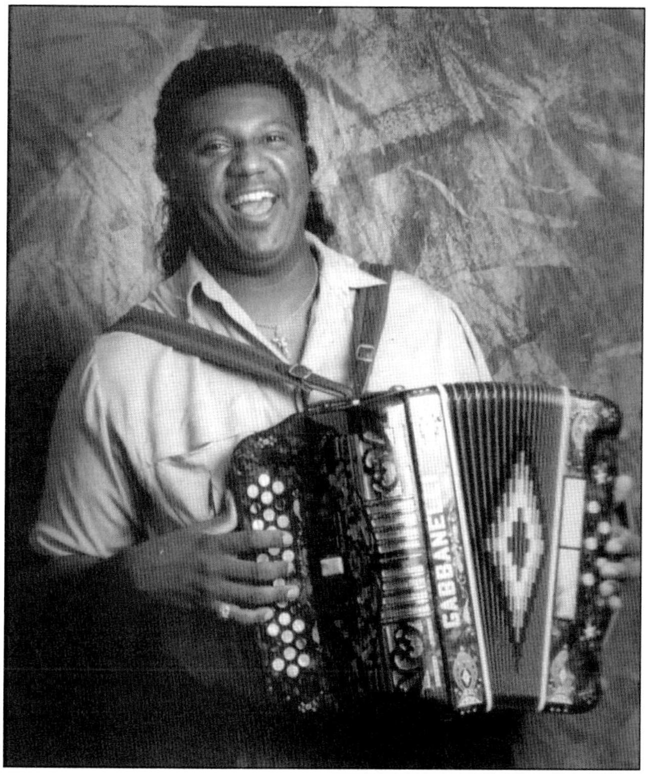

Grammy Winner (Acadia Parish). Longtime zydeco musician Chubby Carrier won the 2011 Zydeco/Cajun Grammy Award and is the third African American from Louisiana to win it. He was preceded by Terrance Simien and Buckwheat Senegal. Carrier was born in Church Point, Louisiana. Carrier's father and grandfather were both zydeco musicians. Chubby Carrier and the Bayou Swamp Band has recorded several albums and performs at many local events. Carrier and his band are a favorite in the music world of zydeco. (Courtesy Edith G. Dupré Library Archives and Special Collections.)

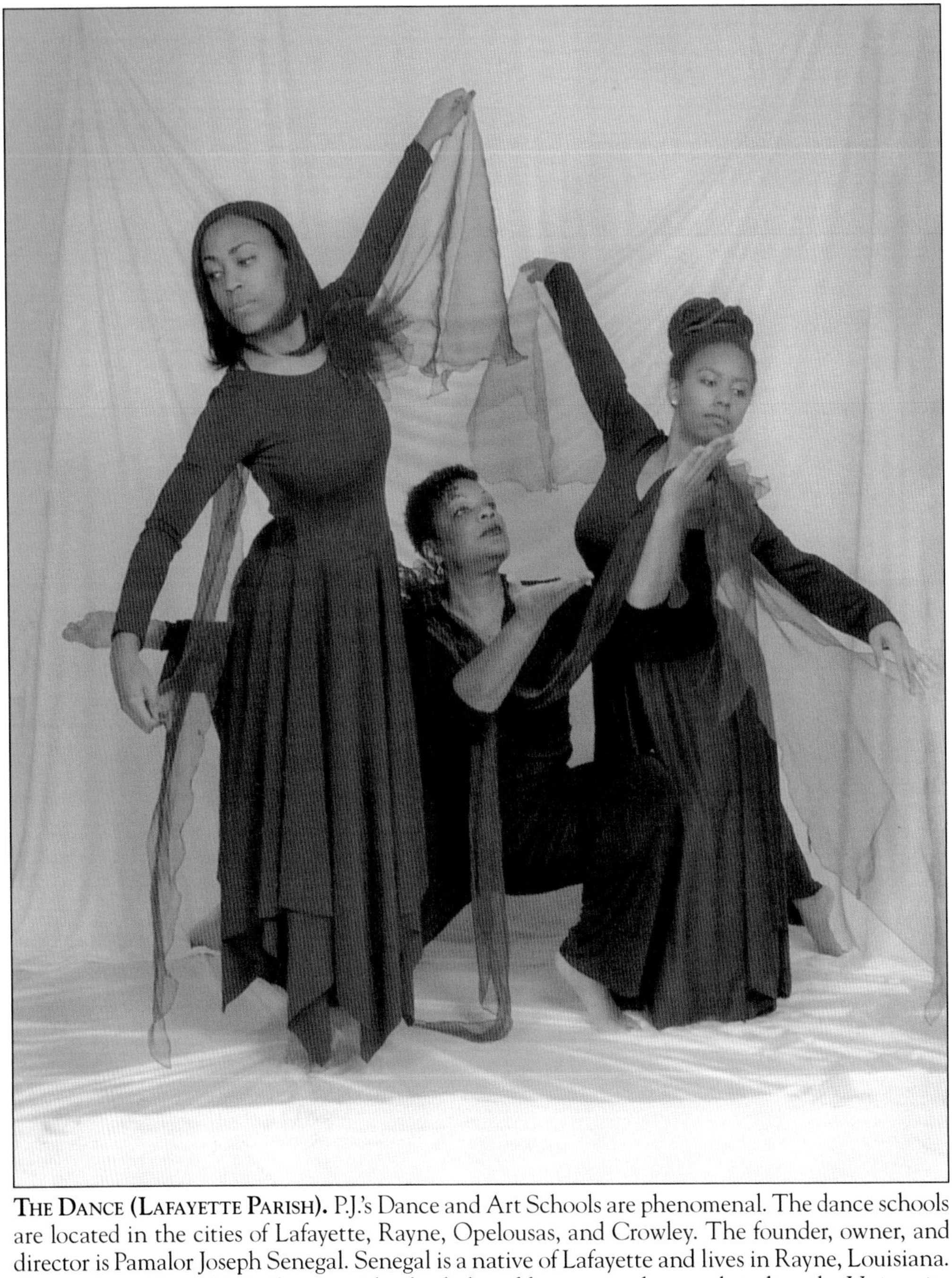

The Dance (Lafayette Parish). P.J.'s Dance and Art Schools are phenomenal. The dance schools are located in the cities of Lafayette, Rayne, Opelousas, and Crowley. The founder, owner, and director is Pamalor Joseph Senegal. Senegal is a native of Lafayette and lives in Rayne, Louisiana. She graduated from UL-Lafayette with a bachelor of fine arts and general studies, the University of Houston-Clear Lake with a master's degree in choreography from, and earned certification as a therapeutic recreational therapy specialist from Eastern Washington University. The schools serve all children but are unique because the focus is on inner-city youth and children with special needs. Senegal serves as a mentor for her students and has received numerous awards for her career as a dance instructor and for her community service. Pictured here are B. Bailey (left), P.J. Senegal (center), and F. Barker performing a liturgical dance. (Courtesy of Pamalor J. Senegal.)

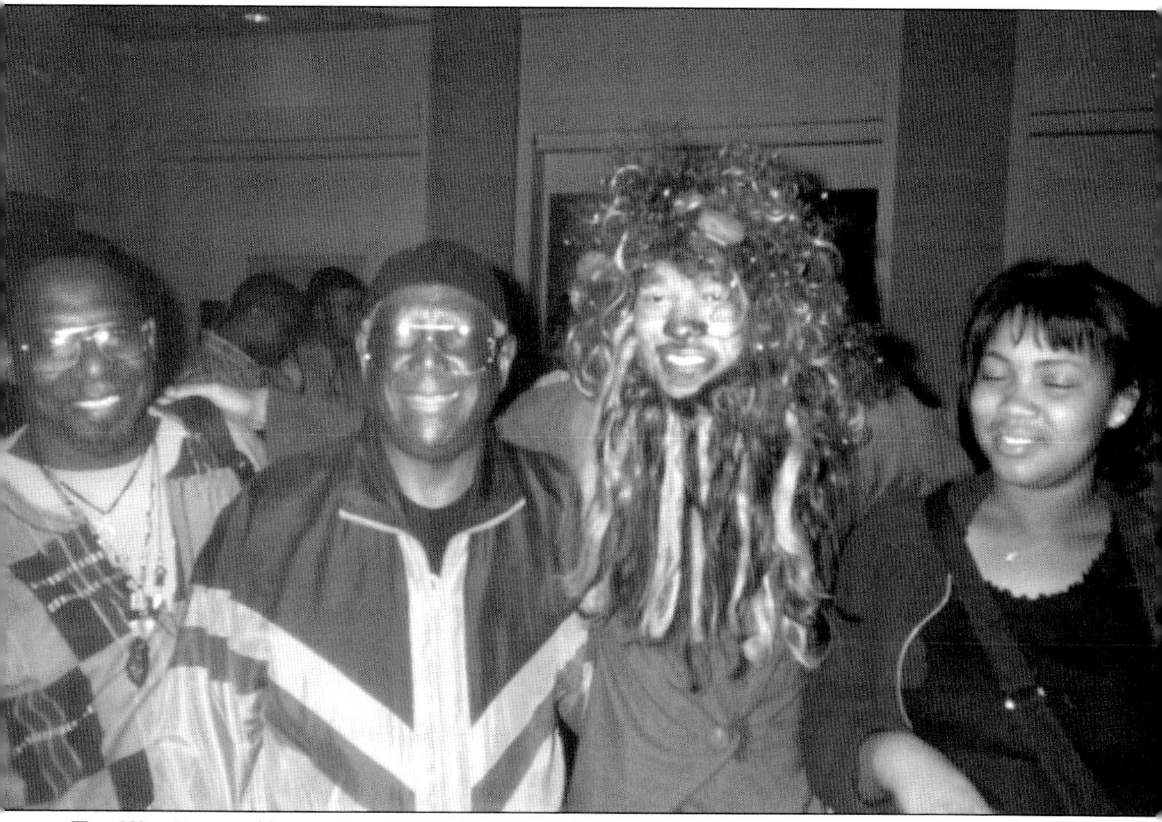

THE WIZ. Pictured here is Dr. Alexander C. Marshall (second from the left) with a group of actors from *The Wiz*, who performed at Dillard University in New Orleans. *The Wiz*, a popular musical, is performed at various theaters across America. Dr. Marshall has directed plays at several colleges and universities. (Courtesy of A.C. Marshall.)

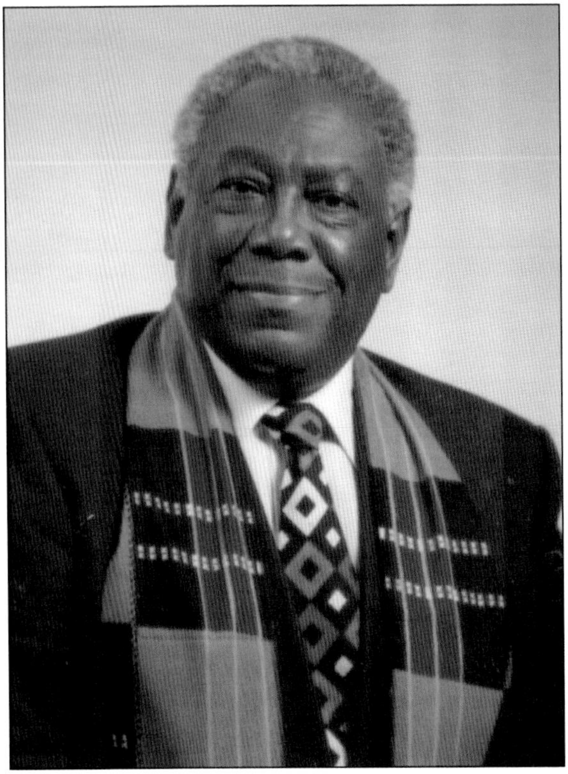

THEATRE ARTS (ST. LANDRY PARISH). Dr. Alexander C. Marshall is the ultimate director of African American plays. He is a graduate of Grambling State University, the University of Denver, and Bowling Green State University. Marshall writes and directs plays that both entertain and educate the community about historical events. His expansive career includes teaching and directing numerous plays at UL-Lafayette, Grambling, Dilliard University, and Bowling Green State University. Marshall has also worked in various community art and theatre productions and directed such plays as *Mam Phyllis, Ms Ever's Boys,* and *The Faces of Emmitt Till.* (Courtesy of Dr. A.C. Marshall.)

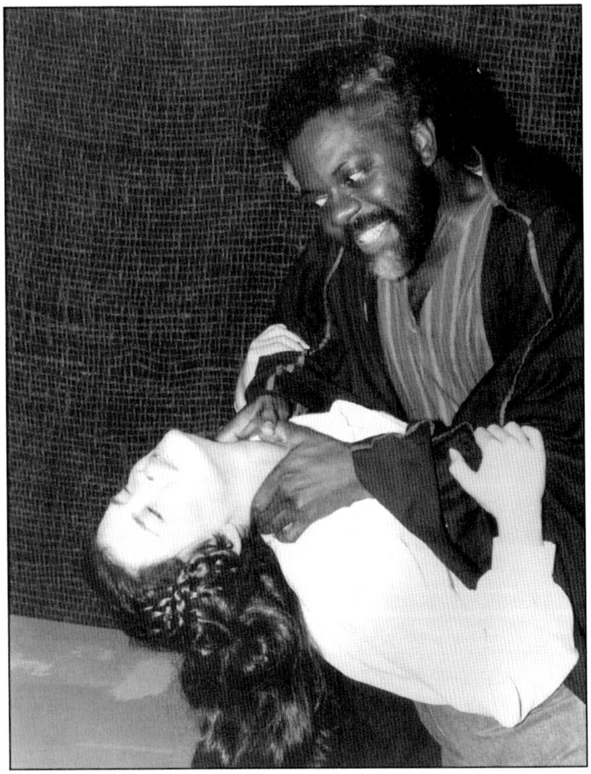

OTHELLO, THE MOOR OF VENICE (LAFAYETTE PARISH). Morris Skipper is pictured here in a scene from *Othello* (performed at the University of Southwestern Louisiana) dramatizing the murder of his wife, Desdemona. He was tricked into believing that she betrayed him, so he killed her and himself. (Courtesy of Edith G. Dupré Library Archives and Special Collections.)

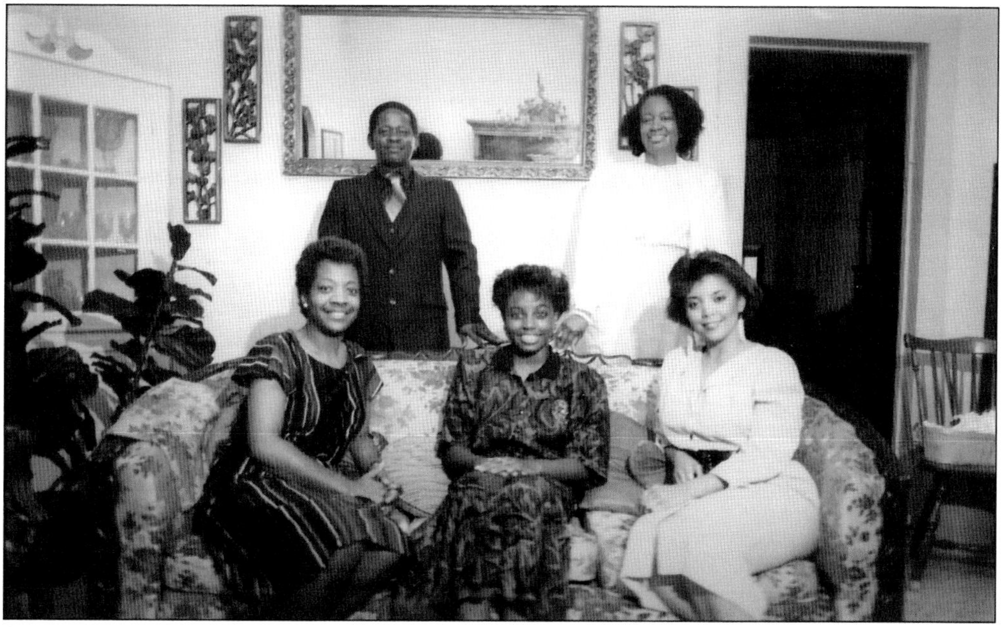

Silent Witness (Lafayette Parish). Attending plays is one of the cultural-arts events that African Americans in Lafayette and southwest Louisiana enjoy. Pictured here are local actors who starred in the play *Silent Witness*. From left to right they are (first row) Mary Lee Delahoussaye, LaMonica Davis, and Alozia St. Julien; (second row) Buster Leopaul and director Annie Johnson. (Courtesy Edith G. Dupré Library Archives and Special Collections.)

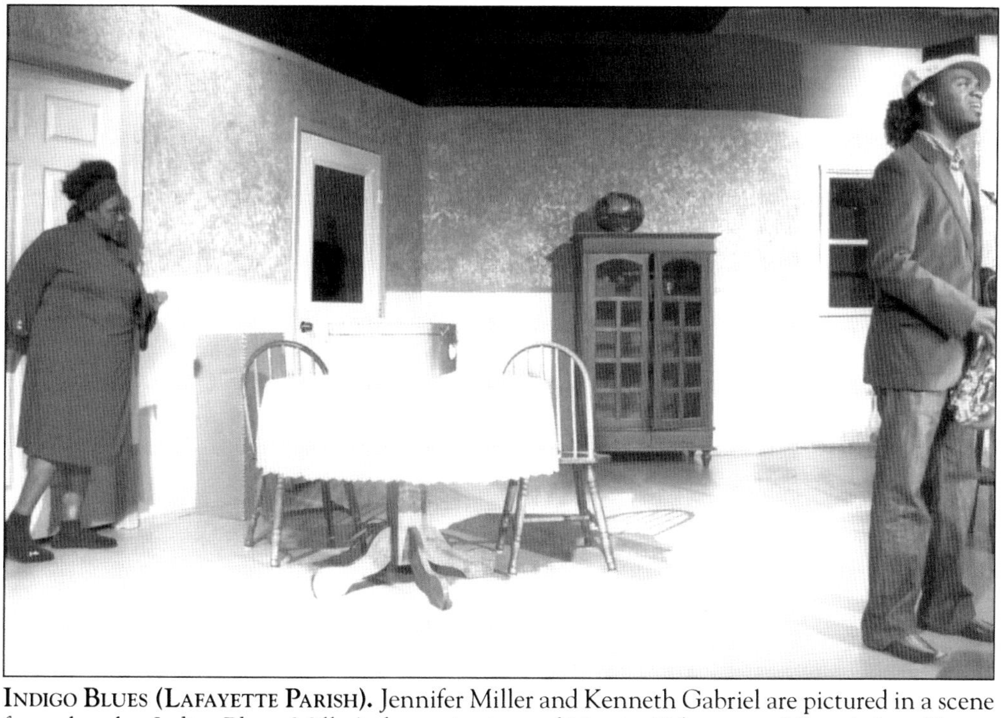

Indigo Blues (Lafayette Parish). Jennifer Miller and Kenneth Gabriel are pictured in a scene from the play *Indigo Blues*. Miller's dramatizations of Harriet Tubman and Fannie Lou Hamer were riveting. The play was directed by Brian Taylor. (Courtesy of Brian Taylor.)

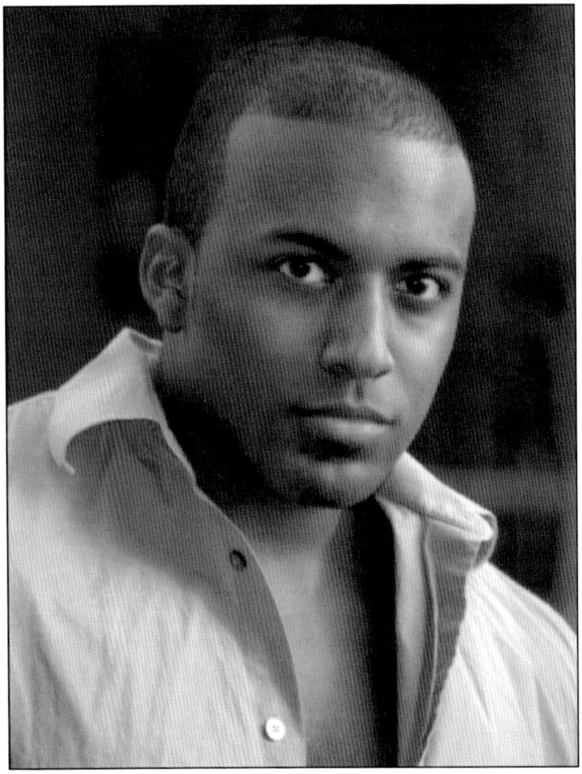

Best Supporting Actor (Lafayette Parish). Nicholas Marshan was recognized as best supporting actor in Louisiana by the American Association for Community Theatre for his role in the play *Two*, which was directed by Dr. Alexander C. Marshall. (Courtesy of Brian Taylor.)

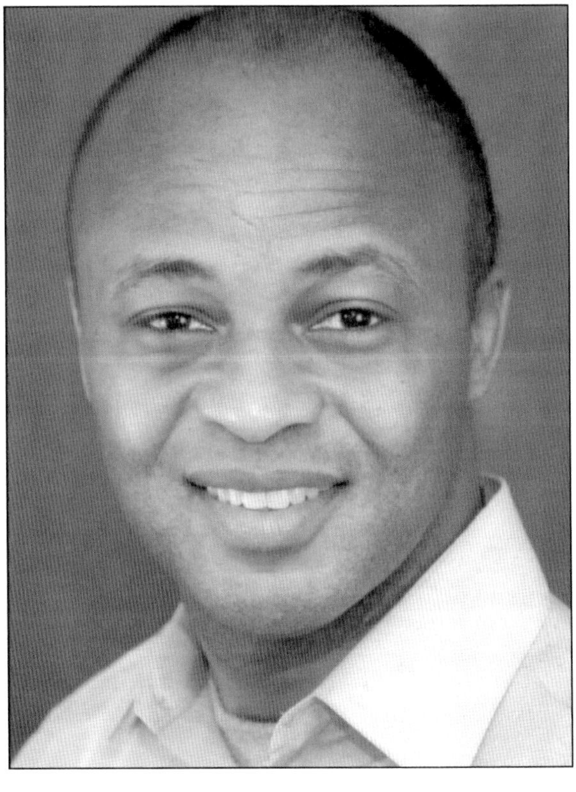

Omni Artiste Inc. (Lafayette Parish). Brian Taylor is president of Omni Artiste' Inc. The company produces diverse productions of live stage, television, and films for multiple audiences in the United States. The company also provides opportunities for local actors to gain recognition. Two of its recent productions have been the movie *Lord Byron* and a television sitcom *Sunday Dinner*, which will air in the fall of 2011. (Courtesy of Brian Taylor.)

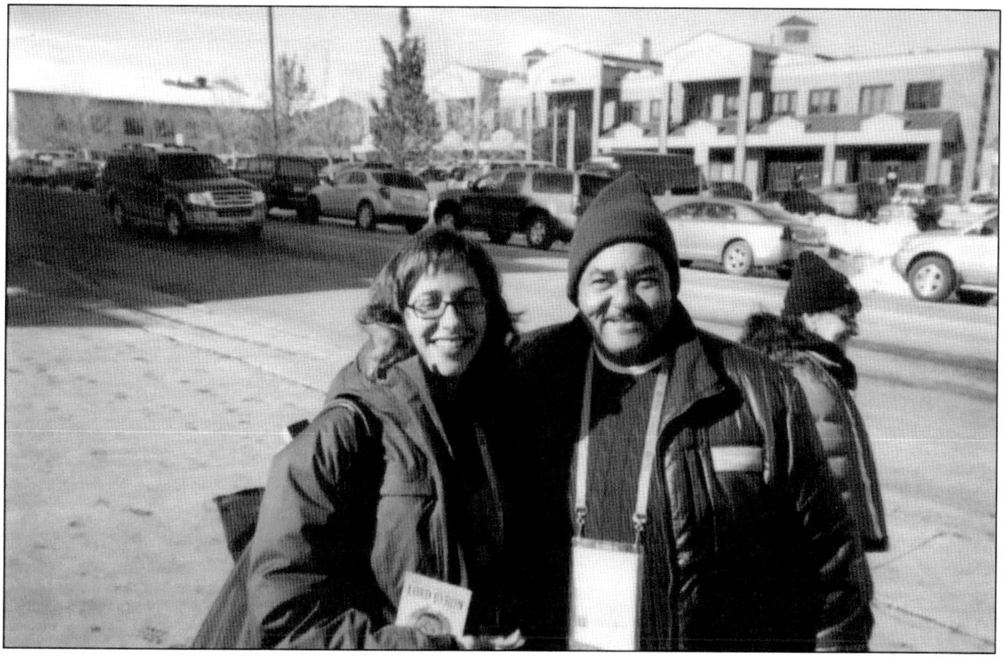

Local Talent (Acadia Parish). Paul Batiste is an artist, actor, and barber who lives in Churchpoint, Louisiana. He recently starred in the film *Lord Byron* and will play a role in the television sitcom *Sunday Dinner*. Batiste is pictured here with a fan who enjoyed the movie. (Courtesy of Paul Batiste.)

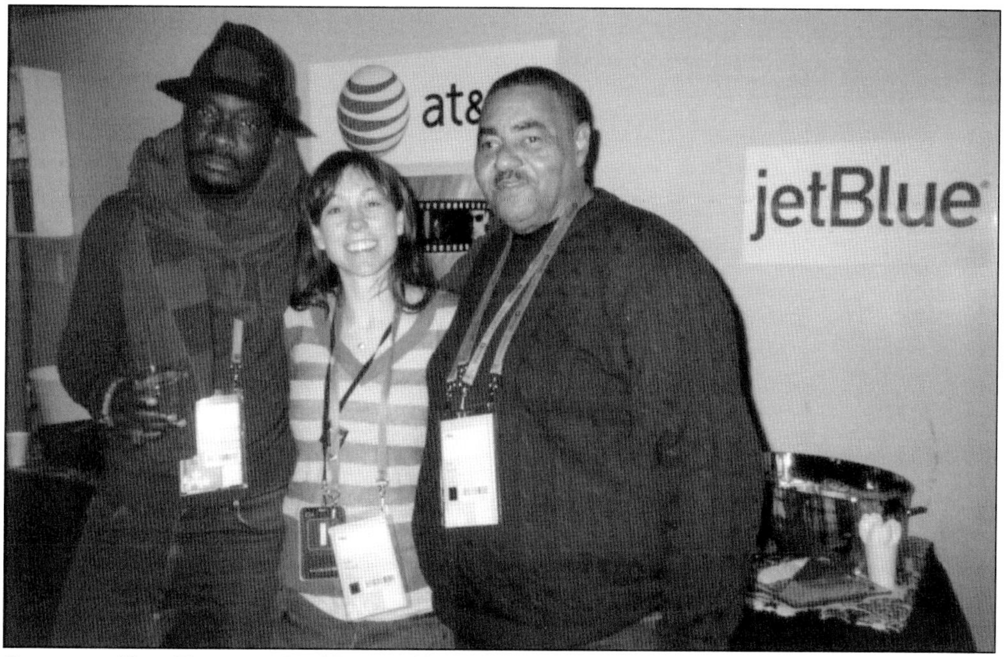

Sundance Film Festival. Paul Batiste (far right) is featured with fellow actors and writers at the Sundance Film Festival in Park City, Utah. The festival is held each year and brings together persons who write, produce, and direct films. It also brings together novice and experienced actors seeking roles for future productions. (Courtesy of Paul Batiste.)

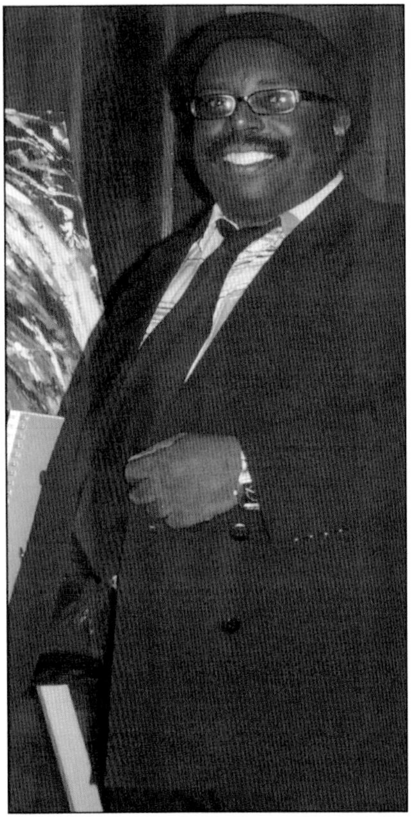

ADRIAN FULTON (LEFT) AND LOUIS ARMSTRONG (BELOW) PAINTED BY ADRIAN FULTON (LAFAYETTE PARISH). Fulton's paintings evolve from many colors to complete their final form. He is an artist with flair who creates paintings, portraits, cartoons, and caricatures. Fulton is also a businessman and the owner of three art galleries: one in Lafayette and two in New Orleans called Adrian Fulton's Fine Art Galleries. He helps to promote art by teaching art classes and showcasing the work of others at his galleries. (Both courtesy of Adrian Fulton.)

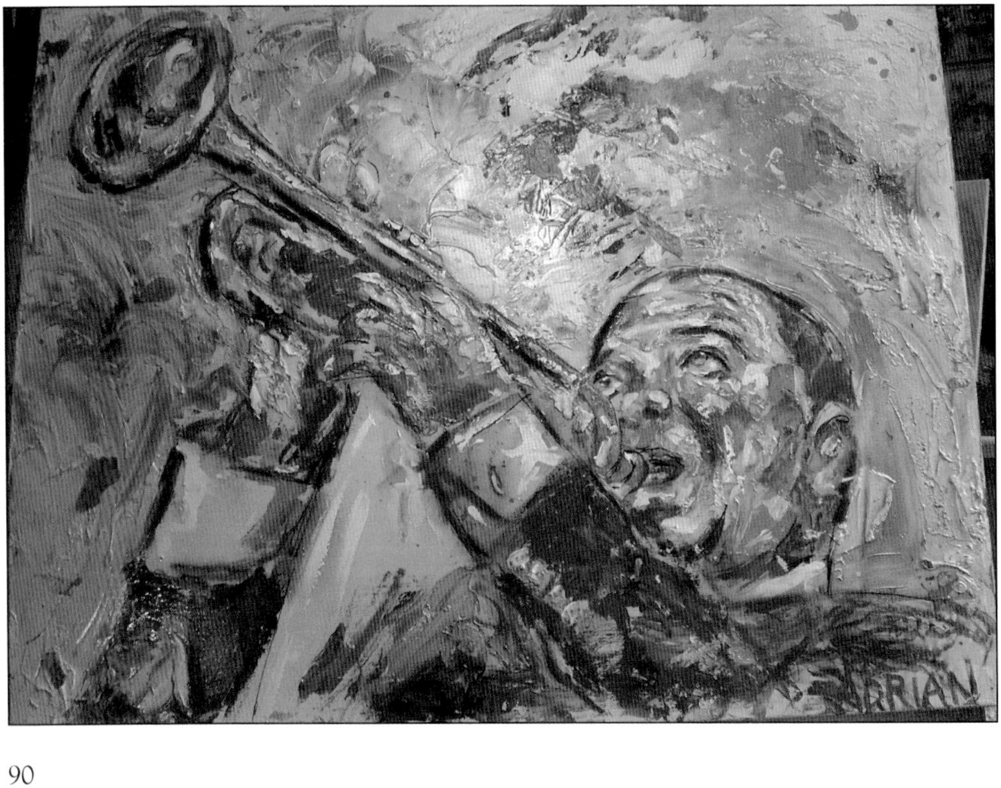

Five

Against All Odds

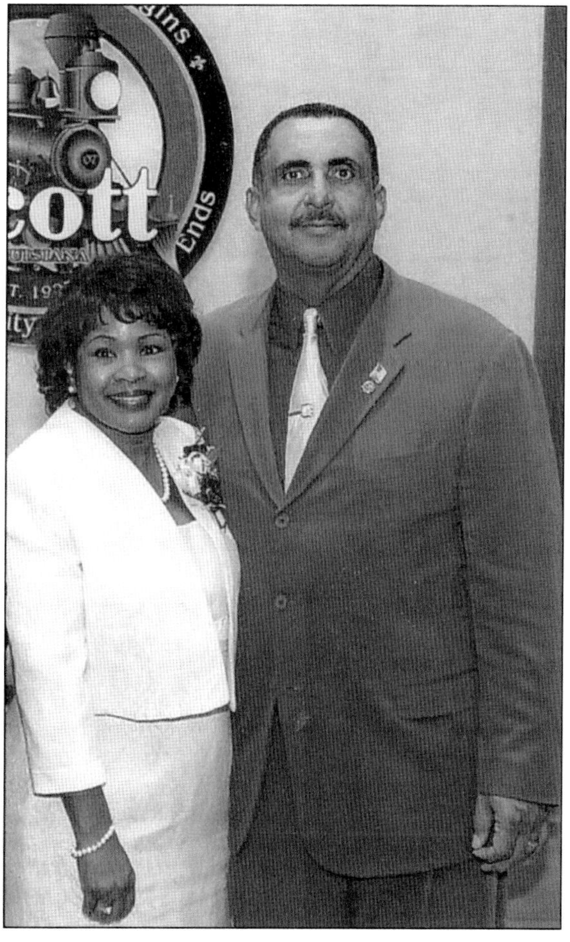

Community Leaders (Lafayette Parish). Mayor Purvis Morrison and Councilwoman Mary Matthews Morrison are residents of Scott, Louisiana. Purvis is the first African American to serve as mayor of Scott, Louisiana. He started his career in politics in 2004 when he ran for Scott City Council and won. Three years later, he ran for parish council in Lafayette and was victorious. Purvis then ran for mayor of the city of Scott and won, becoming the first African American mayor in Lafayette Parish as well as the city. Mary M. Morrison became the first African American female to serve on the parish council in Lafayette. She is completing Purvis's one-year term. The Morrisons have been married for 30 years and have three children: Shanea, Shelly, and Shawn. (Courtesy of Mary Morrison.)

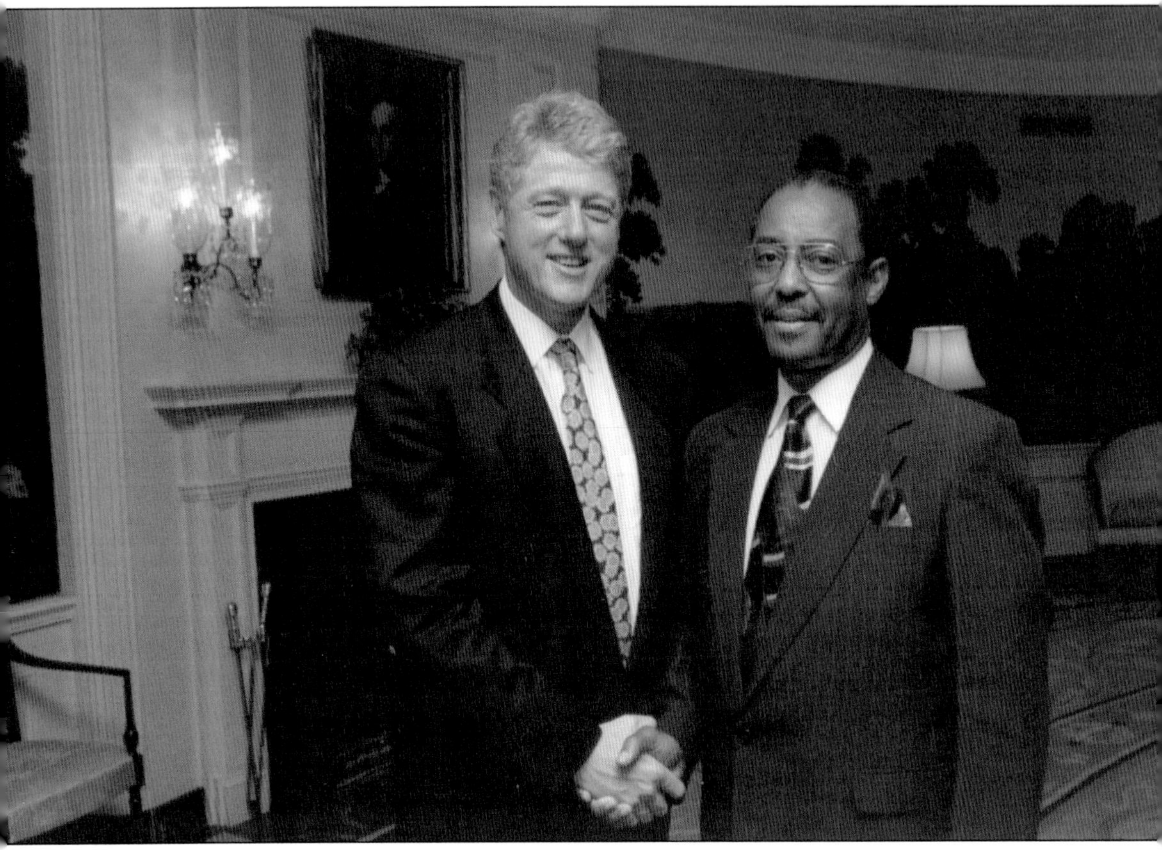

Pres. Bill Clinton with John W. Joseph, the First African American Mayor of Opelousas, Louisiana (St. Landry Parish). In 1989, Pres. Bill Clinton welcomed John W. Joseph, mayor of Opelousas, Louisiana, to the White House. This image was taken in the Oval Office. Mayor Joseph was invited to Washington, DC, by President Clinton to participate in the drafting of a crime bill for the US Congress. Joseph also attended the signing of the congressional bill into law. Because of Mayor Joseph's exemplary leadership, faith was restored in many citizens about the future of the city of Opelousas and the leadership ability of African Americans. Mayor Joseph blazed a trail that opened the door for four more African Americans to become mayor of the City of Opelousas: Michael Thibodeaux, John Vallien, Anna Simmons (first black female mayor), and current Mayor Donald R. Cravins. The city has experienced growth in people and in businesses. It is the third oldest city in the state of Louisiana. (Courtesy of John W. Joseph.)

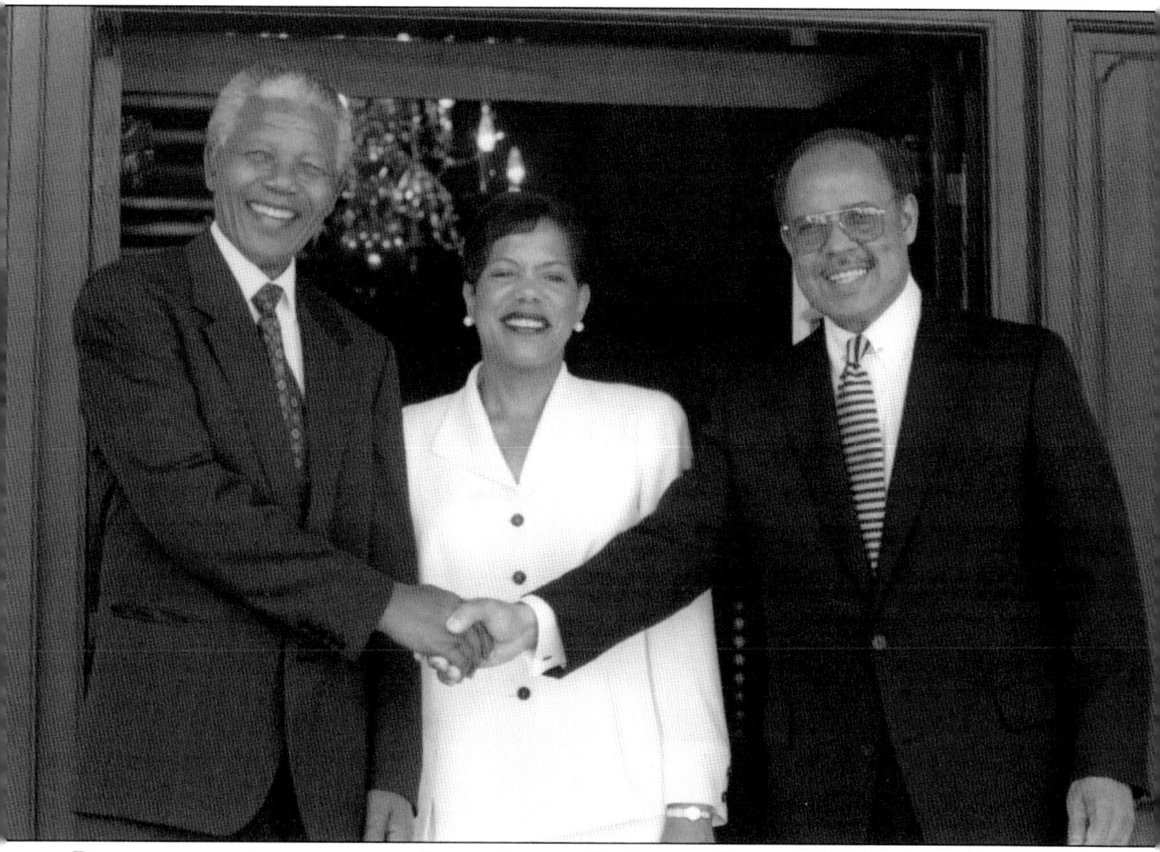

PRESIDENT AND AMBASSADOR TO SOUTH AFRICA (ST. LANDRY PARISH). Nelson Mandela, former president of South Africa (far left), is pictured with James A. Joseph, former US ambassador to South Africa, and his wife, Mary Braxton Joseph (center). Joseph was born and raised in Opelousas, Louisiana. He served as US ambassador to South Africa for four years during the presidency of Bill Clinton. He is the father of two children, Jeffery and Denise Joseph. Joseph is currently a professor at Duke University in Durham, North Carolina, and teaches public policy studies. (Courtesy of John W. Joseph.)

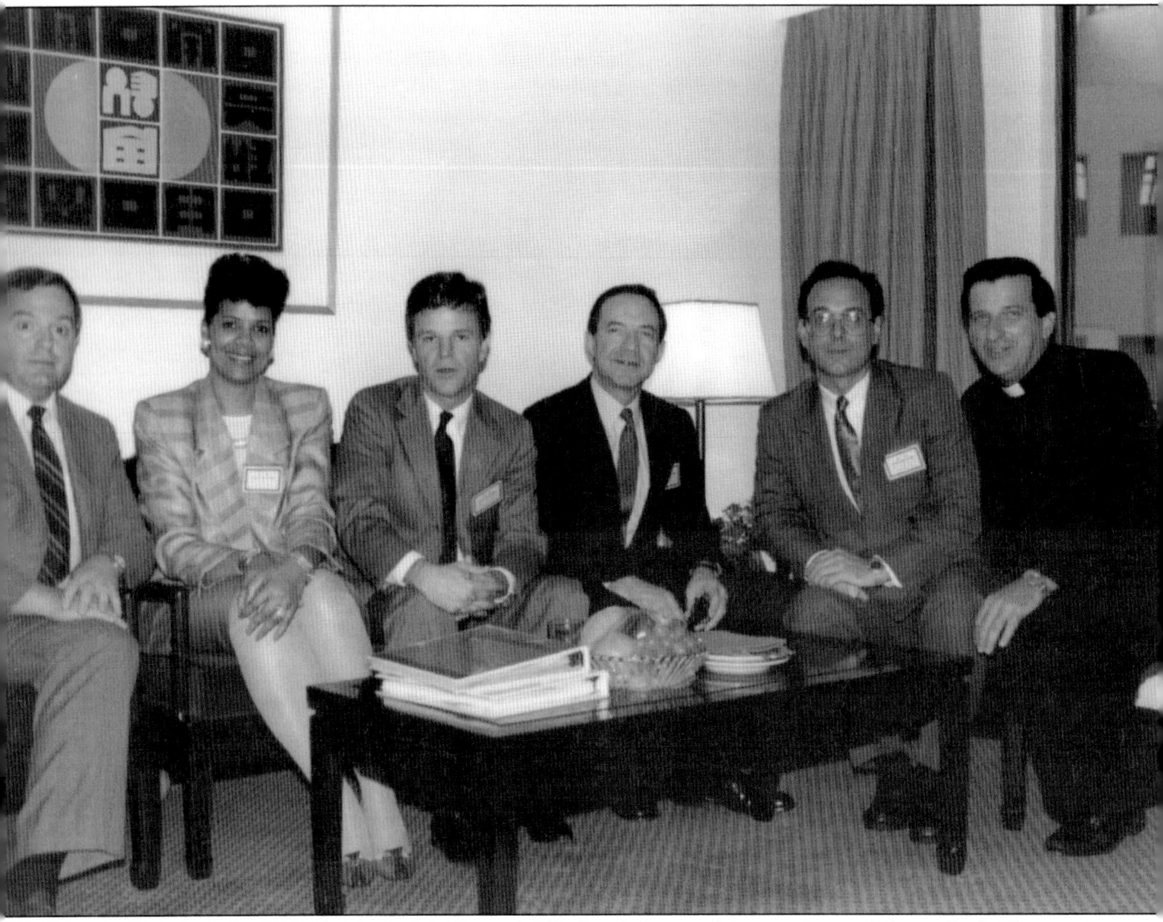

SECRETARY OF LABOR (LAFAYETTE PARISH). Phyllis Coleman Mouton (second from the left) served as the first African American female secretary of labor for the state of Louisiana in Gov. Buddy Roemer's administration (to the right of Mouton). The group attended the Mid-South Governors' Summit in Tokyo, Japan, in 1989. Mouton is a woman of many talents and many firsts. Both her personal and professional lives are inspiring, making tremendous changes that continue to impact the lives of future generations. Mouton is a living success story who is educated, personable, creative, and a community leader. Some of her accomplishments include being vice chancellor of Baton Rouge Community College (1997–present) and the first female and African American president of the Lafayette Chamber of Commerce (1986). (Courtesy of Phyllis C. Mouton.)

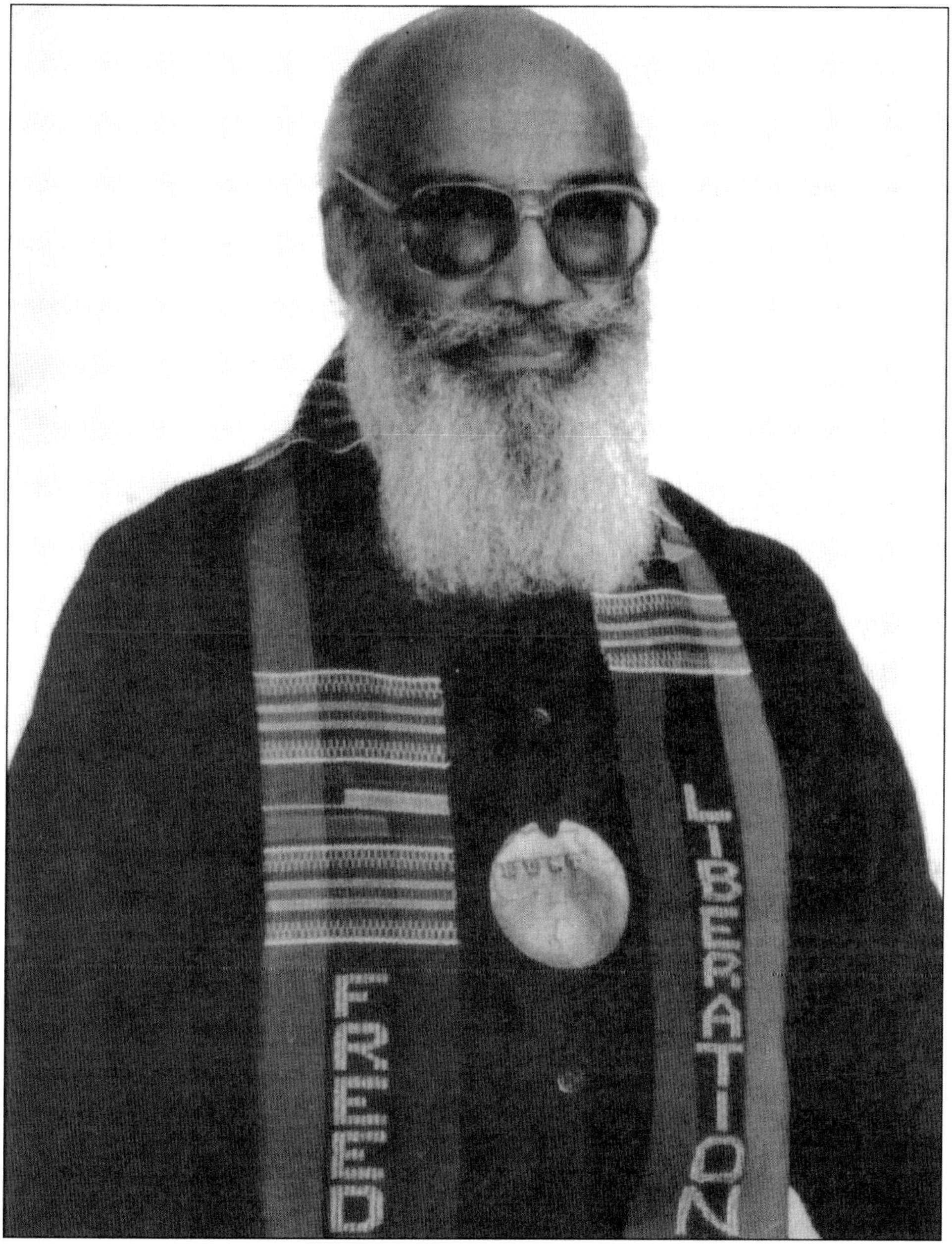

Rev. A.J. McKnight, Sisters of Charity of St. Paul (CSSP). (Lafayette Parish). A history about people, places, and events in southwest Louisiana that does not include Father McKnight is remiss. He is known in communities as Father McKnight, is a visionary thinker and community Leader, and he has worked tirelessly throughout the years to bring about positive changes in Lafayette, Opelousas, and the entire state of Louisiana. In his book *Whistling In the Wind*, McKnight tells the story of his journey to make life better for people in business, education, and Christian worship. Father McKnight acknowledges everyone who worked with him and describes the development, problems, successes, and rewards of building an economic base for African Americans in Louisiana. He was the assistant pastor at St. Paul's Church and the first priest to live with white priests in the rectory in Lafayette, Louisiana. (Author's collection.)

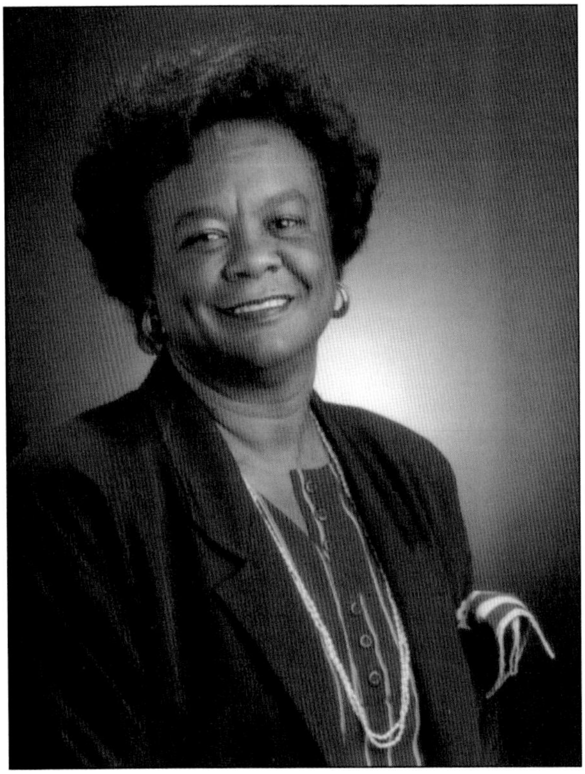

HOME DEMONSTRATION AGENT (ST. MARTIN PARISH). Etta Pearl H. Brew lives in Breaux Bridge, Louisiana, where she worked for 30 years as the first African American home-demonstration agent. In 1974, she was appointed as the extension home economist and worked with youth and adults in St. Martin Parish. Brew's achievements and memberships are numerous and include being parish chairwoman and involved with the Louisiana Home Economics Association, American Home Economist Association, St. Martin Parish Council on Aging Board, and the Cajun Area Agency on Aging, which serves nine parishes. Brew is a community leader who continues to work tirelessly in an effort to make the world a better place. (Courtesy of Etta Pearl Brew.)

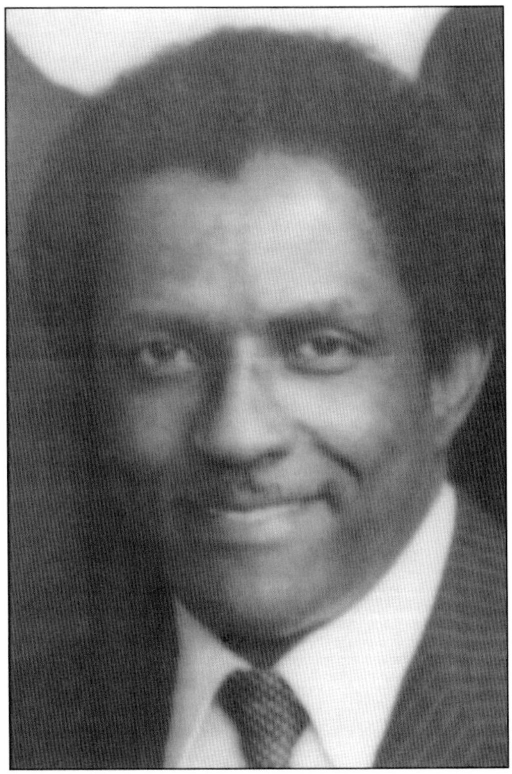

TUSKEGEE AIRMAN (LAFAYETTE PARISH). Mervin Harmon was born and raised in Lafayette Parish. He comes from a family of self-made entrepreneurs. Harmon was educated in a one-room schoolhouse that contained several grades and ages of students. When Harmon was 18 years old, he served in the Army Air Force as a Tuskegee airman. He was stationed in Tuskegee, Alabama, and his military occupational status (MOS) was crew chief. His job was to make sure that everything was in working order before planes would take flight. Corporal Harmon served for three years, was honorably discharged, and returned to Lafayette where he opened a business as an upholster and later a general merchandise store in his neighborhood, the Truman Addition. In 1974, Harmon was the first black citizen elected to serve as a member of the Lafayette Parish Police Jury. He served for 10 years. (Courtesy of Mervin Harmon.)

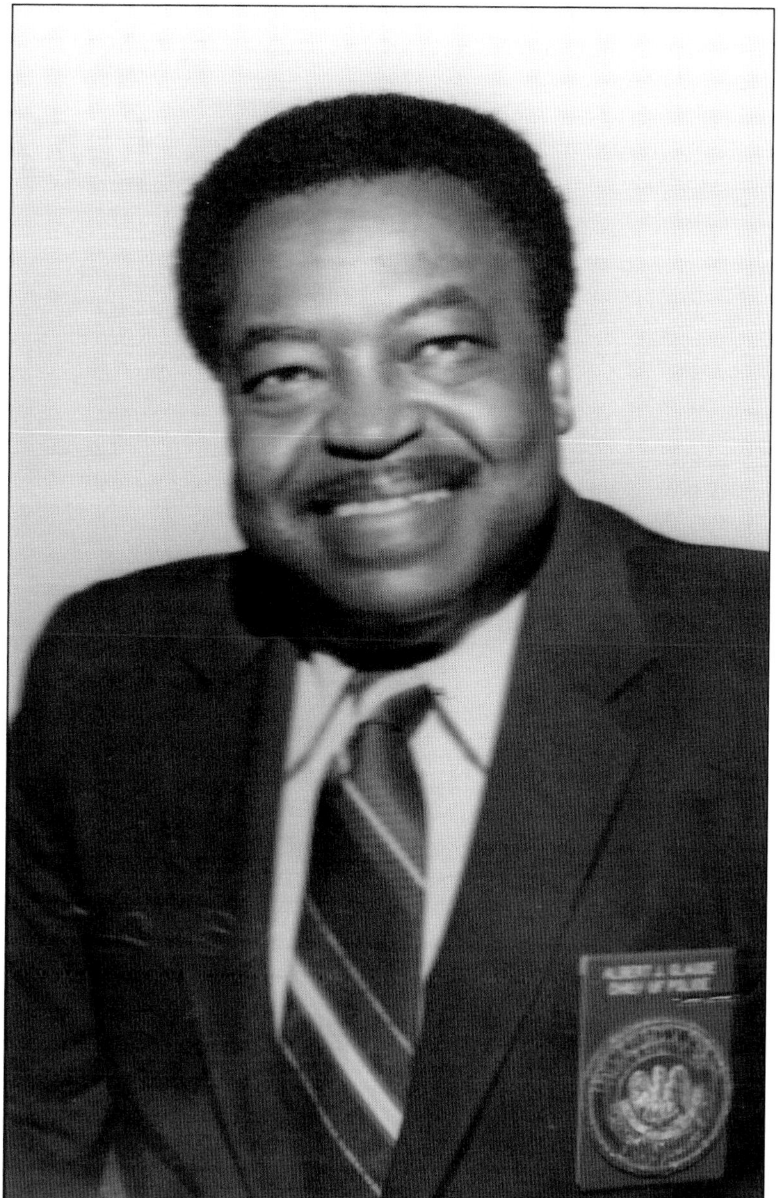

Albert J. Glaude, Chief of Police at USL (Lafayette Parish). Albert Glaude was born and raised in Lafayette, Louisiana. He was educated in the public school system, graduated from Paul Breaux High School, and later served in the Marine Corps. He was the first African American in Lafayette to serve as chief of police of a predominantly white public university, the University of Southwestern Louisiana (now the University of Louisiana at Lafayette). He applied for the job and went through a thorough screening by the search committee before he was hired. They interviewed his high school principal and his assistant principal, reviewed his high school diploma, and talked to his neighbors and friends about the kind of person and husband/family man he was. His state test scores were posted in Martin Hall (the administrative building on campus) on a bulletin board for all to see. After the interviews, he was hired to work for the campus police department. (Courtesy of Albert J. Glaude.)

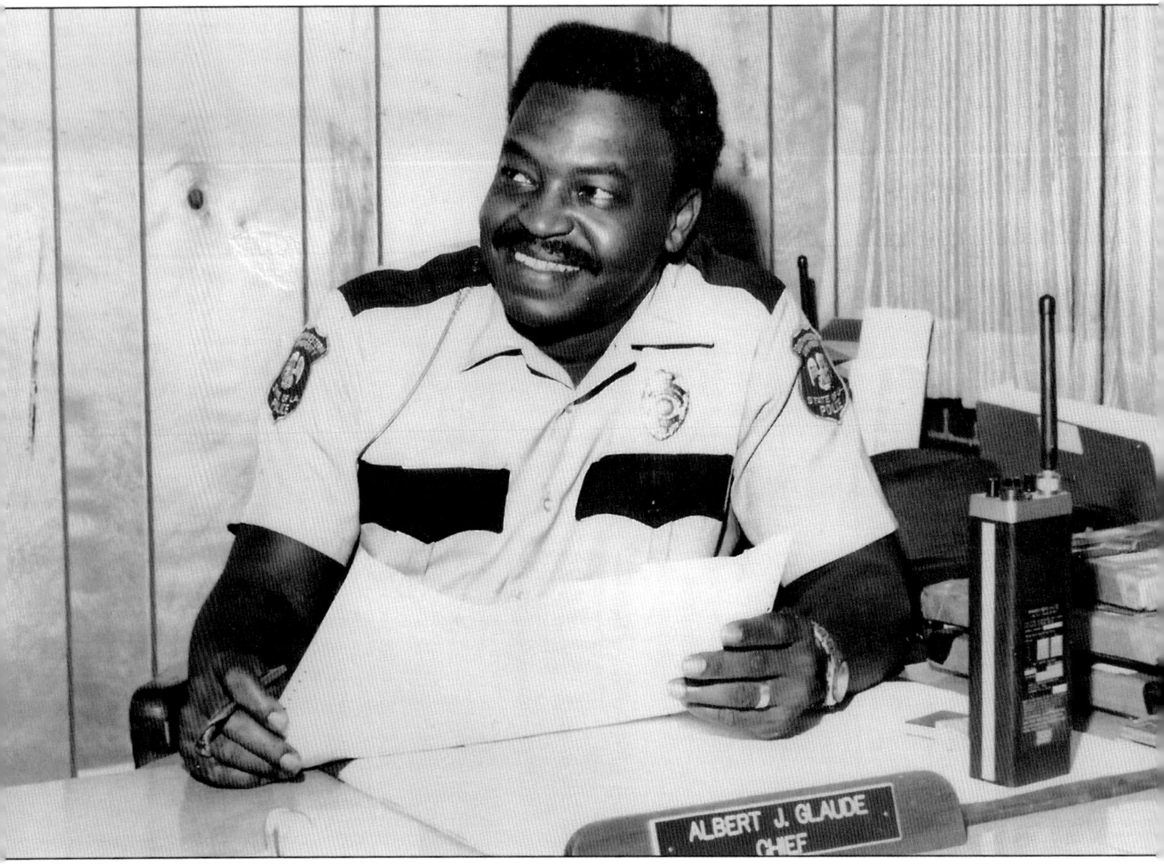

KEEPING THE CAMPUS SAFE. Albert Glaude began his career as a patrolman in the department of campus security and later advanced to patrol sergeant, shifting to supervisor captain. He served as acting chief when the chief was on sabbatical leave. Later, he was appointed to the position of police chief. He wanted the department to have name recognition in relation to the work that officers did on a daily basis. He successfully had the name changed from Department of Campus Security to the Department of University Police. Glaude served the university in law enforcement from 1970 to 1987. He earned a degree in criminal justice from USL in 1978 and continues to work in the community in law enforcement at the Lafayette Parish Sheriff's Office. (Courtesy of Edith G. Dupré Library Archives and Special Collections.)

First African American Graduate (Lafayette Parish). Christiana Gordon Smith was the first African American graduate of the University of Southwestern Louisiana (now UL-Lafayette). She was a teacher for 39 years. The black alumni association, the Christiana Smith African American Alumni Chapter at UL Lafayette, is named in her honor. The white student who was supposed to march with her in the graduation ceremony refused to walk with a black student; Smith walked alone and received her degree in education. She taught school for more than 30 years. Her portrait, donated by Wilfred Pierre and his brother Samuel Pierre, hangs in the Edith Garland Dupré Library. (Courtesy of Carolyn Stemley.)

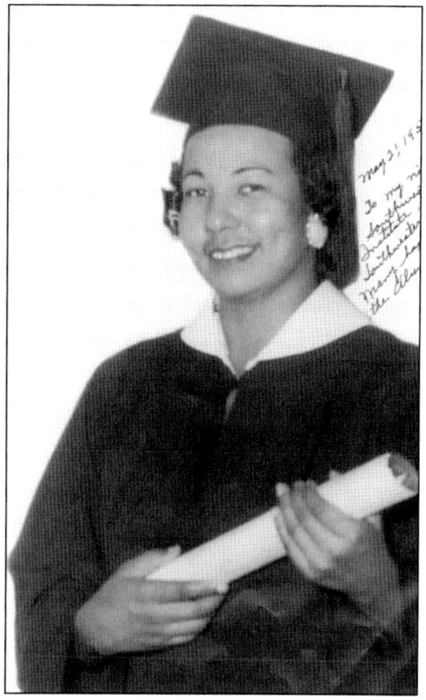

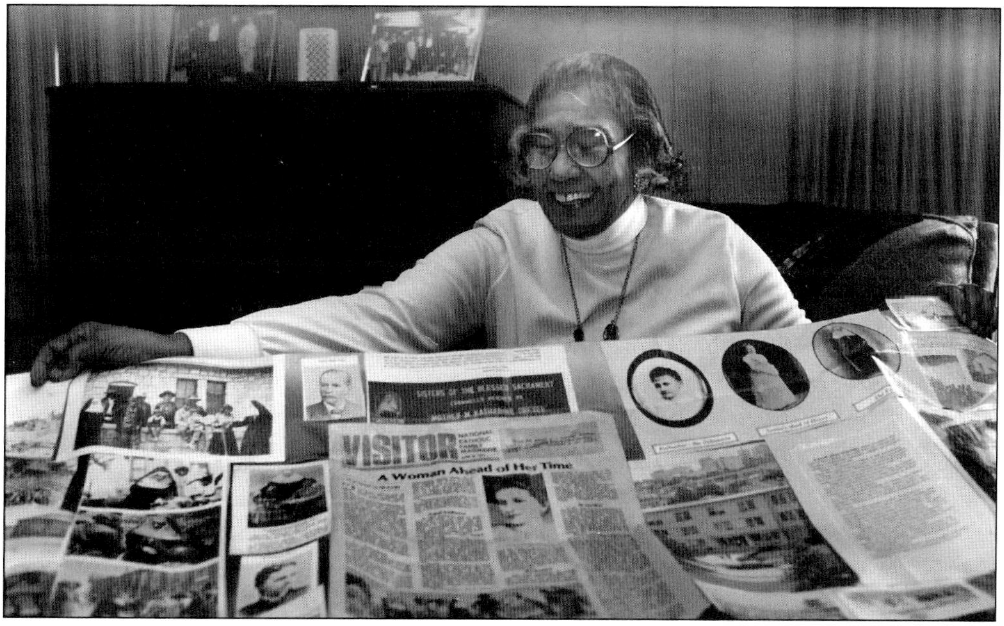

Researching a Mentor. Christiana Gordon Smith (the first black graduate of USL) is shown in this picture collecting articles written about Mother Katherine Drexel. Smith was working on a historical book about the prolific nun who spent her life making education possible for black and Native American children. The Katherine Drexler Elementary School, located in Broussard (Lafayette Parish), is named in her honor. She and the Sisters of the Blessed Sacrament are the founders of Xavier University of Louisiana in New Orleans. It is the only historically black Roman Catholic university in America. (Courtesy of Edith G. Dupré Library Archives and Special Collections.)

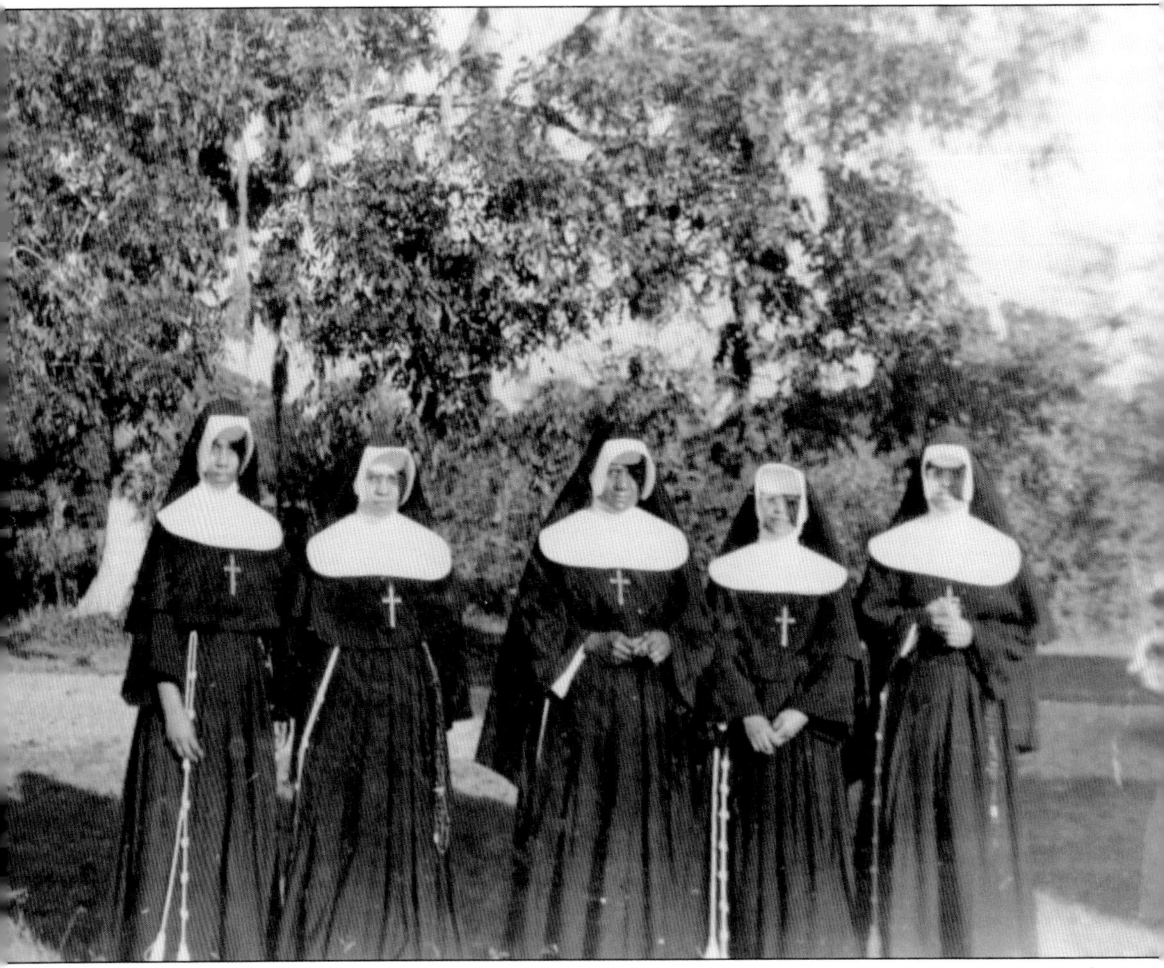

Sisters of the Holy Family (Lafayette Parish). The sisters were teachers and principals and taught black children in Lafayette Parish and other southwest parishes. They arrived in Lafayette in 1903 and began work at St. Joseph's School. Later, they worked at St. Paul's School. They commuted until a convent was acquired for them across the street from the school. (Courtesy of the Lafayette Diocese Archives and Research Department.)

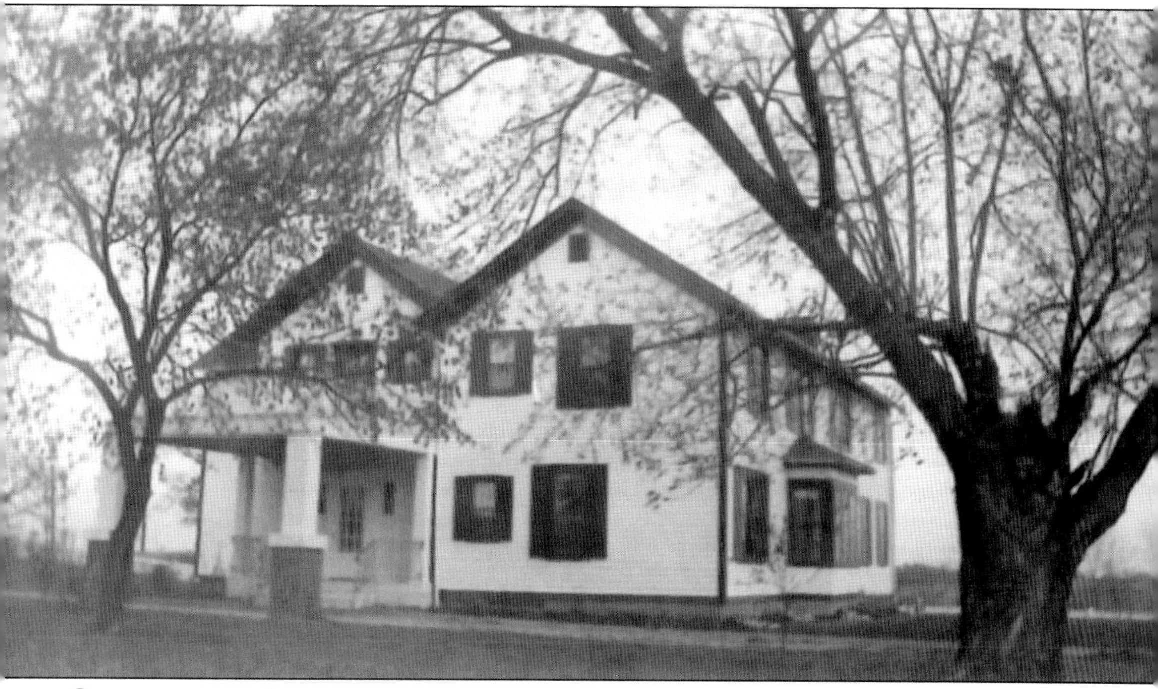

CONVENT OF THE SISTERS OF THE HOLY FAMILY (LAFAYETTE PARISH). The convent was home for many sisters who lived and worked in the community. They were teachers and principals at Holy Family School, Holy Rosary Institute, Immaculate Heart of Mary School, and other schools in southwest Louisiana. Presently, the convent is being converted into a library for the students and faculty at Holy Family School. (Courtesy of the Lafayette Diocese Archives and Research Department.)

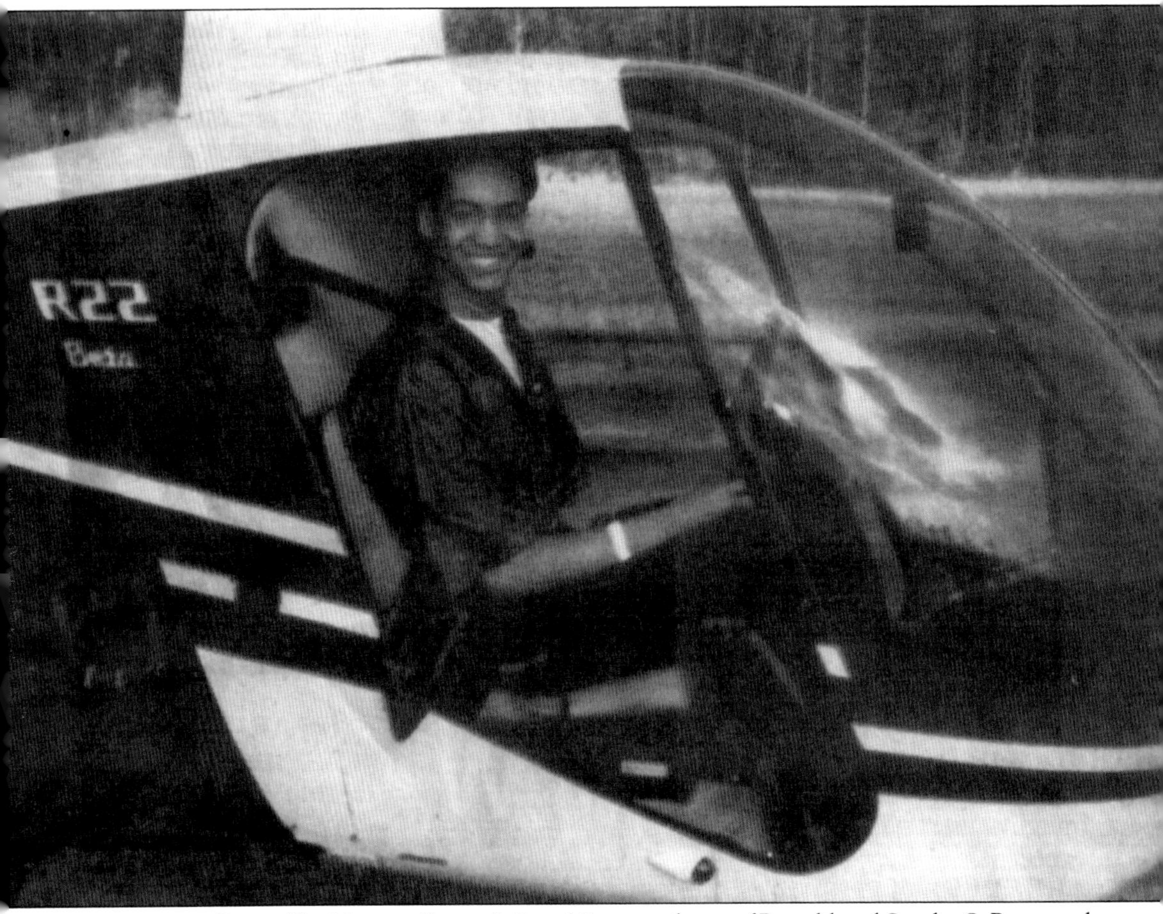

YOUNGEST PILOT (ST. MARTIN PARISH). Jamal Broussard, son of Ronald and Sandra S. Broussard, was one of the youngest pilots to receive a license when he did so in 2003. Jamal wanted to learn to fly airplanes and enrolled in a flight school in Lafayette, where he successfully completed the course to fly helicopters. He was 17 years old when he flew a solo flight before graduating from flight school. (Courtesy of Sandra Broussard.)

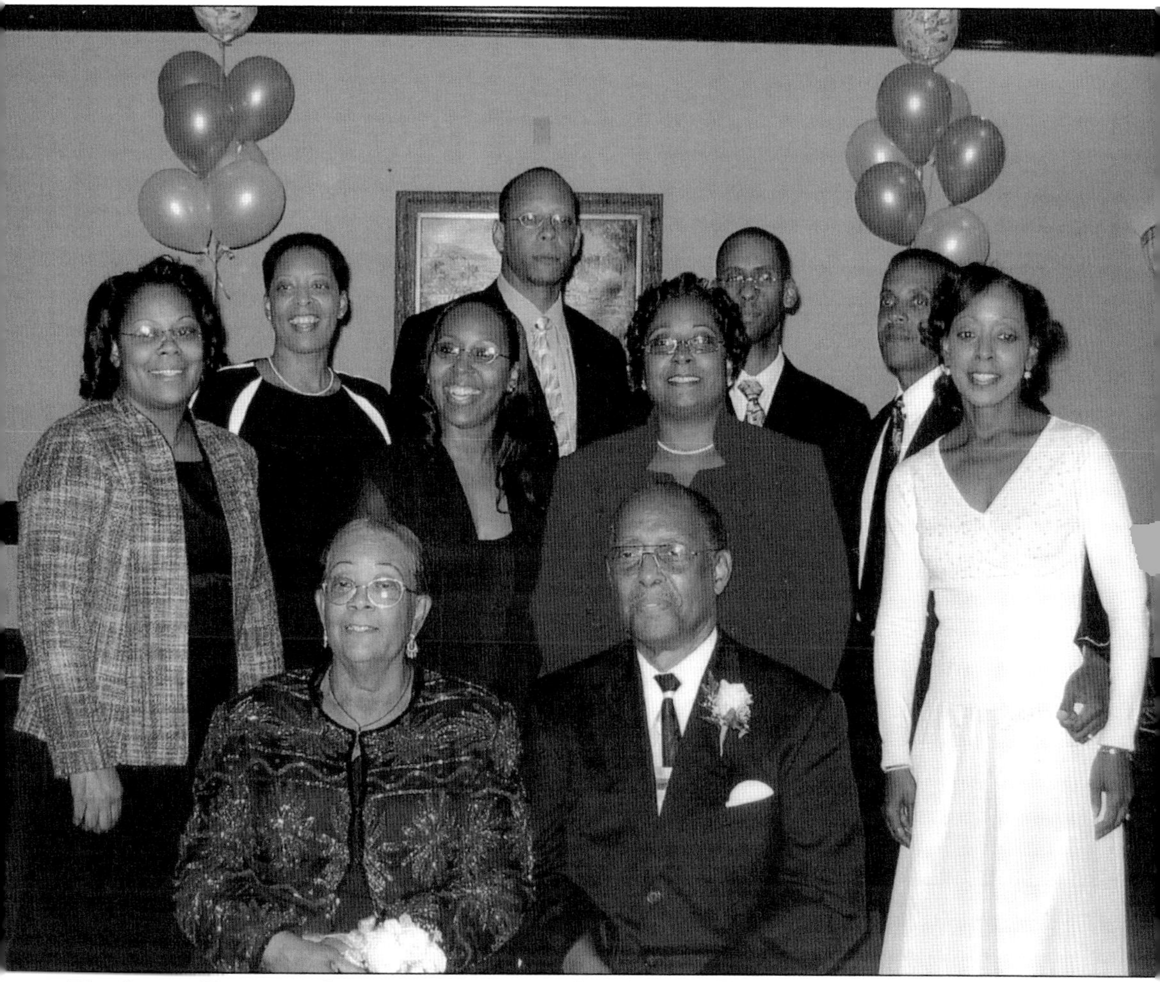

THE JOSEPH FAMILY IN OPELOUSAS, LOUISIANA (ST. LANDRY PARISH). John W. Joseph (seated, right) was the first African American mayor of Opelousas. He is pictured here with his wife, Cecile Joseph (a retired teacher), and their eight children. Cynthia, Sheila, Justina, Brenda, Sonya, Brent, John, and John Keith all graduated from college and have professional careers. Cynthia Joseph Bridges (back row, far left in the black and white dress) is the secretary of the Louisiana State Revenue Department. She is the first African American to serve in the position, which has been under Louisiana governors Mike Foster, Kathleen Blanco, and Bobby Jindal. Bridges. (Courtesy of Cecile Joseph.)

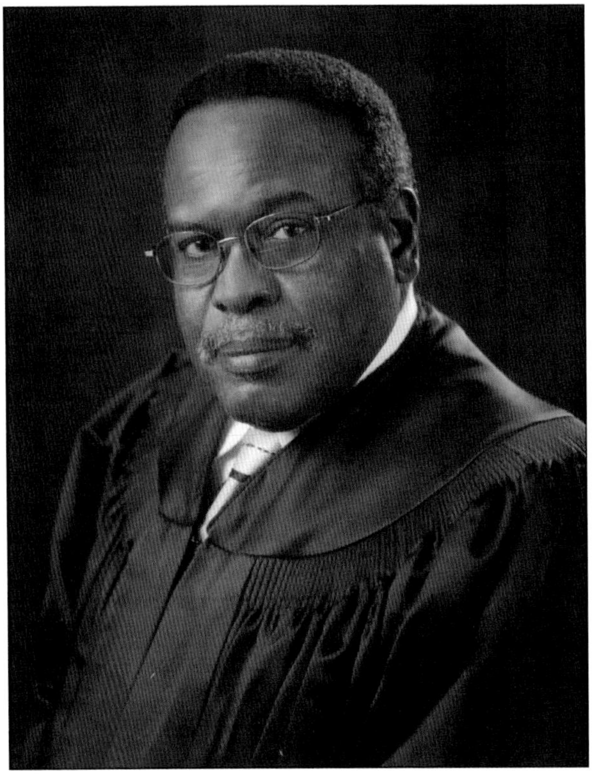

First African American as 15th Judicial District Court Judge (Lafayette Parish). Edward D. Rubin is the first elected African American judge serving Lafayette, Acadia, and Vermilion Parishes in the 15th Judicial District Court. Judge Rubin serves in Division D and has done so for 18 years. He is a graduate of Paul Breaux High School in Lafayette and Southern University Law School in Baton Rouge. (Courtesy of Judge Edward D. Rubin.)

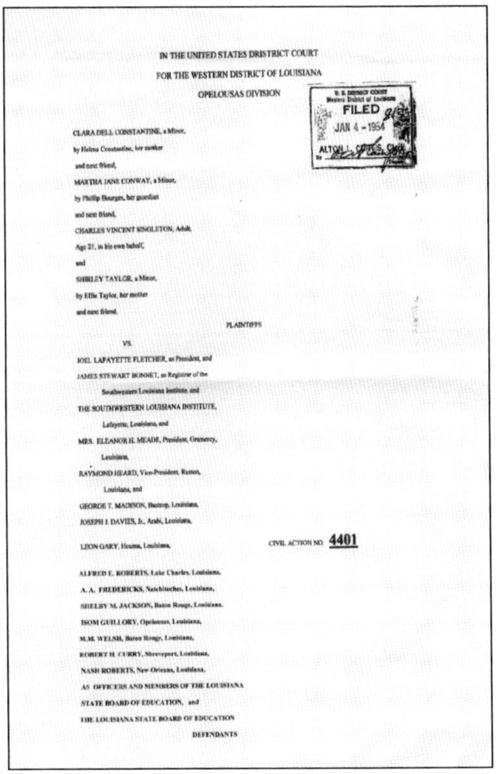

IN THE UNITED STATES DRISTRICT COURT

FOR THE WESTERN DISTRICT OF LOUISIANA

OPELOUSAS DIVISION

U. S. DISTRICT COURT
Western District of Louisiana
FILED
JAN 4 - 1954
ALTON L. COTES, Clerk

CLARA DELL CONSTANTINE, a Minor,
by Helma Constantine, her mother
and next friend,
MARTHA JANE CONWAY, a Minor,
by Philip Bourges, her guardian
and next friend,
CHARLES VINCENT SINGLETON, Adult,
Age 21, in his own behalf,
and
SHIRLEY TAYLOR, a Minor,
by Effie Taylor, her mother
and next friend,

PLAINTIFFS

VS.

JOEL LAFAYETTE FLETCHER, as President, and
JAMES STEWART BONNET, as Registrar of the
Southwestern Louisiana Institute, and
THE SOUTHWESTERN LOUISIANA INSTITUTE,
Lafayette, Louisiana, and
MRS. ELEANOR H. MEADE, President, Gramercy,
Louisiana,
RAYMOND HEARD, Vice-President, Ruston,
Louisiana, and
GEORGE T. MADISON, Bastrop, Louisiana,
JOSEPH J. DAVIES, Jr., Arabi, Louisiana,
LEON GARY, Houma, Louisiana,

CIVIL ACTION NO. **4401**

ALFRED E. ROBERTS, Lake Charles, Louisiana,
A. A. FREDERICKS, Natchitoches, Louisiana,
SHELBY M. JACKSON, Baton Rouge, Louisiana,
ISOM GUILLORY, Opelousas, Louisiana,
M.M. WELSH, Baton Rouge, Louisiana,
ROBERT H. CURRY, Shreveport, Louisiana,
NASH ROBERTS, New Orleans, Louisiana,
AS OFFICERS AND MEMBERS OF THE LOUISIANA
STATE BOARD OF EDUCATION, and
THE LOUISIANA STATE BOARD OF EDUCATION

DEFENDANTS

***Constantine v. Southwest Louisiana Institute* (Lafayette Parish).** This is a copy of the suit filed on January 4, 1954—a courageous move that led to the desegregation of colleges and universities throughout the state of Louisiana. (Courtesy of Edith G. Dupré Library Archives and Special Collections.)

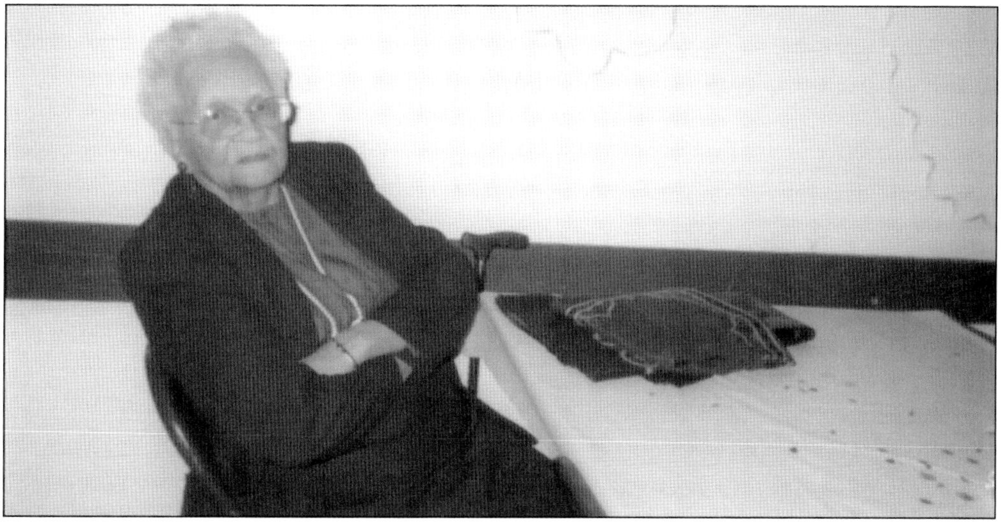

MOTHER OF DESEGREGATION (LAFAYETTE PARISH). Helma Constantine wanted her daughter to attend Southwest Louisiana Institute in 1953, but the all-white school refused to admit Clara D. Constantine because of the color of her skin. Constantine and three students and their parents filed a suit against the university, and the school decided to admit some black students. (Courtesy of Helma Constantine.)

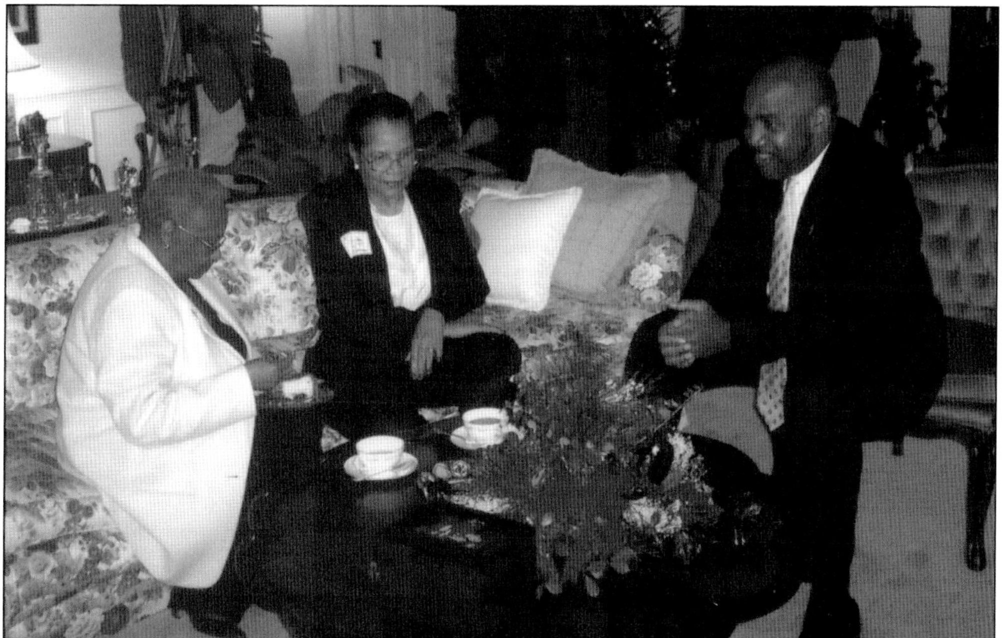

FIRST TO REGISTER (LAFAYETTE PARISH). Clara D. Constantine (seated, left) was the first student to register at SLI, but she was turned away because she was a black student. Constantine and three other students, Martha Conway, Charles Singleton, and Shirley Taylor, were petitioners in a class action suit against SLI. The university opened its doors to the students—but without a welcome mat. The harsh treatment of the students led to them giving up the desire to complete their education at SLI. They did, however, receive honorary degrees in 2004 from the University of Louisiana-Lafayette. (Courtesy of Helma Constantine.)

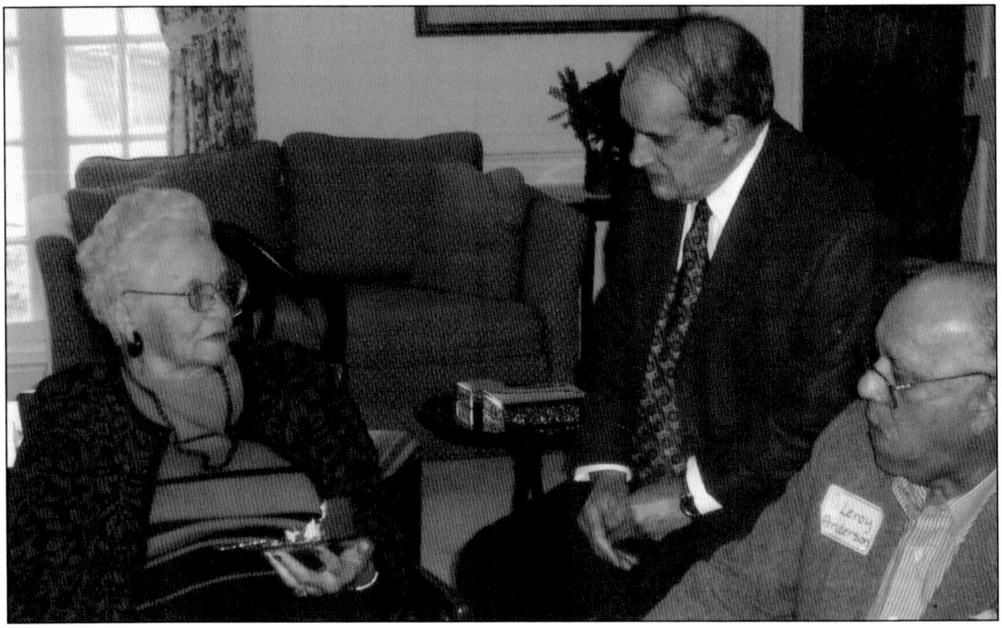

NAACP Secretary (Lafayette Parish). Helma Constantine was secretary of the NAACP in 1953. She and attorney A.P. Turead, J.K. Haynes, and others successfully fought desegregation of the University of Southwestern Louisiana (USL). That movement led to the desegregation of several colleges and universities in Louisiana. Constantine is seated here with former USL president Dr. Ray Authement (center) and Roy Anderson. (Courtesy of Helma Constantine.)

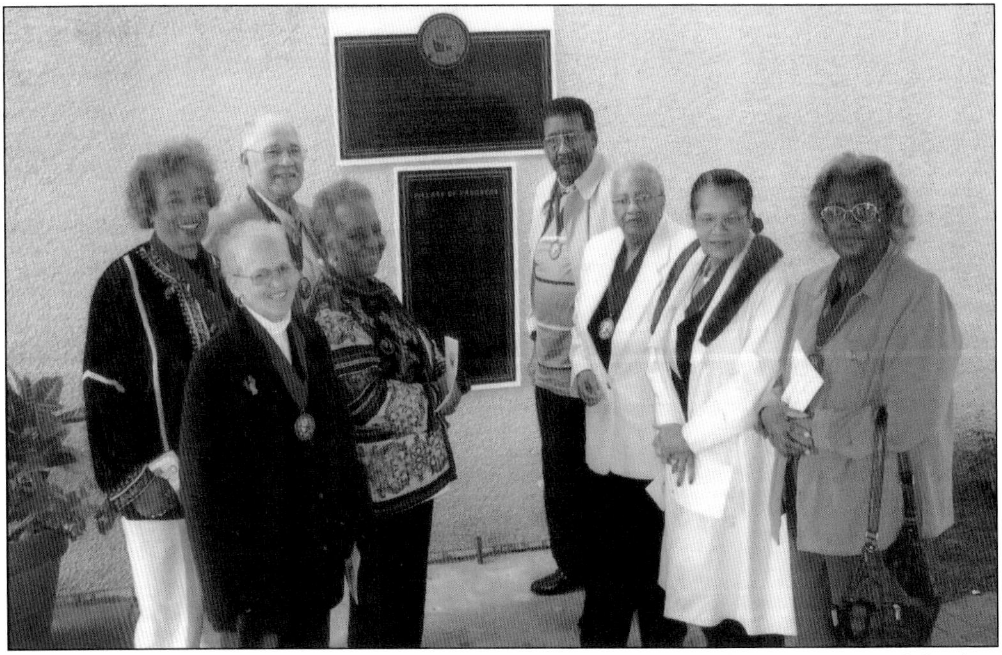

First Black Students (Lafayette Parish). The people pictured here are some of the first black students and graduates of Southwest Louisiana Institute. Pictured are C.D. Constantine, S. Taylor, G.M. Syrie, J.J. Thibeaux, H.R. Gordon, and other students who attended the university. (Courtesy of Helma Constantine.)

Breaking the Barriers (Lafayette Parish). Dr. Ernest W. Kinchen Jr. is a graduate of Paul Breaux High School, Dillard University in New Orleans, and Howard University College of Medicine School in Washington, DC. He applied for admittance to Louisiana State University's medical school program but was denied because of segregation. He is a board-certified general surgeon. In 1971, Kinchen broke the color barrier by becoming the first African American doctor to be admitted to Charity Hospital Tulane Service and the first black doctor in the Charity Hospital System of Louisiana. He performed surgery in some cases that were deemed hopeless and the patients survived. (Courtesy of Barbara Kinchen.)

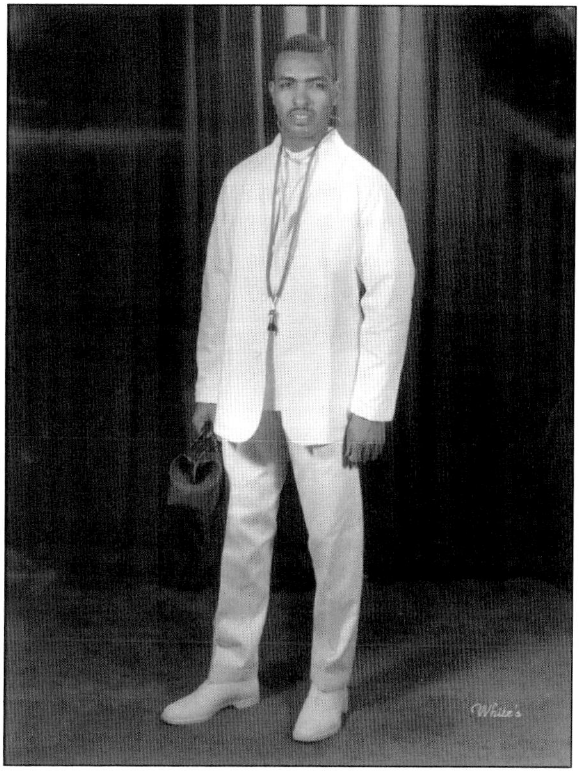

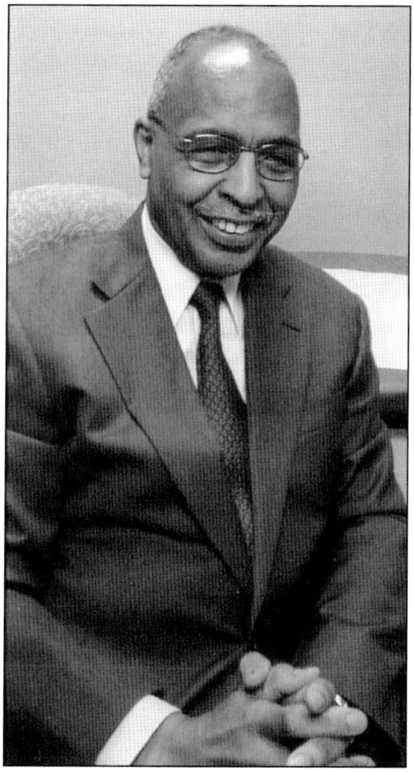

Living Legends (Lafayette Parish). The Joseph Henry Tyler Jr. Chapter of the National Medical Associate is 21 years old, and its members are physicians. Each year, the organization sponsors the Living Legends program and banquet that honors an outstanding black medical professional. The group also sponsors scholarships for students enrolling in medical school. Dr. Ernest Kinchen is the founder of the prestigious organization. (Courtesy of Dr. Ernest Kinchen Jr.)

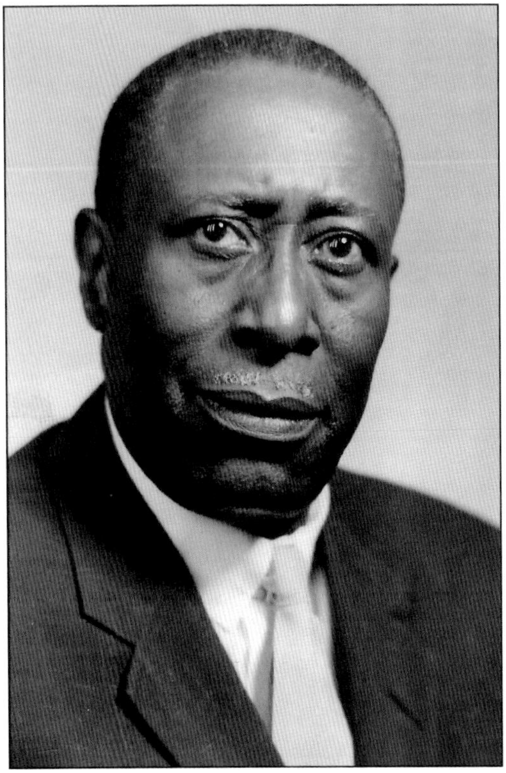

The Doctor (Lafayette Parish). Dr. R.B. Jones was one of the first African American physicians to have a practice in Lafayette, Louisiana. Jones graduated from Knoxville College and from Meharry Medical College in Nashville. Dr. Jones had a medical office but also made house calls to take care of sick patients. He was paid by most patients but sometimes received food items as payment for his services when the patients had no money. He was married to Sarah Edwards Jones, an English teacher. They had two children, Ransom Jones and Yvonne Jones Hightower. Dr. Jones was a member of Good Hope Baptist Church, the Alpha Phi Alpha Fraternity, the Lafayette Negro Business League, was a Prince Hall 32nd Degree Mason, and participated in many other civic organizations. (Courtesy of Edith G. Dupré Library Archives and Special Collections.)

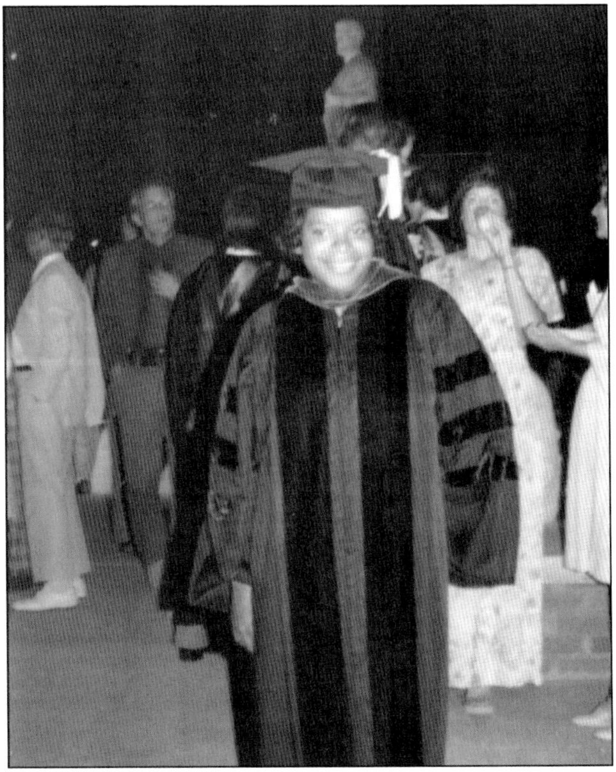

First African American Female Doctor (Lafayette Parish). Dr. Ruth Smothers was the first African American female doctor in Lafayette. She graduated from the University of Arizona College of Medicine. She has a medical practice in nephrology (kidney specialist). Smothers also studied internal medicine at Howard University in Washington, DC, and has an internal medicine practice in Lafayette. (Courtesy of Wilma R. Bowles.)

INTERNIST (LAFAYETTE PARISH). Dr. Clinton Young is a graduate of Grambling State University and Louisiana State University School of Medicine in New Orleans. He practiced internal medicine in Lafayette for 32 years. Dr. Young received his certification in sleep medicine and currently has a practice in the field. He is married to Lula Young, and they have three daughters: Courtney, Lindsay, and Constance. (Courtesy of Lula Young.)

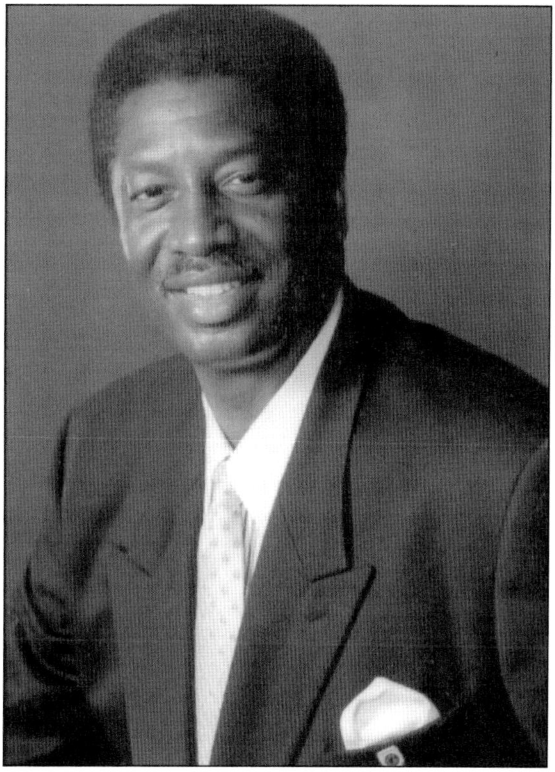

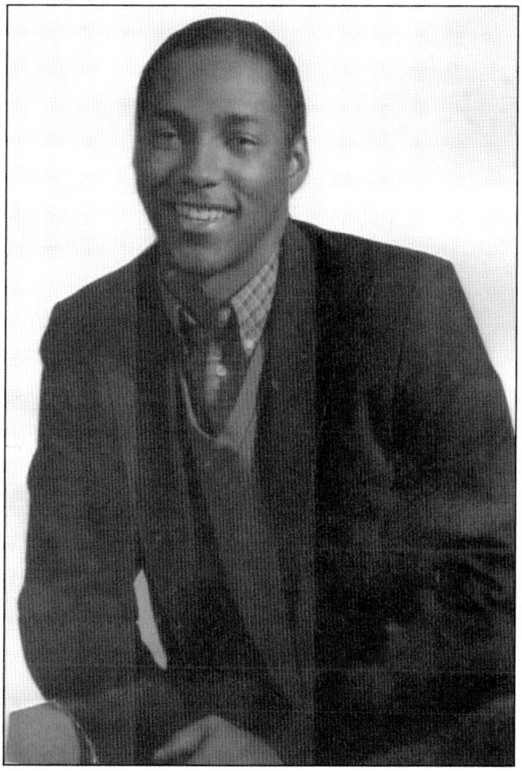

ONCOLOGIST SURGEON (LAFAYETTE PARISH). Dr. Emery Minnard was born and raised in Lafayette. He is a graduate of Holy Rosary Institute and Meharry Medical College in Nashville, Tennessee. He is an oncologist surgeon and has a practice in New Orleans. (Courtesy of Adele Minnard.)

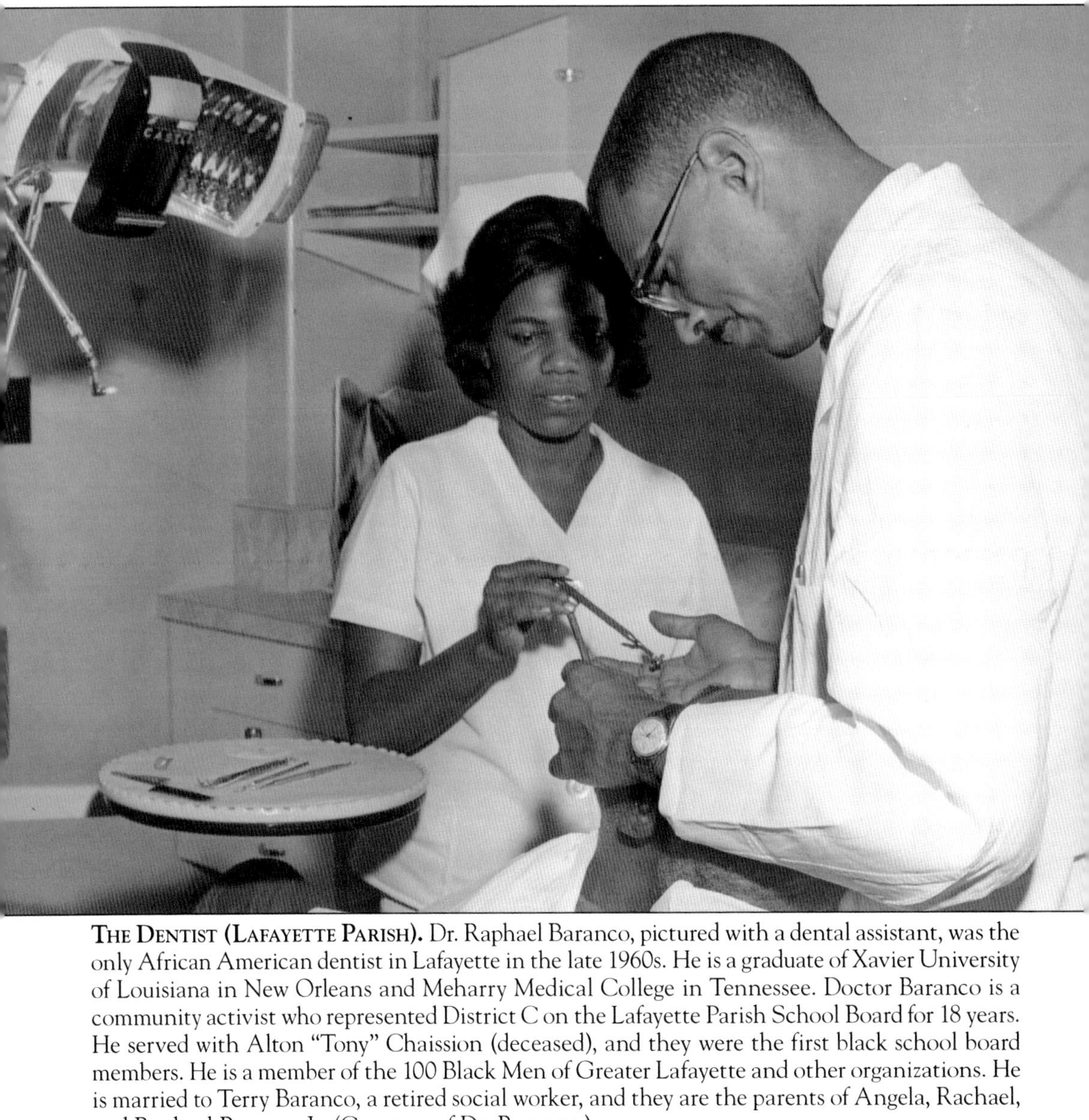

The Dentist (Lafayette Parish). Dr. Raphael Baranco, pictured with a dental assistant, was the only African American dentist in Lafayette in the late 1960s. He is a graduate of Xavier University of Louisiana in New Orleans and Meharry Medical College in Tennessee. Doctor Baranco is a community activist who represented District C on the Lafayette Parish School Board for 18 years. He served with Alton "Tony" Chaission (deceased), and they were the first black school board members. He is a member of the 100 Black Men of Greater Lafayette and other organizations. He is married to Terry Baranco, a retired social worker, and they are the parents of Angela, Rachael, and Raphael Baranco Jr. (Courtesy of Dr. Baranco.)

Army Veteran and Medical Doctor (Lafayette Parish). Dr. Robert Louis was born and raised in Lafayette, Louisiana. Louis graduated from the premed program at the University of Southwestern Louisiana (now UL-Lafayette) as well as Meharry Medical College in Nashville, Tennessee. Louis lives in Houston, Texas, and has been a medical doctor for 45 years. (Courtesy of Merline Herbert.)

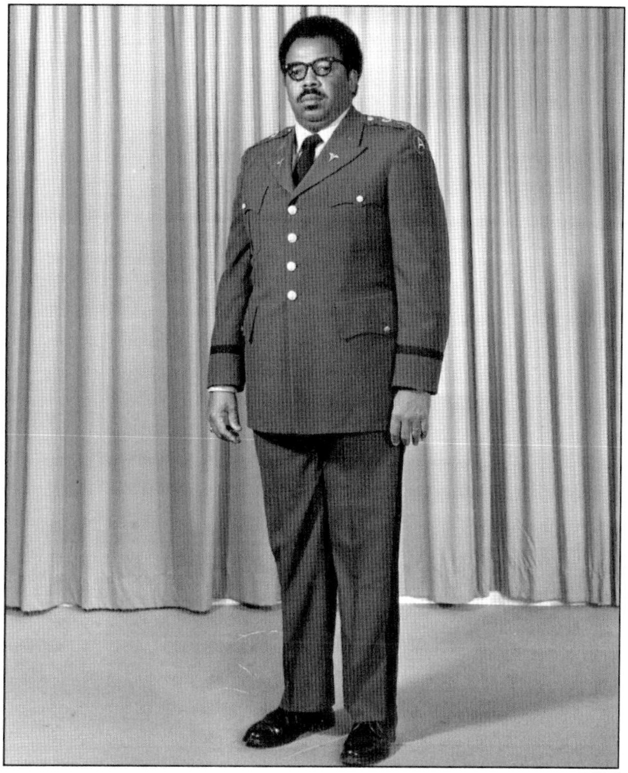

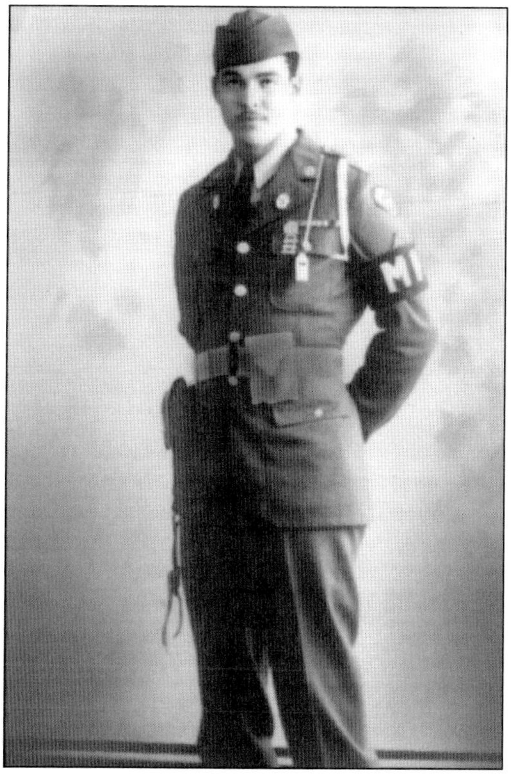

World War II Veteran (Lafayette Parish). Denris Mouton, a World War II veteran, served in the US Army and was stationed in Cottingham, England, during the war. He is currently in his 90s. During the war, he worked as a military policeman and served for 14 months from 1943 to 1944. He was also stationed in Normandy and Cherbourg, France. He served at the rank of provost sergeant. (Courtesy of Denris Mouton.)

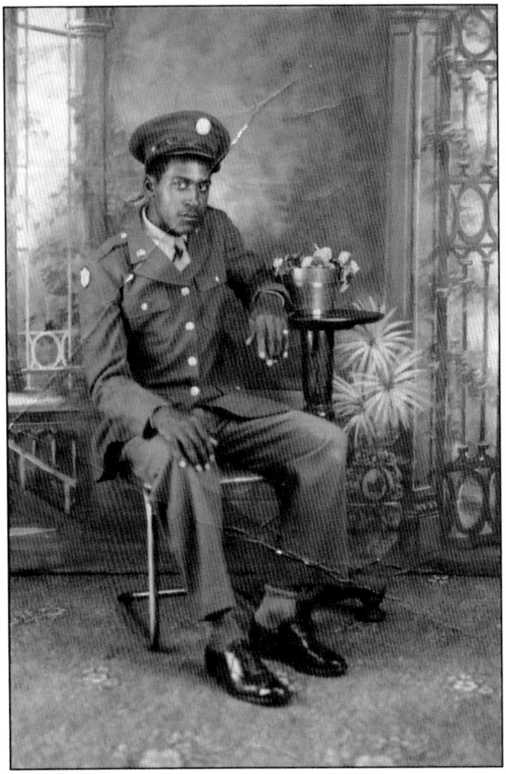

Drafted World War II Veteran (Lafayette Parish). Gilbert Broussard Jr. served two years, five months, and 21 days in the US Army. He was stationed overseas at South Hampton, England, and in Normandy, France. He received several medals, including the Good Conduct, ATO Med, EAMETO Med, and World War II Victory Medals. He was honorably discharged and returned to Lafayette. He worked for Gulf States Utilities and retired after 33 years. (Courtesy of Deborah Broussard.)

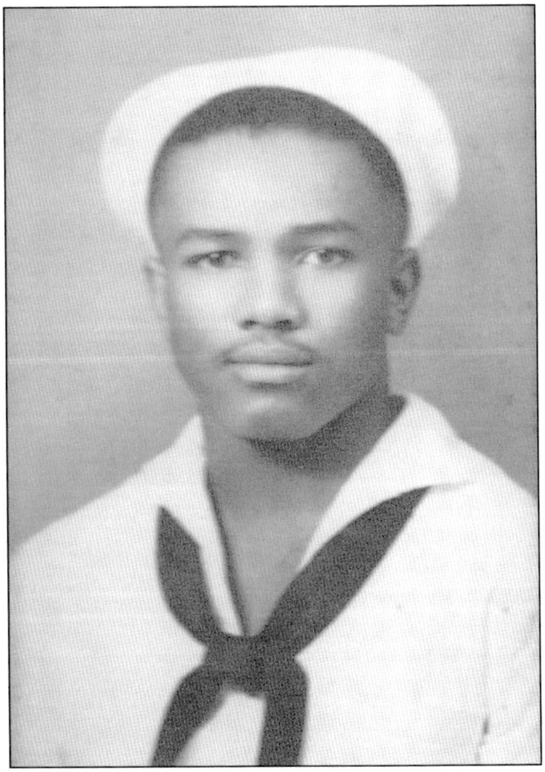

Pearl Harbor Veteran (Lafayette Parish). Alex Taylor, Seaman 2nd Class, served in the US Navy for seven years, 11 months, and 29 days. He was a First Class Cook on the USS *Dobbin*. Taylor was 18 years old when he enlisted. Black seaman performed such duties as cooking, sweeping, mopping, washing dishes, and shining shoes. A cook's job was one of most prestigious jobs for black seamen. Taylor served during the attack on Pearl Harbor. He is proud of his service time and the places where he traveled: Australia, Hawaii, and Japan. Taylor is married to Hazel Taylor, and they have two daughters. (Courtesy of Alex Taylor.)

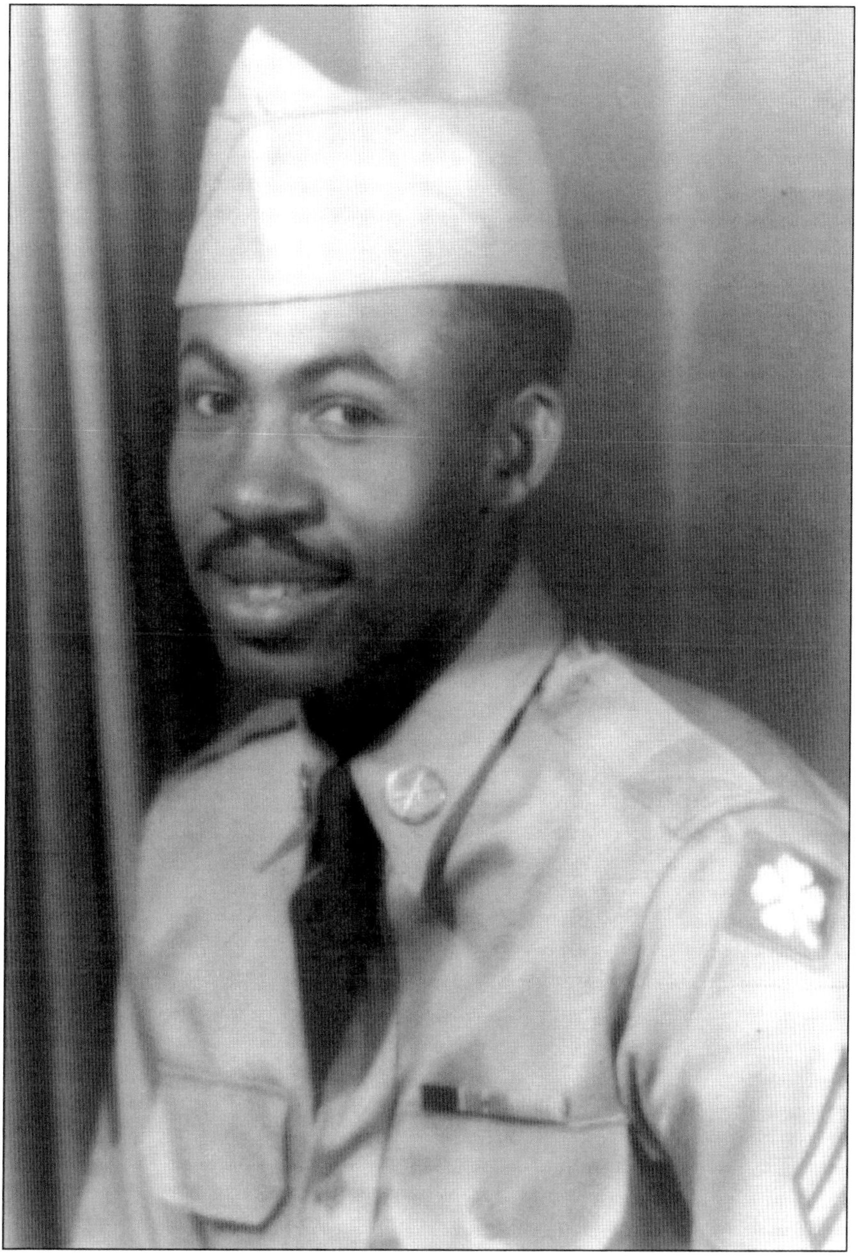

KOREA WAR VETERAN AND COMMUNITY ACTIVIST (LAFAYETTE PARISH). Joseph "Joe" Dennis is a Korean War veteran. He was wounded and received the Purple Heart fighting in North Korea. He returned to a segregated America and to his home in Lafayette. He retired from the Diamond Crystal Salt Company in New Iberia, Louisiana, where he worked for 33 years. Dennis began to work for change for black people in Lafayette as soon as he returned from military service. He collaborated with Father McKnight, Alfred McZeal, and several other community citizens in the Black Alliance for Progress to get black citizens elected to public offices, such as the Lafayette Parish School Board, the police jury, and Lafayette City Council. They were successful in securing all three positions that were served by first-time black elected officials. Dennis is married to Mildred J. Dennis, and they are the parents of four sons. (Courtesy of Joseph Dennis.)

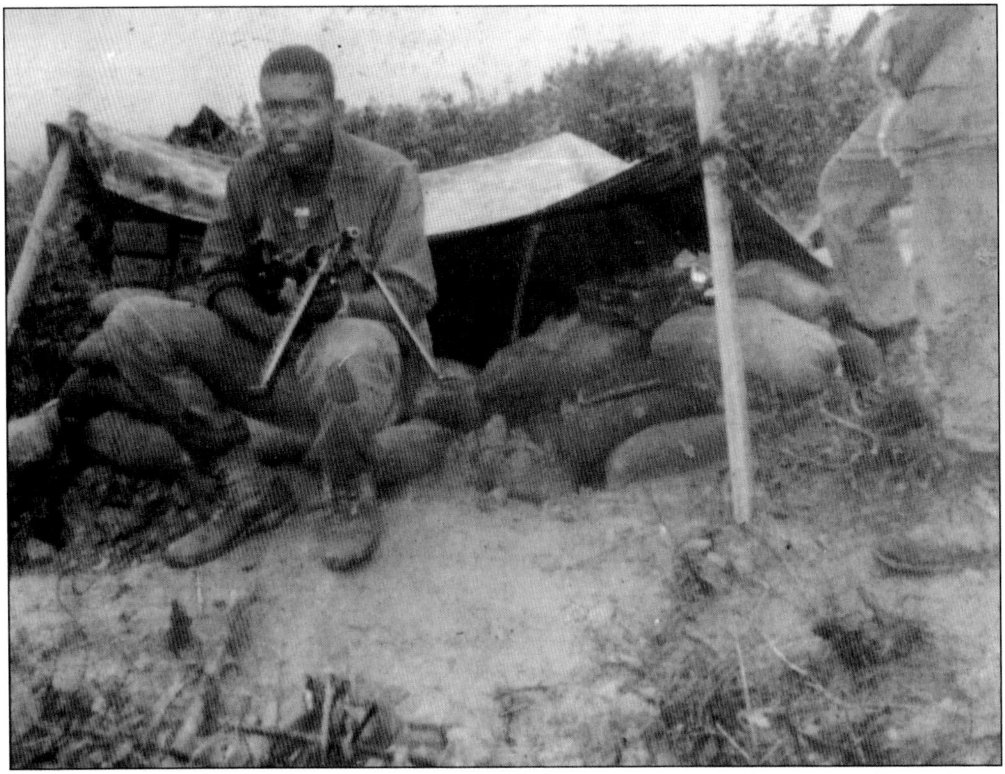

Vietnam Veteran (Lafayette Parish). Cpl. J. Kennedy Green enlisted in the US Marine Corps when he was 19 years old and served in the northern part of South Vietnam at Quang Tri Province with Hotel Company 26. He was injured and received the Purple Heart. (Courtesy of J. Kennedy Green.)

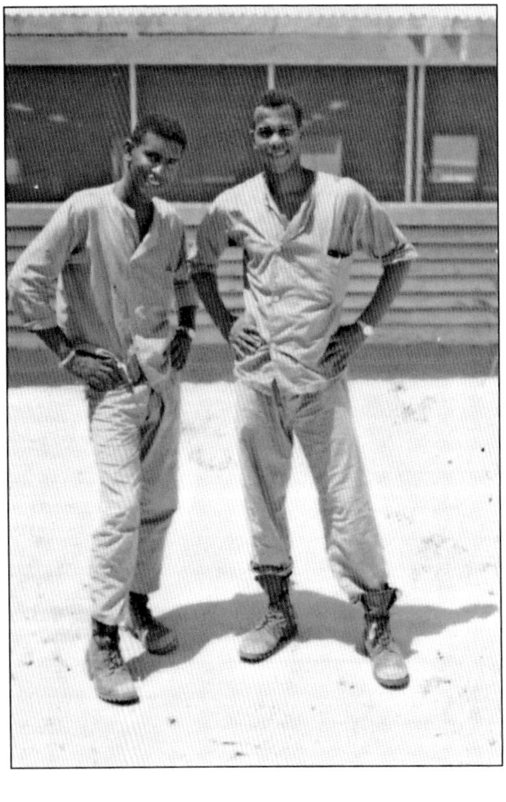

Vietnam Veterans at Cam Ranh Bay, Vietnam, 1967 (Lafayette Parish). J. Kennedy Green (left) and Gerard Gabriel were not only military personnel serving in Vietnam, they were cousins, friends, schoolmates, and teammates at Paul Breaux High School. Green and Gabriel are wearing hospital-issued clothing in this picture while recovering. Green was a corporal in the US Marine Corps. Gabriel (deceased) was a soldier in the US Army. (Courtesy of J. Kennedy Green.)

Six

MOVERS, SHAKERS, AND HISTORY MAKERS

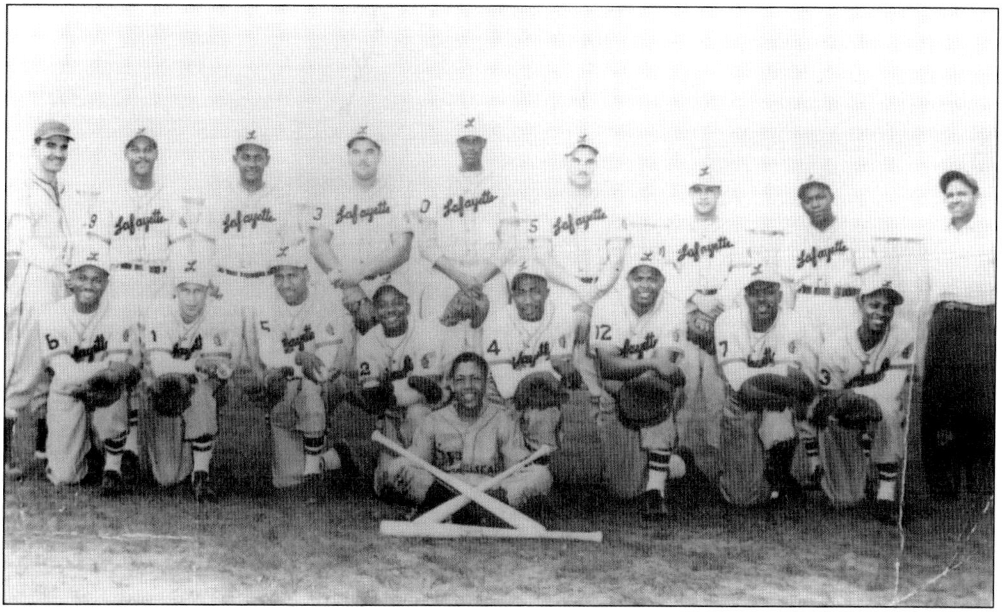

THE LAFAYETTE BIG CHIEFS BASEBALL TEAM (LAFAYETTE PARISH). The semi-professional Lafayette Big Chiefs was a powerful team in the late 1940s and 1950s. Wallace "WaWa" Mouton was the manager of the team. His brothers Stanley and Denris Mouton played on the team as well. The team was scheduled to play against the New Orleans Creoles, whose team had a female player, Toney Stone, known as the "Girl Wonder"; Stone played second base. Crowds of 8,000 packed the stadium to see the team play. Forrest Langlinais was the team's owner. (Courtesy of Louis J. Perret, clerk of court, Lafayette Parish.)

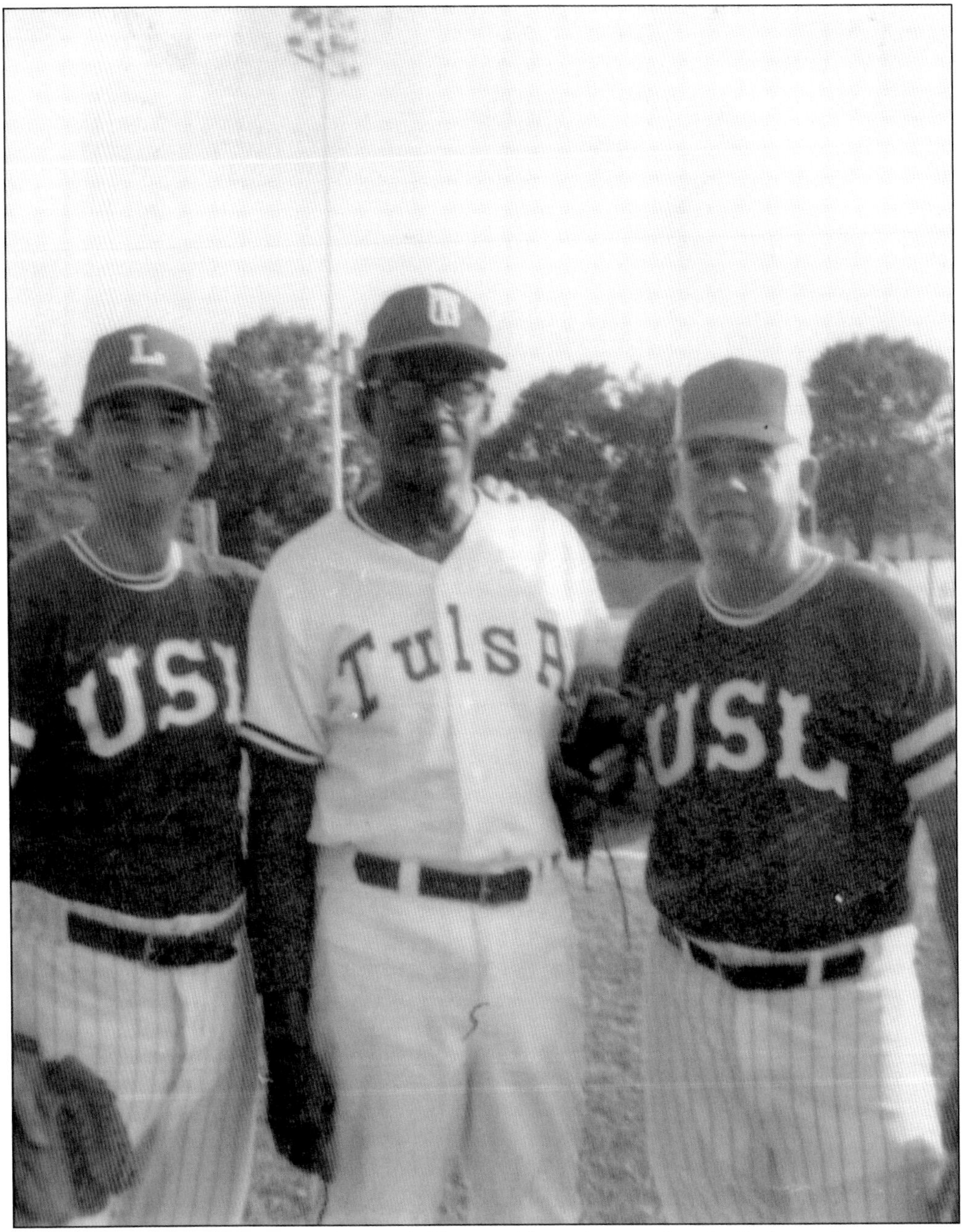

Baseball Players (Lafayette Parish). Famous Negro League baseball player Satchel Paige (center) is flanked by a former USL baseball player (left) and local favorite baseball player Stanley Mouton (right). Mouton was considered one the best players in Lafayette and in the league. He was almost selected to integrate major-league baseball because of his excellent skills but was not chosen because of the light complexion of his skin. Jackie Robinson was instead picked, and America had its first African American major-league baseball player in 1947. Robinson played for the Brooklyn Dodgers, and in his first game the Dodgers won 5-3 with Robinson manning first base. It was the beginning of the destruction of segregation in America for such entities in American professional sports and other organizations. (Courtesy of Lyle Mouton Sr.)

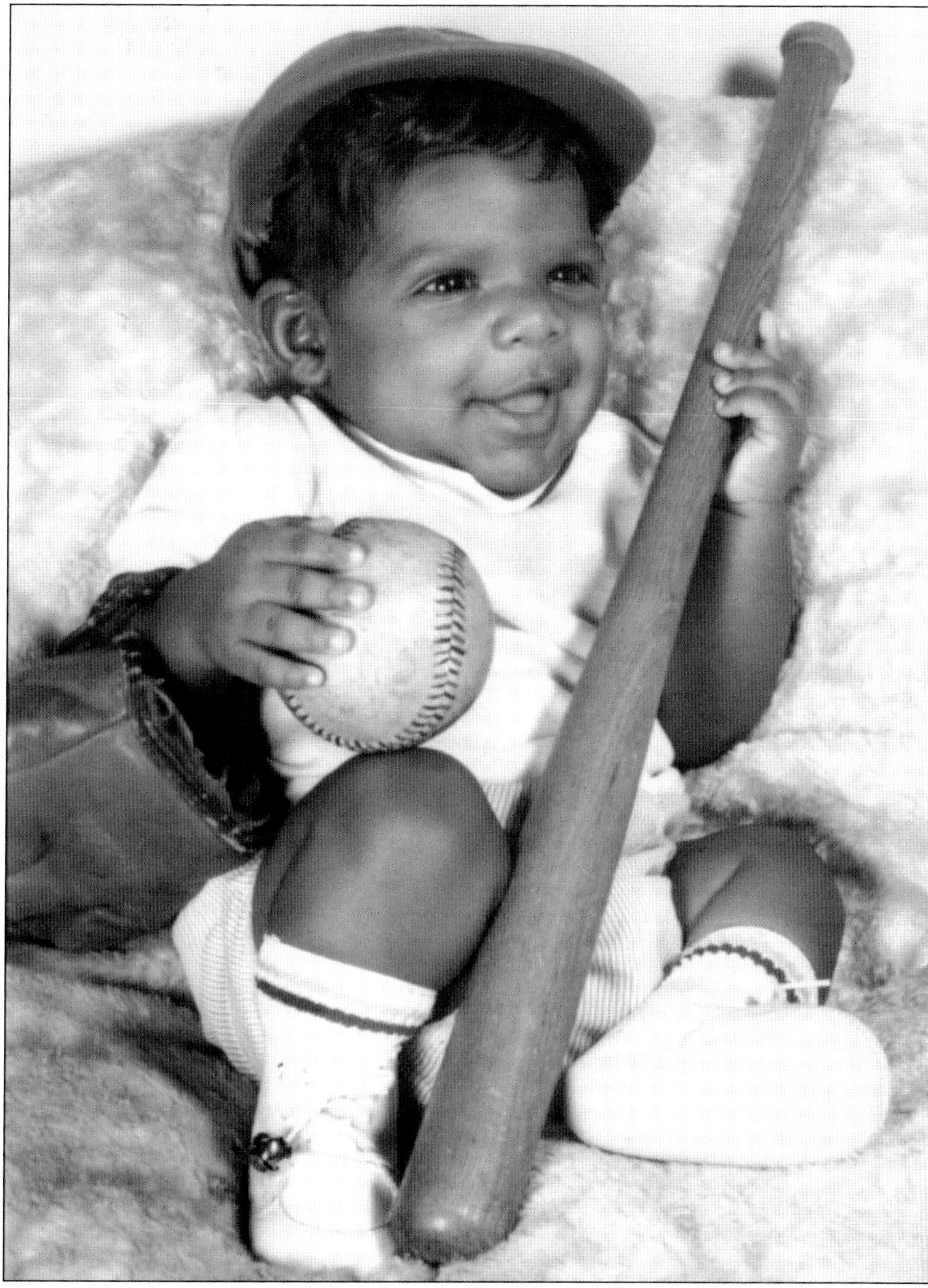

BABY LYLE MOUTON JR. (LAFAYETTE PARISH). Destined for greatness in sports, Lyle Mouton Jr., the son of Phyllis and Lyle Mouton Sr., is two months old in this photograph and is holding a baseball glove, bat, and ball. He grew up to play basketball and baseball in high school and in college at LSU. His baseball career blossomed into playing for several professional baseball teams, including the Chicago White Sox, Baltimore Orioles, Milwaukee Brewers, and Florida Marlins. (Courtesy of Phyllis Mouton.)

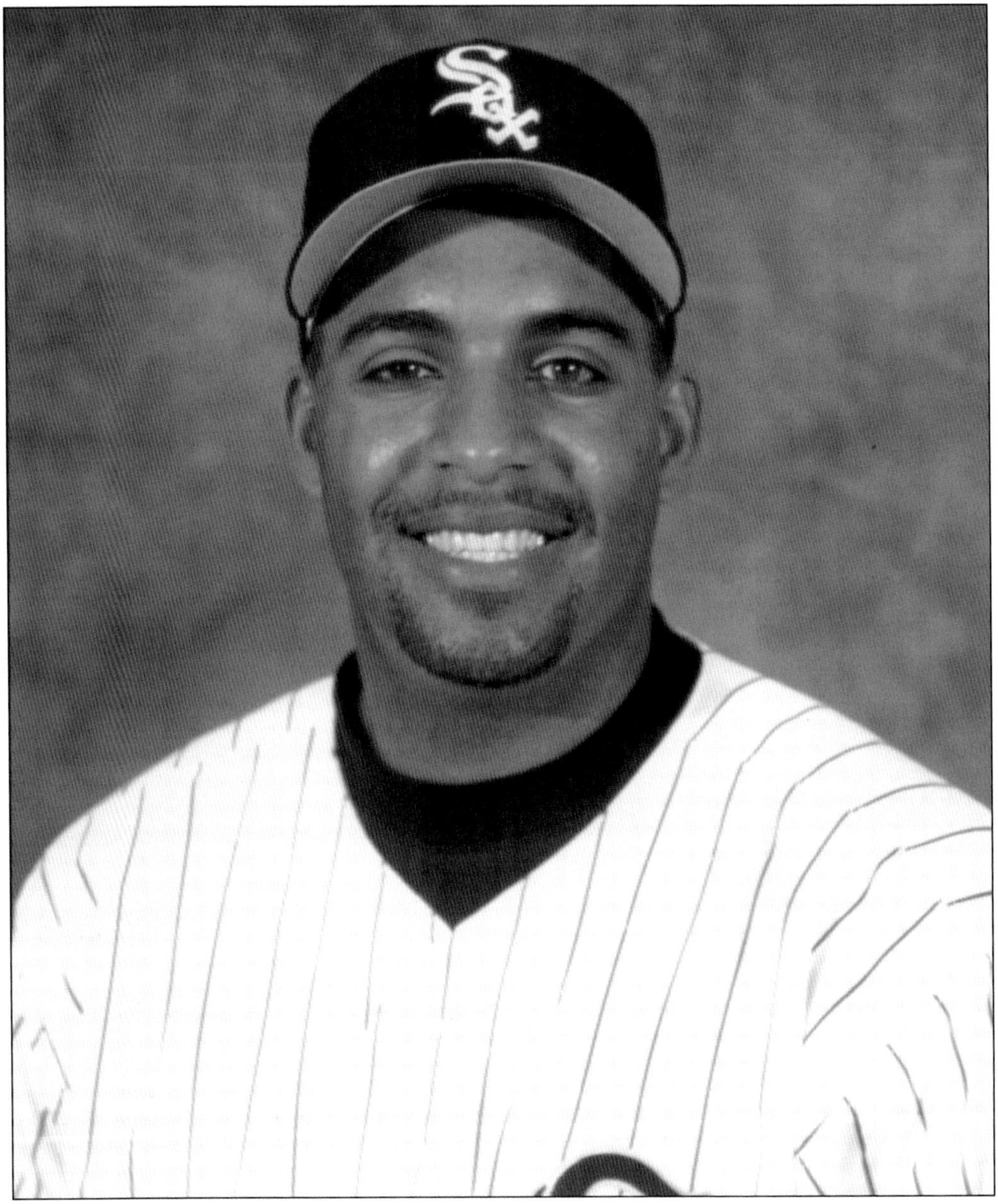

The Chicago White Sox and Lyle Mouton Jr. A St. Thomas More High School graduate, Lyle Mouton Jr. had a lustrous career as a professional baseball player. He played basketball and baseball in high school and in college at Louisiana State University. He had the athletic ability to play all three outfield positions in college and played in the outfield in the major leagues. Lyle's father (Lyle Mouton Sr.), his grandfather (Wallace Mouton), and great uncles (Stanley Mouton and Denris Mouton) all played baseball in school and on semi-professional teams. Mouton was Mr. Basketball in Louisiana in 1987, as well as an All-American, and both of his uniform numbers (in basketball and baseball) have been retired. His major-league career stats total a .280 overall batting average, 22 home runs, and 116 RBI. (Courtesy of Lyle and Phyllis Mouton.)

PLAYING THE GAME. Lyle Mouton Jr. (no. 21) is seen here playing basketball for Louisiana State University in Baton Rouge, Louisiana. In baseball, he helped to lead the Tigers to three College World Series Tournaments and the 1991 championship during his tenure as a student-athlete. (Courtesy of Lyle and Phyllis Mouton.)

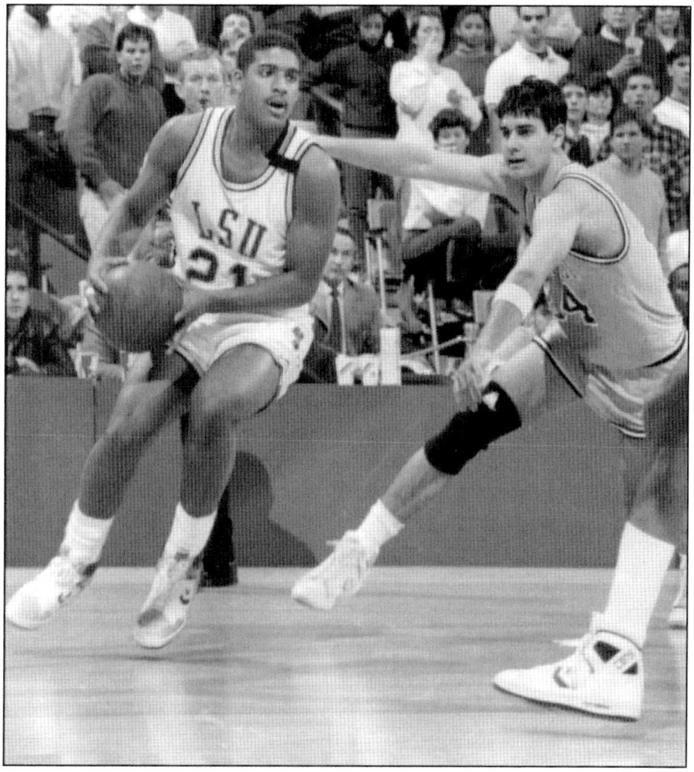

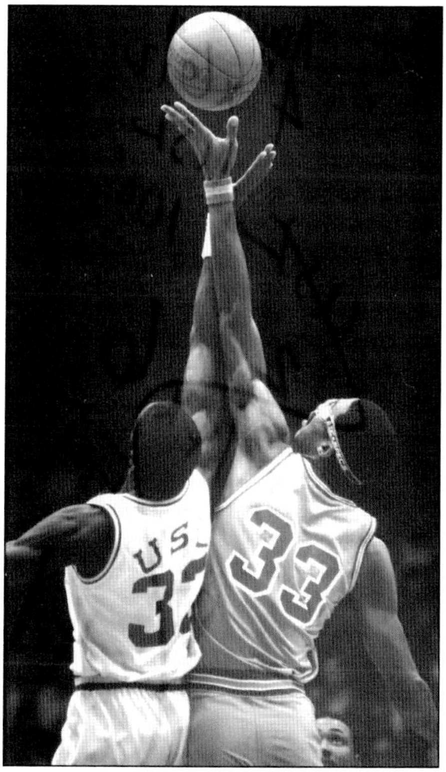

BASKETBALL PLAYERS (LAFAYETTE PARISH). Several players in earlier years graduated from USL and played professional basketball, including Dwight "Bo" Lamar, Andrew Toney, and Kevin Brooks. The University of Southwestern Louisiana (now UL-Lafayette) had two African American basketball coaches, Jessie Evans and Robert Lee. Most of the players in recent years have been predominately African American. The sport is a favorite among students, faculty, staff, and the Lafayette community. (Courtesy of Edith G. Dupré Library Archives and Special Collections.)

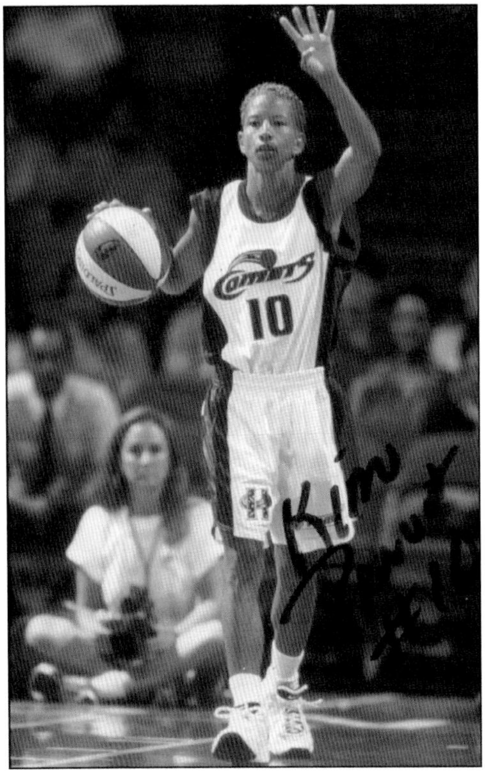

WOMEN NATIONAL BASKETBALL ASSOCIATION CHAMPION KIM PERROT. (LAFAYETTE, PARISH). Kim Perrot was born and raised in Lafayette, Louisiana. She was the youngest child of six children born to Consuella Perrot. She began playing basketball at an early age and showed passion, potential, and professionalism for the game. She played basketball at Acadiana High School in Lafayette, Louisiana, for the University of Southwestern Louisiana, and became a professional basketball player with the Houston Comets. Perrot was only five feet, five inches tall, but she was a powerful player who averaged about 30 points per game in 1990 in college and an astounding 58 points one game during that season. Perrot's record at UL-Lafayette is 2,157 points, and it still stands today. Her no. 12 jersey was retired, and she remains the guiding influence for the women's basketball program at UL-Lafayette. Perrot joined the Houston Comet's team in 1997 and played in the position of point guard. The Houston Comet's won two consecutive WNBA titles in 1997 and in 1998 under her leadership. (Courtesy of Loretta Perrot.)

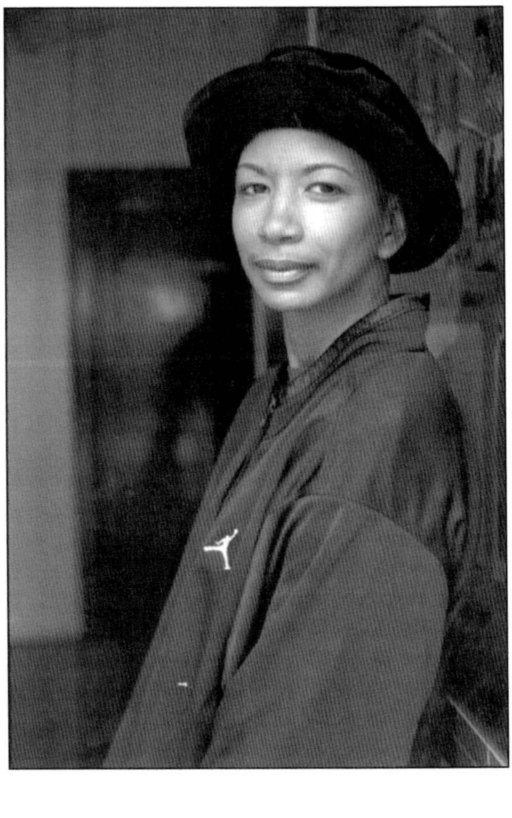

WOMEN'S PROFESSIONAL BASKETBALL ASSOCIATION TEAM, THE HOUSTON COMETS (LAFAYETTE, PARISH). Kim Perrot grew up in the Truman Addition neighborhood, attended school at Truman Elementary, and graduated from Acadiana High School. She showed her athletic ability at a young age, as she had a passion for playing basketball. During her motivational speeches, she encouraged students to follow their dreams. Unfortunately, she passed away in 1999 at the young age of 32. Despite her short life, she left a permanent mark of success on women's sports. (Courtesy of Loretta Perrot.)

CHANDA RUBIN, WTA SINGLES CHAMPION (LAFAYETTE PARISH). Chanda was a seven-time WTA singles champion, and at one point she rose to a no. 6 world ranking. Chanda ended 2003 ranked no. 9 in the world. She is an avid supporter of the Women's Sport Foundation and the United Negro College Fund. (Courtesy of Bernadette Rubin.)

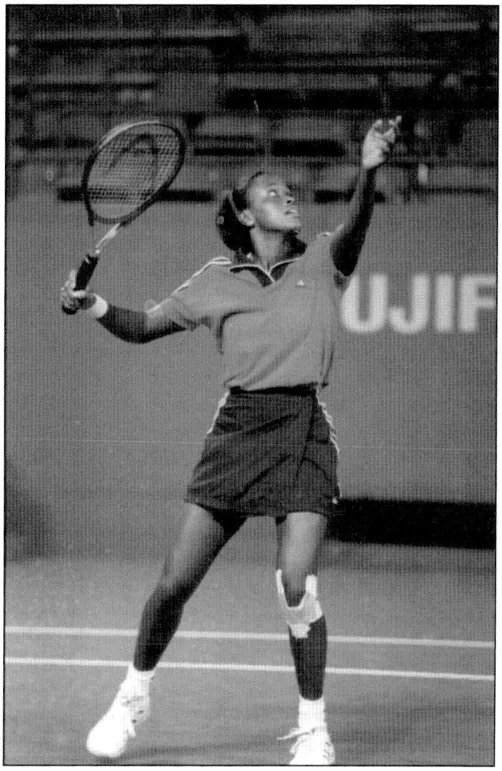

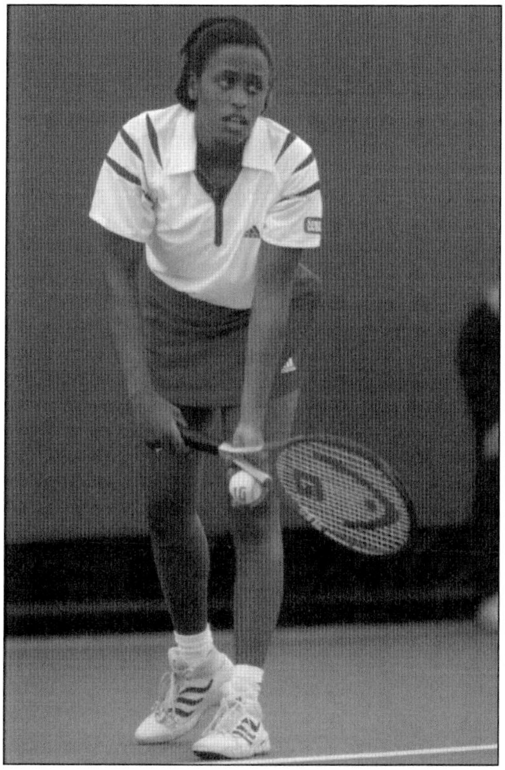

CHANDA RUBIN (LAFAYETTE PARISH). Benny Sims was Rubin's coach, and he introduced her to Arthur Ashe, a legendary professional tennis player. The three formed a friendship that lasted until Ashe's death in 1993. (Courtesy of Bernadette Rubin.)

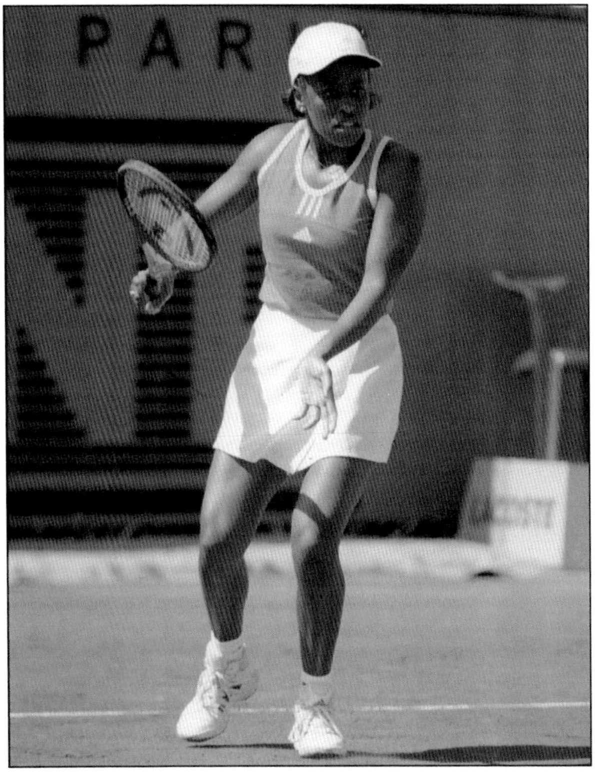

Chanda Rubin, Tennis Champion (Lafayette Parish). Tennis champion Chanda Rubin was born, raised, and educated in Lafayette, Louisiana. She is the daughter of Edward and Bernadette Rubin. She has one sister and one brother. Rubin attended elementary school at Holy Family Catholic School. She graduated high school from Episcopal School of Acadiana. She began her career as a tennis player when she was 15 years old and played in the US Open several times. Rubin was a seven-time WTA singles champion on tour and was as high as sixth in the world rankings at one point in her career. Rubin is actively involved in local and state communities and often conducts tennis clinics. She is a member of Athletes Against Drugs, the Children's Museum, the American Heart Association, and other charitable organizations. (Courtesy of Bernadette Rubin.)

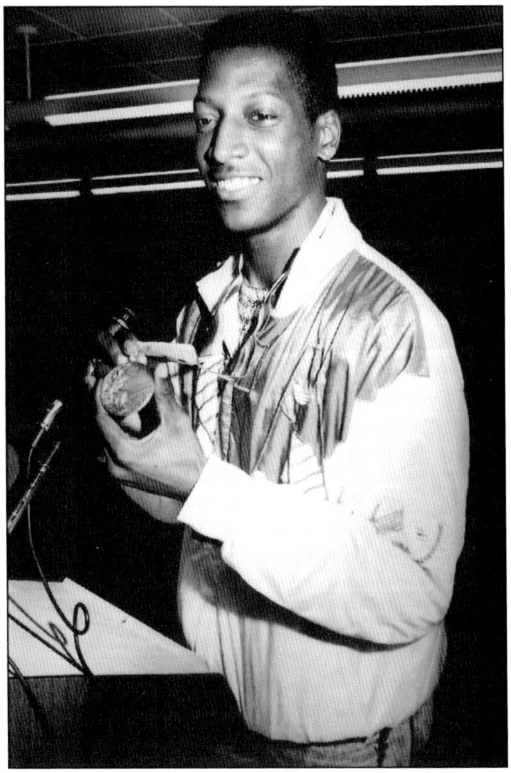

An Olympic Athlete (Lafayette Parish). Hollis Conway is presently a minister and motivational speaker, but he left records in track and field that remain unbroken. Conway is an All-American and two-time Olympic medalist, with a personal high-jump record of seven feet, 10.5 inches. He was no. 1 in the world in 1990 and 1991. He is a member of the Louisiana Sports Hall of Fame. Conway is a University of Southwestern Louisiana graduate, and he worked as an academic counselor and Champs coordinator at UL-Lafayette. He is the founder of Overcoming Obstacles, Inc. (Courtesy of Edith G. Dupré Library Archives and Special Collections.)

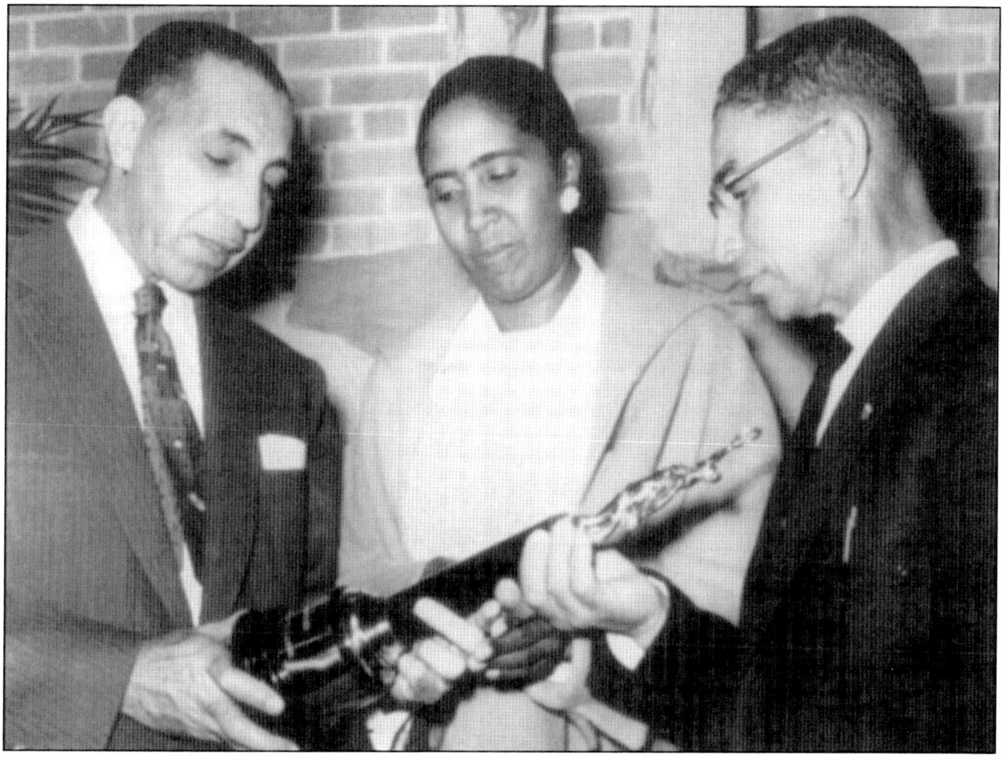

The Award (Lafayette Parish). Dr. Felton G. Clark (left) presented the Best Farmers Trophy to Clarence J. and Mathilda Green Broussard in 1957. Clark was the president of Southern University Agricultural and Mechanical College in Baton Rouge, Louisiana. The Broussard farm was located in Lafayette Parish and grew cotton, sugarcane, sweet potatoes, peppers, and okra. (Courtesy of John A. Broussard.)

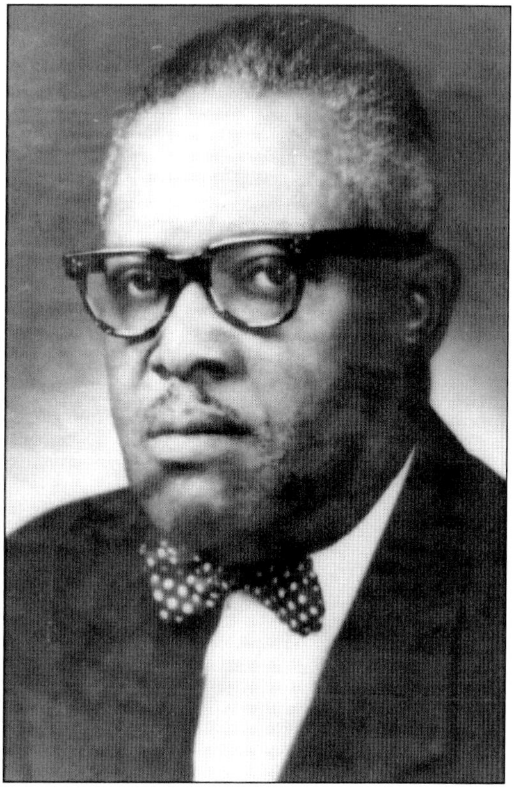

Civic Leader (Lafayette Parish). Doremus Dorsey was an influential leader in the Lafayette community. He worked at Heymann's Department Store and helped some people gain employment at the store. He was one of the leaders of Lafayette's Mardi Gras Festival and served as president. He was King Toussaint L'Ouverture of the 1962 Mardi Gras Ball. Dorsey was a mason, and the Masonic Hall in Lafayette on Twelfth Street was named in his honor. Dorsey was married to Ethel Dorsey, an English teacher, in Lafayette Parish. (Courtesy of Louis J. Perret, clerk of court, Lafayette Parish.)

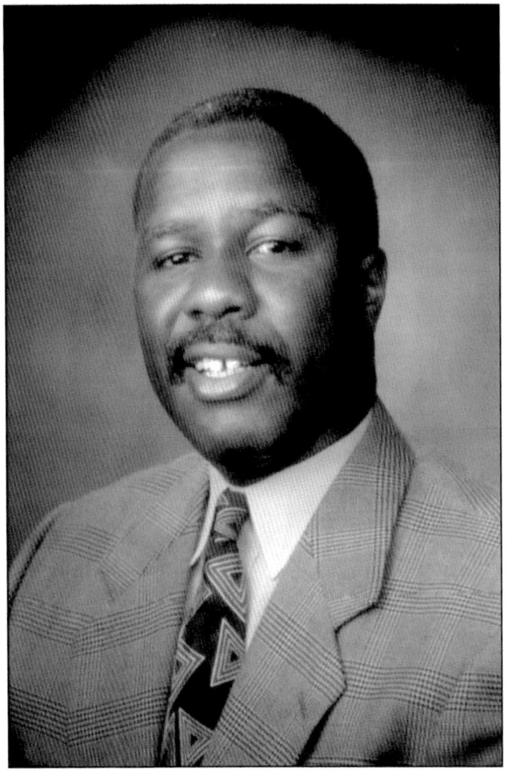

Parks and Recreation (Lafayette Parish). Gerald R. Boudreaux is the first African American director of Parks and Recreation in Lafayette Parish and has served in the position for 26 years. He is a graduate of Northside High School and the University of Southwestern Louisiana. Boudreaux is a board member of the MLK Holiday Committee, Our Lady of Lourdes Regional Medical Center, and Miles Perret Cancer Services Center. He is married to Carlos C. Boudreaux, and they are the parents of three daughters: Brittney, Whittney, and Hallie. (Courtesy of Gerald R. Boudreaux.)

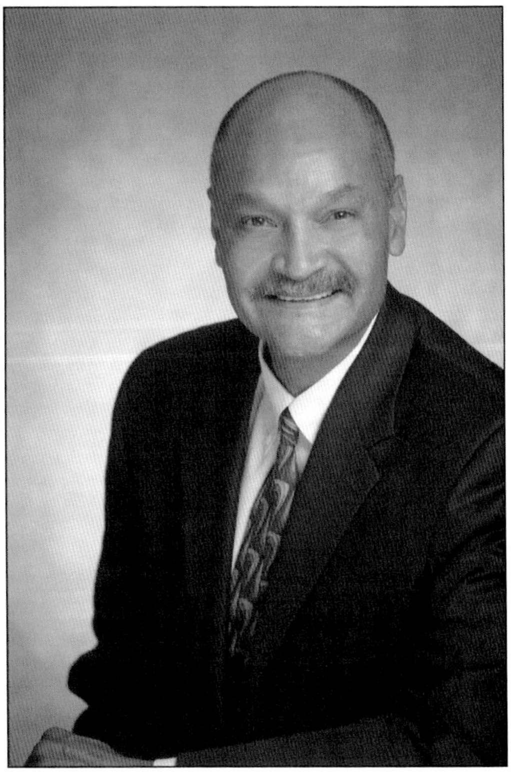

Lafayette Civic Center (Lafayette Parish). Greg Davis is the first African American executive director of the Cajundome and has held the position since 1993. Davis currently serves as chairman of the Louisiana Post-Secondary Education Commission and is a board member of the Council for a Better Louisiana (CABL), Education's Next Horizon, the Evangeline Area Boy Scout Council, Education Committee of 100 Black Men of Greater Lafayette, and Greater Lafayette Chamber of Commerce. (Courtesy of Greg Davis.)

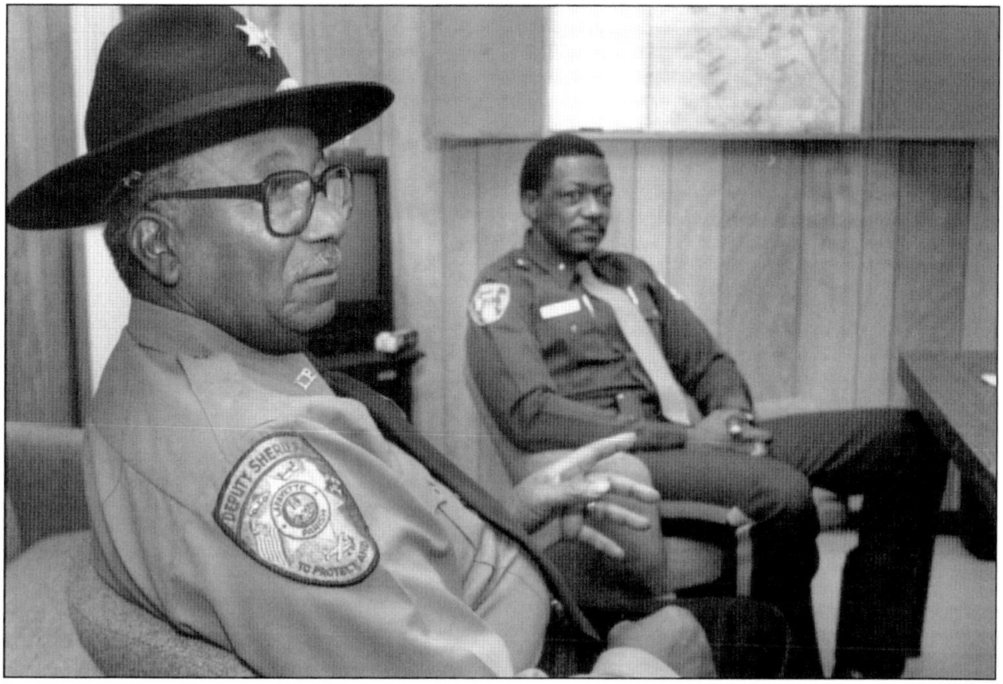

Policemen (Lafayette Parish). James Benoit (at left above and at right) and Oscar Benoit (at right above) were father and son and both worked in law enforcement. James, who has since passed away, was the first black deputy with the Lafayette Parish Sheriff's Office, and he and Johnny Mitchell were the first African American police officers in Lafayette in 1953. The officers had badges but could not wear their uniforms downtown, were not allowed to arrest white people, and had no police cars; however, black people were proud of the officers and respected and trusted them. When a warrant was issued for a black person, he or she would go to the home of Officer James Benoit, turn themselves in, and he would take them to the jail. Oscar is the first African American park police chief in Lafayette and is respected by the community as he works to keep the parks and recreational facilities safe and enjoyable for citizens of Lafayette Parish. His son James Benoit is also a police officer with Troop I Louisiana State Police (Lafayette), making history with three generations of law enforcement officers in the Benoit family. (Both courtesy of Oscar Benoit.)

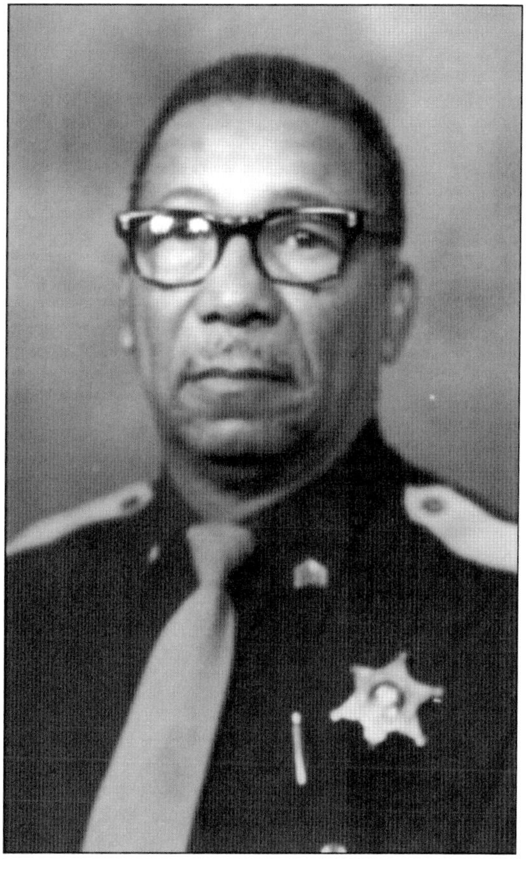

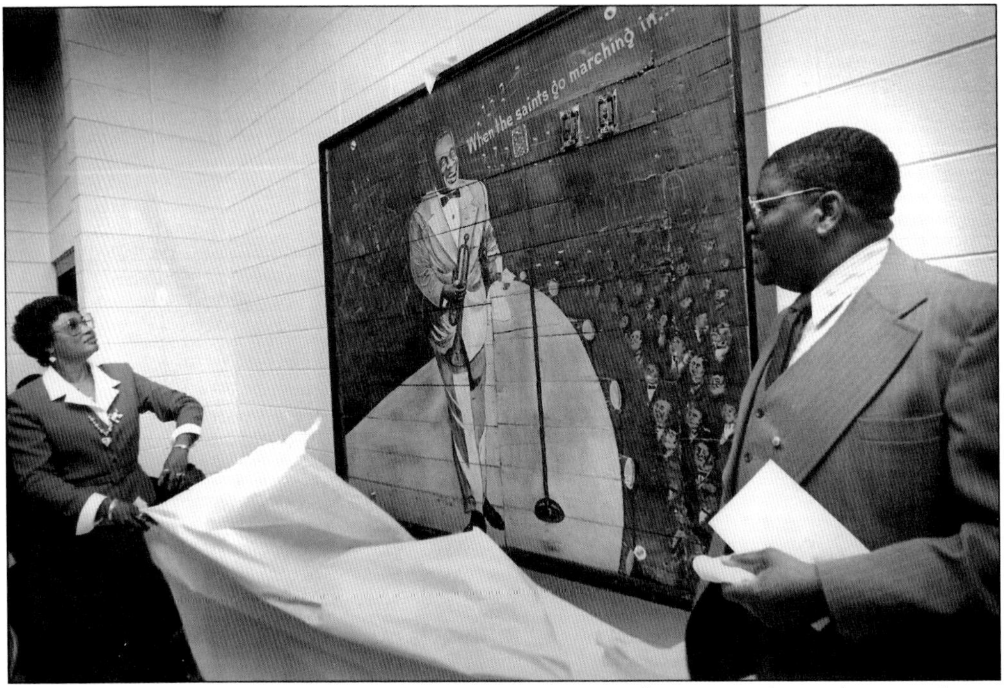

The Mural (Lafayette Parish). Theresa Ventroy Davis (longtime educator) is unveiling a mural with her husband, Wesley Hezekiah Davis, who was a band director at Paul Breaux High School with the Lafayette Parish School System. The painting was commissioned by the City of Lafayette and created by artist Wilson Davis, who was the brother of Wesley H. Davis. (Courtesy of Edith G. Dupré Library Archives and Special Collections.)

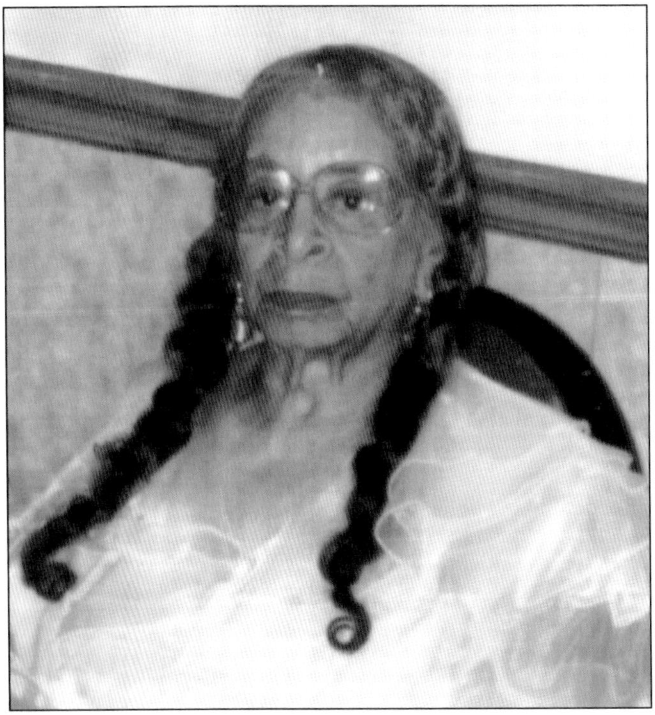

African American Centenarian (Lafayette Parish). Lilly P. Abrams is 105 years old and was born on July 1, 1906, in Loreauville, Louisiana (Iberia Parish), to Odelia and Willie Porter. She is the fourth of 14 children. She was married to Alcide Abrams and is the mother of six children (four living and two deceased). She has lived through 19 presidents, numerous wars and hurricanes, the joys of life, and through the election of the first African American president, Barack H. Obama. (Courtesy of Nelson Abrams.)

Bibliography

Brasseaux, Paul, Keith Fontenot and Claude Oubre. *Creoles of Color in the Bayou Country*. Oxford, MS: University Press of Mississippi, 1996.

Dell, Eula M. *Little Zion Missionary Baptist Church*. Opelousas, LA: self-published, 2002.

Donnan, James H, ed. *Creoles of Color of the Gulf South*. Knoxville, TN: University of Tennessee Press, 1996.

Joseph, John W. *From Farm Boy to First Black Mayor*. Opelousas, LA: self-published, 2006.

McKnight, A.J. *Whistling In the Wind: The Autobiography of the Rev. A.J. McKnight*. Lafayette, LA: Southern Development Foundation, 1994.